PETER
THE APOSTLE

William Thomas Walsh

PETER
THE APOSTLE

SCEPTER

LONDON – NEW YORK

This edition of *Peter the Apostle* is published:
in England by Scepter (U.K.) Ltd., 21 Hinton Avenue, Hounslow
    TW4 6AP; e-mail: scepter@pobox.com;
in the United States by Scepter Publishers Inc., Lockbox, PO Box 72073,
    Cleveland, OH 44192; e-mail: info@scepterpub.org

This title was first published as *St Peter the Apostle* in 1948 by The
Macmillan Company, New York.

ISBN 978-0-906138-67-0

Cover: *Domine quo vadis?* Annibale Carracci (1560–1609), National
Gallery, London.

Cover design, text revision and typeset by ISV Intermedia, and printed in
the EU.

Preface

For many years I have wondered why there were so few books about Saint Peter, compared to the vast number on Saint Paul. The Apostle to the Gentiles has had a perennial fascination for writers, even for those – one is tempted to say especially for those – of sceptical bent. The Apostle to the Hebrews has found many champions and opponents, but few chroniclers.

This book is not offered as an exhaustive or definitive survey of the material, much less as an authoritative interpretation of it. I am too well aware of my own limitations to make any such attempt. Yet if painters and sculptors are permitted to imagine how the Prince of the Apostles looked under various circumstances, perhaps a writer who makes no claim to be an exegete or a theologian may endeavour at least to paint his portrait in words, not in this or that incident merely, but in the whole range of his unique and adventurous life, against his own social and historical background. Such a purpose, considering the subject, does not justify fictionalizing, but it does require considerable liberty to imagine and to conjecture. This, I infer, is licit so long as the reader is not led to mistake suppositions for facts.

It has been a great help to have the permission of the Macmillan Company to quote freely from the New Testament of Our Lord and Saviour Jesus Christ, translated into English from the original Greek by the Very Reverend Francis Aloysius Spencer, O. P., (New York, 1943); for many facts about Saint Peter are made clearer in the Greek text than in the Vulgate or its Douay derivative. Quotations from the Old Testament are from the Douay Version. I have followed the Hebrew spelling of proper names (Isaiah, for example) rather than the Latinized form of the Vulgate (Isaias); though I have called Peter's father Jonas to distinguish him from other Johns in the narrative.

The geographical and other settings are the composite result of a great deal of scattered reading. It would be pedantic and unnecessary to weight a work of this kind with the enormous bibliographies accessible in any good library. Where some special acknowledgement seemed called for, I have indicated the source of my material in brief notes.

William Thomas Walsh

The Author: William Thomas Walsh (1891-1949)

William was born in Waterbury, Connecticut on 11 September 1891, and through the years was given a sound Catholic education that would inspire him in later years with a fierce desire to defend it. After acquiring a B.A. from Yale, he worked as a reporter at various newspapers for a few years, taught one year in a Hartford public high school, and in 1910, published his first book, *The Mirage of the Many*. Walsh wrote it as a warning to those who would follow Socialism. In 1914, he married Helen Gerard Sherwood. Four years later he became head of the department of English at Roxbury School, and in 1933 professor of English at Manhattanville College, New York City.

It wasn't until twenty years after his first book that Walsh finally wrote and published a second. *Isabella of Spain*, which was translated into Spanish (and later into French and German), was published six years before the advent of the Spanish Civil War. *Philip II*, a massive volume that covers anyone who was anyone from the years 1527-1598, was published one year after the initiation of the war against the Catholic Faith in Spain. *The Times* regarded it as more gripping than fiction. *The New York Times* claimed that, "*Philip II* is so thoroughly documented that it must stand as a calm and realistic portrayal of a man and an era, often more exciting to the imagination than fiction, while the suavity of his impeccable literary style offers constant delight."

One can get a good look at Walsh's personality through the introductions of the books he wrote. He said of the history he sought to clarify, "It is a tale so dramatic, so fascinating, that it needs no embellishing or piecing out with the wisdom – or folly – of another age. To probe the inner cosmos of men and women long dead by the light of a pseudo-science, to strip away with pitiless irony all noble or generous appearances, to pry open with an air of personal infallibility the very secret hinges of the door to that ultimate sanctuary of the human conscience which is inviolable even to father confessors – that is an office for which I have neither the taste nor the talent; and if I have fallen unawares into any such pitfalls of the devils of megalomania, I beg forgiveness in advance."

Walsh's obsession for an accurate historical record led to publishing *Characters of the Inquisition,* which came out just a few years after *Philip II.* "No one sees Catholics today burning unbelievers, even in Ireland and Portugal, where the population is almost entirely Catholic; nor does any man of sense foresee the likelihood of a future persecution involving Catholics – except, perhaps, as victims. Yet vast numbers of persons continue to associate the word "Inquisition" with vague notions of Catholic dogma; as though the thing were essentially and peculiarly Catholic, and began and ended in the Catholic Church."

Continuing his clean sweep of the historical era that so wrapped his attention and energy, Walsh's final major work on this historical era was a fresh look at St. Teresa of Avila.

"Years ago," Walsh wrote, "when I read an English translation of Saint Teresa's *Autobiography,* as it is improperly called, I wondered whether a woman in whom the divine and the human so strikingly met could really have been as banal, as priggish, as self-consciously 'literary' as she often appeared in those pages. Later, when I was able to read the Spanish text, I discovered that the irritating qualities were not hers, but her devout translator's. What a vital book to be embalmed in so much stuffy rhetoric! I would make my own translations, and as literally as possible, even at some sacrifice of euphony; not excluding the occasional slips in grammar, faulty reference and vigorous colloquialisms of one who wrote with no eye to bookish effect, but just as she spoke – rapidly, tersely, now and then quite awkwardly ... When I came to her letters and later treatises, there were some good translations at hand, notably the excellent ones by the Benedictines of Stanbrook Abbey, England."

Walsh received an honorary degree from Fordham University. In 1947 he retired to devote more time to writing, but he passed away in White Plains, New York, on 22 February 1949. One of his six children became a Sister of Mercy – Sister Mary Concepta – at the Sacred Heart Convent in Belmont, North Carolina.

1

"O God, my God, look upon me: why have you forsaken me?"
The voice of the young teacher continued with the rest of the Psalm. Simon and the other boys, sitting cross-legged in a semi-circle on the rug, stared at him a little sleepily, for the lesson had been long and it was nearly time to go home. Their eyes wandered from his fine hands, as he unrolled the parchment scroll a little more with each line, to his long chaluq which fell to his ankles, and back to the oddly twisted sudar on his head.

"... I am a worm, and no man, the reproach of men, the outcast of the people. All they that saw me have laughed me to scorn ...

They have like-a-lion my hands and feet. They have numbered all my bones ... They parted my garments amongst them: and upon my vesture they cast lots ..."[1]

The teacher looked up from the scroll and said:

"These words of David clearly refer to the messianic age to come, and to the sorrows of the Jewish people from which our glorious King will liberate us. As for the figure of speech, 'They have like-a-lion my hands and feet', many learned rabbis and doctors of the Law have expressed their opinions. All agree, as this note in the margin states, 'like-a-lion' must signify 'dug' or 'pierced'. But no one knows why the inspired prophet used such a strange expression. Possibly there is reference to some trial that will be inflicted upon Israel before the glory that is promised. There is no end to the rabbinical commentaries that have been written about this line. But as I have told you before, 'all prophets prophesied only of the days of the Messiah.'"

He rolled up the parchment, tied the scroll, and said:

"That is all for today."

The boys filed out and then scattered more briskly from the small house near the white-walled synagogue that rose from black basalt foundations near the shore. Simon and his brother Andrew, if we may continue to imagine this unrecorded scene, scuffed along the beach toward the suburb of Bethsaida, the fishing port of Capharnaum, where the house of their father Jonas stood on the hillside, overlooking the marvellously blue waters of Gennesareth

---
[1] Ps 21

or Galilee.

It was a fair-sized, typically middle-class Jewish home, made of white limestone. It would include a living room some twelve feet square, a dining room of the same size or a little larger with very high ceilings, and farther back, three or four bedrooms opening upon a court surrounded by a covered walk or portico. An outside stairway led to the flat roof, made of brick or tile, with a balustrade around it about three feet high.

Here at certain hours Jonas the fisherman, a Galilean of the tribe of Napthali, would betake himself alone to pray. Or he would go to read in the sky and the winds the prospect for tomorrow's fishing, or tonight's. Or he would sit idly watching his neighbours, who were similarly engaged, and feeling thankful that he lived there, and not in Pontus or Illyricum, where he might have been a serf, or might be dragged to Rome to fight the wild beasts in the arena. For Jonas was a thoughtful man, as the blue-eyed toilers of the sea and the farms frequently are, and it would be a great mistake to infer from his occupation that he was ignorant, much more illiterate. Physical labour was held in honour among the Hebrews. The rabbis encouraged even the rich to learn some useful trade, even the poorest to master reading and writing. For some reason they had a particularly high respect for fishermen. It may well be, then, that Jonas had a fairly definite idea of what the world was, and a shrewd notion that only here, in a small corner of it, did the sun still shine with something like the clarity with which it had opened the first flowers in the Garden of Eden, and darkened the white flesh of Eve. Only here in Palestine did it seem to have more than a natural radiance, like the gleam of the Shekinah on the wall of the Temple of Solomon. Crossing the sparkling waters of the inland sea that lay like a pear-shaped jewel set in the silver-green of olive groves and the pale saffron of wheat fields, it was warm and life-giving, and it told him that he was one man in millions, richly blessed by God. He was glad that his ancestors for centuries past had dragged their living from that deep and dangerous water.

Of Jonas we know little enough; of his wife, not even her name. Yet she was the one who made the first and most lasting impression upon the mind of Simon. It was the mother who began the important work of educating a Jewish boy from the time he was "separated unto God" at his circumcision until he was about six years old. "Knowledge of the Law," observed the rabbis sagely, "is to be sought in those who have sucked it at their mothers' breasts."

And women in Palestine were not mere concubines and child-bearing slaves as in most parts of the ancient eastern world. They were the queens of real homes, and the companions of their husbands. The wife of Jonas the fisherman, whatever her beauty and intelligence or lack of them, had surely been taught from her cradle to take as her models the wonderful mothers of Israel – Rachel and Sara, the chaste Suzanna, the tender Ruth, the fearless and resolute Esther, the heroic mother of the Maccabees. She must have had in some degree the qualities of that valiant woman of the *Book of Proverbs*, who rendered her husband good and not evil all the days of his life, who stretched forth her hands to the needy, and walked in strength and beauty with laughter on her lips and wisdom and clemency on her tongue, while her children called her blessed and her husband trusted and praised her. It was from such a mother that Simon learned the ancient prayers of his people, and the more simple of the psalms.

"O Lord, our Lord, how admirable is your name in the whole earth!" she would chant with him. "... I will behold the heavens, the works of your fingers: the moon and the stars which you have founded. What is man that you are mindful of him? or the son of man that you visit him? You have made him a little less than the angels, and have set him over the work of your hands. You have subjected all things under his feet, all sheep and oxen, moreover also the beasts of the fields: the birds of the air and the fishes of the sea, that pass through the paths of the sea ..."

Simon remembered what she said, but even more vividly what she did. Long years after she had gone to Abraham's bosom, he would see her patient hands preparing the sabbath meal, and setting aside part of the dough as she kneaded the bread for that weekly ritual. He would always think of those hands when he saw anyone lighting a sabbath lamp. He would never forget the shy and reverent gesture with which she would caress the *Mezuzah* (a little folded parchment attached to the doorpost, with the name of the Most High written upon it) and then kiss the fingers that had touched it. Afterwards she would hold him up to do likewise.

His next teacher was his father, who drilled him in the *Torah* or first five books of the Bible (believed to have been written by Moses himself) until he was ten. The men of Israel took this duty so seriously that they went without food or sleep, if necessary, to fulfil it. Even the worst of them regarded one who would neglect to give his son the fundamental truths about God and His chosen people as no better than the heathen or the publican. So Simon began to learn, very early, the history of the world by the light of the only wisdom that made it understandable. Both in the classical Hebrew, and in the rougher Aramaic dialect of Galilee, he heard how God had made all things; and of man's disobedience and punishment; and of God's promises to Abraham and to Moses; of the great flood, and the burning of filthy Sodom; of the flight from Egypt, and the forty years in the desert; of all the strange and moving history, the joys and sorrows, the sins, the punishments, the rewards and triumphs of the children of Israel. He could recite parts of the book of Deuteronomy when he was six or seven, and all of the Great Hallel (Psalms 113-118) before he was ten.

It was probably from his father, too, that he learned to write, commencing at the end of a line and moving laboriously toward the left, as in most eastern languages. The Jews used various kinds of materials for this. They wrote on paper made of palm leaves, of ground walnut shells, of pomegranate rind. They had learned from the Egyptians to make a good strong parchment out of papyrus. They used reed pens sharpened with pumice stones, dipping them into a black ink made of soot, or of gum arabic and vitriol; or into coloured inks of various vegetable substances. Most commonly, however, they employed a tablet such as that on which the priest Zacharias, deprived of speech, wrote the name of his son, the future Baptizer. This was fashioned of thin pieces of wood, glued or strung together and heavy waxed. The writing was done with a stylus of iron, pointed on one end to scratch letters in the wax, and blunted on the other to rub them out. With one of these instruments Simon began to set down, in large wobbly characters, the names of things about him: man; dog; fish; boat; water.

This was all very well, but it could become tiresome, and something to sigh over: especially after that wonderful day when Jonas first taught him how to sail a boat. It was only a short walk from their house to the wharves of Bethsaida, where he owned one of the biggest hulks that lay tugging at their hawsers, swinging their dark masts back and forth against the blue sky. Soon they had pushed off; the sails were unfurled and began to flutter and to belly out, the water swished around the high prow, and sometimes came flying up in spray over their heads. Every day Simon and Andrew learned a little more about the handling of that beautiful curved symmetry that carried them as delightfully as if they were flying birds. They learned to tack and to reef, to read the language of the wind and of the stars, to know every bend and inlet of the incredibly clear lake that stretched for thirteen miles between green banks and white beaches. In those days there were nine or ten cities along the shores, their wharves reverberant with shouts and laughter, their lights sparkling in a great arc along the shore at night; and hundreds of sails glided back and forth, flapping in the realm or careening in a stiff blow.

Simon was not likely to forget the first storm he experienced. Lying nearly seven hundred feet below the level of the Mediterranean, the Sea of Galilee (or Tiberias, or Gennesareth) can be as flat and motionless as glass; then almost in a moment a sudden gust from some ravine can lash it into a madness of frothy towering waves and howling wind. This sometimes continues through a night of terror mingled with the strange fascination that men find danger. Sometimes it ends as suddenly as it begins, leaving the deep more unruffled than before.

Fishing on such a lake was rare sport, and furnished a good livelihood for thousands. It was said that fish bred there faster than anywhere else in the world. Almost at will a man could pull in a good-sized flounder with hook and line. But Jonas usually operated on a larger scale. He was a drift-net fisherman, and when the weather was promising, he and his sons and neighbours, naked as the day they were born and sunburned almost to blackness, would go out at nightfall to try their luck. Setting his sails according to the wind, he would let his boat drift idly along, usually with a partner, his friend Zebedee, some distance away, and a heavy net dragging and bulging behind them. If it happened to encounter a shoal of fishes, it grew heavy and sagged; and when they got it near the beach, they lugged it ashore with shouts of triumph. It was a rare night when there were not enough silvery victims in the meshes to make their labour worth while. Occasionally a boat would bring in a haul of six hundred pounds.

Marketing, for a boy at least, was not so interesting a part of the performance. After the smallest fishes had been thrown back into the sea, the largest ones were slung on rings or on loops of twin and thus carried to the market at Bethsaida, or to Capharnaum, while good but smaller ones were taken there in baskets or casks. It was probably Simon's unsolicited job to fill these. And if there was anything likely to be more boring, it was the slow scrubbing and scraping of the nets after each expedition – a task that Jonas readily deputed to his two sons and his hired men. A good business, fishing! Everybody ate fish, especially with the sabbath meal. The Jews loved it fresh, dried, pickled, roasted; and they usually washed it down with imported beer, rather than with the wine they drank with meat; so at least the rabbis advised.

The rabbis knew almost everything, it seemed. When Simon was ill, his mother would give him one of their various prescriptions. Some of these sound as if they might have had therapeutic value. Others suggest that even a chosen people could not always escape the influence of neighbouring pagan idolaters, with their magical formulae and other superstitions. One cure for a cold in the head, for instance, was to "pour slowly a quart of the milk of a white goat over three cabbage stalks, keeping the pot boiling, and stirring with a piece of Marmehon wood." Simon's mother would undoubtedly try that rather than the one consisting of "the excrement of a white dog mixed with balsam." In any case, the cold always passed away after it had run its due course.

The rabbinical teachings must not be judged, however, by such aberrations or exaggerations. Their function under the guidance of the High Priests in the Jewish theocracy was to explain and keep alive and pure the knowledge and love of the one true God. And to render better this priceless service to Israel and to the world, the rabbis had established all over Palestine, either in the synagogues or if need be in the open air, a remarkable system of free public schools, where all children of six or over were obliged to study. It was unlawful, in fact, for a family to live where there was no school. Such a place, the rabbis taught, deserved to be destroyed or excommunicated. Undoubtedly, then, Simon attended one of these schools, either, as already suggested, in the white synagogue whose ruins have been found in Capharnaum, or in the open fields near Bethsaida.

If Jewish education tended to become too narrow and rigid in its multiplication of ceremonial precepts and needless prohibitions, it was very comprehensive in another way. The Old Testament, in the hand of a good teacher, offered a compendium not merely of theology, the queen of all sciences, but of rhetoric, history, hygiene, architecture, law, both civil and criminal, and a great deal of the most sublime poetry ever written. What his father had begun with the Torah, the rabbis continued with other books of the Bible. No doubt, too, they examined many fine points too subtle for the mind of Jonas the fisherman. When Moses began the *Book of Genesis*, for example, with the words, "In the beginning God created heaven and earth," why, since there is only one God, did he use the plural form of the word, Elohim, instead of Eli?[2] The rabbis disputed this point endlessly. Why, likewise, did the Lord God say, "Behold, Adam is become as one of us"?[3] This mystery also had remained unsolved thus far, but was faced honestly. Nor would they ever presume to change one iota of the inspired text, not even the "like-a-lion" of Psalm 21.

After the Torah came the far more intricate studies of the *Mischna*, that vast accumulation of commentaries on the traditional or secondary Law, explaining and supplementing the Mosaic Law – the commentaries that in the course of two or three centuries were to become what we know as the *Talmud*. There was already noticeable in this body of man-made legislation a tendency to depart from or to obscure some of the essentials of the Law divinely revealed in the Pentateuch; and to attach more importance to rabbinical commentaries on the Scripture than to the revealed truth itself. The total weight of small observances had already become so overpowering that no Jew could possibly observe it in its entirety.

It is hardly likely, however, that Simon went very far in these higher studies. He had a good solid knowledge of the Law and the Prophets, and could quote them accurately all his life. He probably learned some Greek also, for Hellenism had captivated Jerusalem as well as Rome, and was having no slight effect even in Capharnaum. On the whole, judging from his later words and actions, he could not have been a brilliant student, or one whose parents ever thought seriously of having him trained to be a scribe or a doctor of the Law. It seemed likely enough that he would spend his life as a fisherman on the Sea of Galilee. A good, strong, honest lad, loyal, warm-hearted and dependable, quick to anger and quick to forgive, he probably knew as much at twelve as he would ever need to know. So at least the neighbours thought.

Ritual itself is a powerful teacher. An average boy like Simon was likely to understand and remember the history of his people much better when he saw it re-enacted and commemorated year after year in the great cycle of festivals. Every night during the midwinter feast of the Dedication of the Temple an extra candle was set in the window of each house until there were eight to recall the triumph of Israel over the Assyrians under the lion-hearted Judas Maccabeus; so would the holy flame of Israel expand and fill

---

[2] Gen 1:1
[3] Gen 3:22

the darkness of a sodden world. There was keen fun at the springtime feast of Purim, when they celebrated the deliverance of God's People through Esther. The Passover mood was quite different. All the older people were away, at Jerusalem. The children noticed that there was no leaven in their bread, and eating the paschal lamb prepared with bitter herbs, they learned that it commemorated the awful sacrifice their ancestors had offered to God on the night before they fled from Egypt, while the angel of death struck down the first-born of their persecutors. There was a warm and fragrant smell of summertime in the memory of the Feast of Weeks, when the first and best fruits were dedicated to the Lord, and carried up to Jerusalem in procession. There was something as mysterious and heavy as death in the autumnal solemnities of the New Year, a suggestion of the final accounting man must make to God, of the last judgment of the world, and the closing of the books of destiny forever. Who could forget the day of the Atonement with its stark fasting and dismal music? Yet children always hark back to happy endings; there was the winter feast of Tabernacles to look forward to throughout the year – that fantastic week of revels in thanksgiving for harvests and other blessings, when people lived in leafy booths, and lost themselves in laughter and careless singing.

All this was bound to impress deeply upon the heart of a rather slow honest boy like Simon a sense of dedication, of mystery, which was both consoling and disturbing, and not easy to put into words. Deeply rooted in the consciousness of every Jew was an awareness of belonging in some special manner to the Lord God, as a member of his chosen people. He had promised their ancestor Abraham that his descendants would be as numerous as the sands of the sea; that in his seed all nations should be blessed. To be a Jew was to feel the full force of this promise, and to know that whatever misfortunes might have to be faced – and what miseries had Israel not survived? – God could never forget or withdraw what he had pledged. Under an impression of insecurity, of conflict, of being an exile and a stranger in an unfriendly world, there lived always in the Jewish heart a sort of unquenchable hope. To be an Israelite was like standing on a rock in the midst of fickle winds and a variable sea. But the rock was deeper than the sea, and more lasting than the world, and when the sea dried up, it would still be there.

2

Simon's greatest desire was to see Jerusalem. All his aspirations had been directed toward the place where the only clean and acceptable sacrifice in the whole world was offered to the one true God. The mount of Sion was more than a symbol to him. It was the home, the centre, the beginning and the end of all Hebrew life and thought, the capital of Judaism, the unique doorway to all that was holy and eternal. The dispersion of the children of Israel to the farthest corners of the known earth had done nothing to chill this loyalty. Distance and separation, on the contrary, had warmed it to the point of fanaticism. Jerusalem was an international hub to which millions of Jews came trekking at incredible expense, danger, and inconvenience. Three times a year they offered sacrifices of goats or doves before the Holy of Holies. If possible, they went there to enjoy their Passover lamb with unleavened bread, bitter herbs and red wine. "If I forget you, O Jerusalem, let my right hand be forgotten; let my tongue cleave to my jaws, if I do not remember you."[1] Every Jewish boy could quote it.

It was no common day in Simon's life when at the age of twelve or thirteen he began the adventurous journey he had so long dreamed of. Preparations had been carefully made. The women, if there were any in the party, would be mounted on mules, while the men stalked along beside them; and there would be another mule or ass laden with provisions and clothing, for even in good weather, the caravan would be four or five days on the road. It was only sixty miles, as the crow flies, from Bethsaida to Jerusalem. As a man walks, however, there were two long circuitous routes. The shorter passed through Samaria, west of the Jordan, and then ascended the bleak rocky Judean plateau. But to avoid being insulted if not beaten and robbed by the heretical Samaritans, most Jewish pilgrims from Galilee took the more disagreeable one along the bank of the Jordan.

All the mysterious past of Simon's people seemed to have become woven in some way with the changeful music of this remarkable river, this Swift-Flowing, that divided Palestine in half from north to south as it raced from its source in a cave on snow-capped Mount Hermon, down through the Sea of Galilee, and then,

---

[1] Psalm 136 (137).

ploughing out a deepening gorge in the soft limestone for another hundred miles, widened again into the salty waters of the Dead Sea. Running thus for some thousands of years, an inseparable part of the scenic background of Jewish history, it had cut two beds for itself. The narrower one, the Ghor, was never dry; and it was only seventy-five feet wide in the north, and at most two hundred and twenty-five in the south. Down through this serpentine passage all the year flowed the cream-coloured waters hidden from the road by dense thickets of oleanders, acacias and willows. In the wider bed, the Zor, there were many wheat fields and olive groves where now one sees but stark clumps of *spinae Christi*. Only in the spring, when the waters were swollen by the melting ice of Mount Hermon, did this channel become impassable under a raging flood. Its temperature was tropical, in summer reaching 120-140°F (60-65°C). Seven hundred feet below the Mediterranean at the Sea of Galilee, it dropped to more than thirteen hundred at the Dead Sea.

For two or three days the pilgrims from Bethsaida would slowly make their way, with increasing discomfort from the heat, along the road that skirted the eastern edge of the Zor, sleeping on the higher ground or in wretched little inns where animals were stabled and sometimes offered for sale, until at last they came to a certain ford. Crossing this, picking their way from stone to stone, they left the river bed and followed a road to the west. And soon they saw, rising out of the green plain against the dark cliffs of Mount Quarantania, the ancient city of Jericho, so often lost and won in the wars of Israel. Simon's father told him how its walls fell down before the trumpet blasts of Joshua, and how the sacred Jordan, even in the full flood of the latter rains of April, dried up to allow his army to cross. This was the very spot where the tawny waters rose up like a rampant lion.

A beautiful city, Jericho; but how hot it was even at night under the sultry moon of the nearby desert and the Dead Sea! As the family of Jonas went wondering and gazing through its gates, the tropical air was almost too sweet and heavy to breathe, with its unnamed perfumes of many sorts, some from the matchless rose gardens that lined every street, some from the clumps of myrrh, henna and balsam, that merchants came seeking from afar. Marc Antony had once given those beautiful groves of palms to Cleopatra. Later the princely gift had passed into the keeping of Herod the Tetrarch, who had died there a dozen years ago, alone, miserable, and despised, among the marble columns, the statues, theatres, hippodromes, public edifices and pagan temples he had built. Nothing remains of them. Even then there was something stifling about the place, and the Galileans were glad, no doubt, to leave it behind.

From Jericho they climbed a steep rocky road that wound to the south-east, through a high mountain pass to the uplands of Judea. Now the air was easier to breathe, and the nights especially were cooler. And although the general aspect of the hills was more barren and rugged, the valleys were often chequered with little farms, vineyards, and olive groves, as in Galilee, and some of the slopes were speckled with grey and white, where the lean sheep nibbled their slow way. It was another good day's journey before they came to a certain hilltop where Simon's father, shielding his eyes from the afternoon sun, would point out to him, on a distant eminence, a flash of snowy white, like an angel's finger tipped with fire, pointing to heaven. There it was! That was the Temple of God, standing high above Jerusalem. Yes, it was all of purest marble, and the roof of the Holy of Holies was actually of solid gold.

Passing the village of Bethany and crossing a slope called the Mount of Olives, they soon saw the whole city sprawling on its hills, its domed roofs glistening, its square walls dark and forbidding against the glare of the afternoon sun which shone full in their eyes. Just outside the old walls, on a small rise, there might be seen, as they drew near the gate, a couple of crosses, with human bodies sagging limply from the arms, for it was there that the Roman garrison executed thieves, murderers and such. Then, most likely, and appropriately, too, they would pass through the Fish Gate. Doubtless some of the sea-food on sale came from the waters of Galilee.

Now they found themselves in a bewildering labyrinth of streets, very narrow and twisted, often mounting or descending by stone steps, and honeycombed with shops and bazaars of all kinds. Outside some of these sat artisans finishing their day's work in the meagre light that remained; grave cobblers stitching sandals, and philosophically discussing the affairs of the world; tailors sitting cross-legged in their immemorial posture; wool-combers, flax spinners, metal workers. At this corner or in that little court were movable booths in which grocers or fruiterers were arranging their displays. Hucksters with baskets or push-carts. skilfully manoeuvred their way among the crowds, hawking their wares. Now and then an ass laden with goods would lurch braying between the

narrow walls, or a camel would sway past with grotesque undulating stride.

On certain streets there were more spacious and elegant shops,
where luxuries were sold – rare essences, perfumes, jewels
imported from the East; silk purchased at its weight in gold, purple
wool double-dyed and put out at fantastic prices; exquisite cups and
vases, linens, glassware, clothing of all sorts from Arabia, Persia,
India, Media, Greece, every corner of the Gentile world. A fine lady
could buy anything from a false tooth to an Arabian shawl or a pair
of crystal vases.

It was absorbing for a boy who had never been there before to
observe the variety of faces and of costumes that made their
progress through these ancient thoroughfares. Simon saw devout
Jews in the garb of every land in the world pushing their way
patiently toward the Temple, or stopping to inspect the wares of this
or that bazaar. He marvelled at the babel of so many different
tongues – "Parthians and Medes and Elamites, and inhabitants of
Mesopotamia, of Judea and Cappadocia, of Pontus and Asia and the
country of Libya about Cyrene, and visitors from Rome, Cretans
and Arabians"[2] A Roman legionary, one of those great hulks in
gleaming armour from Pontus or from beyond the Ganges, saunters
by with lazy assurance, helping himself perhaps to a peanut or a
banana from one of the stalls, as he nods patronizingly to the
hucksters. He is the Law, so far as this sodden age is concerned; but
it will not always be so. That dignified man with the quill over his
ear is one of the scribes, perhaps even one of the *Sopherim*. The
people step aside as he sweeps by with his wide robes, and call him
Rabboni; he is a teacher of the Law, an honoured *Chakham* or wise
man of Israel. That is a Levite, a priest empowered to offer
sacrifice. The man with wide phylacteries is a doctor of the Law,
obviously a pharisee. That woman in the chariot must be one of the
idle aristocrats of Jerusalem, being driven through the streets, to the
peril of everyone, by two of her slaves; notice the jewelled spangles
and bracelets on her wrists and ankles, the vague seductive
fragrance that lingers after her exquisitely draped and elaborately
coiffured figure has gone by. Perhaps the fisherman hurries a little
faster with his two sons, so that they will not dwell too long on the
sight of one so different from their mother. What a vast, noisy,
complicated, fascinating thing a city is! It is a stupendous thought
to the visitors from Bethsaida that a quarter of a million people

---

[2] Acts 2:9-11

ordinarily live in Jerusalem; during a great feast there might be a million or more.

The speech of these native Jerusalemites was hard for Simon to understand at first. Most of the upper classes, in those days of Hellenistic impenetration, spoke Greek. The Aramaic of the commoners was rather affected, and quite different from the patois of Jonas and his family. In fact they were not long in town before they became aware that they were objects of curiosity and derision. The Judeans had always looked down on the Galileans. The rabbis and others of the intelligentsia had written many pungent proverbs at their expense. "No prophet comes from Galilee." "Can any good come out of Nazareth?" The rough brogue of Jonas and his sons caused many a smile or wink.

The first concern of the newcomers, however, was food and lodging. These were ordinarily cheap and plentiful, and must have given the Galilean visitors much to think about: even in times of pilgrimages the law of supply and demand was curbed by a system of price-fixing established under the Jewish theocracy. Special inspectors went about the public markets, testing weights and measures, sampling food and drink, and establishing or lowering prices. Now and then, if need be, they would emphasize their decisions with a few judicious blows of a stick over the back of an offending huckster. Wages also were low, but not disproportionately so. For example, an unskilled labourer could earn the equivalent of about fifty pence a day; but with that sum he could purchase seven and a half pounds of good meat, and the revered Rabbi Hillel is said to have supported his family on less than a third of the amount. Corn, wine, fruit, and oil were plentiful. A workman could get himself a small unfurnished lodging for a week at the price of less than one day's labour. The newcomers from Galilee probably fared pretty well, unless they were among the latest arrivals.

On the second day they would inspect the great city in more leisurely fashion. Simon learned that the rich lived on the western hillside in stately marble mansions and villas rising tier after tier among beautiful terraces pied with the colours of many fragrant gardens. That sombre pile of stone with the three high towers, standing far above the spacious flower-beds and walks that surrounded it, was the palace of Herod the Tetrarch, may his name be forgotten. There was the palace of the Maccabees, blessed forever. Yonder was the palace of Ananias the High Priest. That was the Tyropean Bridge, and below it the Valley of the Cheesemongers. More gruesome memories clung about the Valley of Hinnom, where for a century and a half the apostate Jews of old had driven their own children through the flames of Topheth to appease Baal or Moloch. Yet the chief event of the day, naturally, and one never to be forgotten, would be the visit to the Temple.

This was the third Temple which had stood upon that holy ground. Simon's father said that under King Solomon the children of Israel had levelled off Mount Moriah, east of the city, on the very spot where Abraham had prepared to sacrifice his son Isaac, and then for seven years had toiled to raise upon it a fitting house for the Tables of the Law, and the sacrifice that every Jew was obliged to offer three times a year to the Most High. That was nearly a thousand years ago. That first Temple had stood for four centuries until it was destroyed by Nabuchodonosor. When the Israelites returned from their Babylonian captivity some fifty years later, Zorobabel rebuilt it, but much less magnificently, according to those who had seen the Temple of Solomon. Finally, in 19 B.C., a very few years before Simon's birth, King Herod had destroyed it to raise in its stead the incredible splendour that now shed its soft golden light on their faces. It was not yet finished, in fact: eighteen thousand workmen, hardly noticeable in its vastness, were still engaged upon it. But it was complete enough to lend some weight to the boast of Herod that he had exceeded the magnificence of Solomon.

Simon went slowly with his father and a host of other pilgrims, a few carrying goats and lambs purchased on the Mount of Olives or elsewhere, through the South Gate of the Temple. Presently he found himself on a huge rectangular platform called the Court of the Gentiles. Through this, under the watchful eyes of the guards on the four corner towers, the pilgrims followed a great semi-circular path to the north side, until they passed, through another gate, into that part of the edifice reserved for Jews alone. At a market just inside or close at hand they could purchase doves, goats, or lambs for the sacrifice, if they had not done so before; but they had to pay also a small fee for inspection.

Some of the poor pilgrims and the Galileans grumbled at the prices. Indeed, the temple hucksters managed at times to raise them outrageously; once, for example, they hawked the cost of two pigeons to a Roman gold denar, until a member of Hillel's family intervened and forced it down again to a quarter of a silver denar. A favourite charity of rich Jews was to pay for the sacrifices of the poor. On a certain occasion when the greedy merchants had left the Temple court almost without beasts, Rabbi Baba ben Buta out-witted them by driving in 3000 sheep, thus breaking the market so that the commoners might fulfil their obligations.

Seated at many tables on the Porch of Solomon, certain alert and hard-faced men were busily exchanging the currency of various countries into half-shekels of the sanctuary, for the payment of the annual tax. For this service they charged a fee of one *mash*, or from ten and a half to twelve percent of the amount that each Jew was obliged to contribute for the up-keep of the Temple. Naturally there was plenty of murmuring. Often over the clattering of coins arose the clash of angry voices.

As Simon and his father left this uninspiring scene behind, they mounted flight after flight of broad marble stairs to the inner courts, past a sign threatening death to any Gentile who might dare invade that holy place. There was one extraordinarily majestic doorway called the Beautiful Gate or the Gate of Nikanor, all covered with Corinthian brass; here it was that the Levites stood to blow their long trumpets when the sacrifices were about to begin. It was through this gate, too, that the pilgrims entered the Court of Women, on the east side of the Temple, and thence trooped on to the upper and holier places. On the way Simon saw the room for the purification of lepers and Nazarites, the one containing the sacri-ficial oils and wines, the storehouses for wood used in burnt offerings, and the apartment where the High Priest bathed and vested himself.

Perhaps he was even fortunate enough to catch a glimpse of that august person in all his magnificence, a little horn on his brow, the striped ephod on his breast. At that time he was one Annas, or more properly Ananos, son of Seth, and he had just recently been appointed. How holy he must be! The golden bells and pomegran-ates on the fringes of his blue seamless tunic represented thunder and lightning. The twelve rich stones that hung from the ephod stood for the tribes of Israel; and his fine linen mitre was girded by a crown graven with the Name of Names.

If the outer courts of the Temple had left the boy from Galilee almost breathless with wonder, they were nothing compared to the inner and higher portion that arose in a rectangular mass of marble, sternly undecorated and severe, to the flat roof of gold glistening far above. It was this building, the very one he had glimpsed from a distance intercepting the sunlight, that housed the Sanctuary, the Holy Place, and the Holy of Holies. Simon never looked at it without emotion. No matter how often he saw it, he wondered how human hands could have set such massive blocks one upon another.

And now just outside the Sanctuary door he could see the smoke rising from the stone altar where lambs, goats, or doves had been offered to the Most High God. At one corner of this, on the backs of several brass oxen gleaming like dull yellowish fire, was a basin called the Molten Sea or the Brazen Sea, containing water in which the priests washed their hands and feet. Just beyond, and facing the cast, a massive double door of wild olive wood led to the Sanctuary, where the Tables of the Law were kept. Over this door hung a tremendous veil of which Simon's father had plenty to tell him. Woven craftily of the choicest wool in the world in various rich colours, thick as the palm of a man's hand, it was so long and heavy that it took three hundred priests to hang or rearrange it. How could anyone have embroidered that tremendous bunch of grapes that stood out from its surface in rich purple – grapes, the symbols of Israel, and each grape the size of a man! Here was the goal of all the 210,000 persons who at such times crowded into the Temple courts; here was the end, the crown, the purpose of all that vision of snowy white and glittering gold that rose out of a morning sea of mist, terrace upon terrace and pillar after pillar, to where blood was poured out in homage to the Creator of all life, and smoke, like a prayer made white and visible, curled into the vast blue of his sky, as if from the hands and hearts of all his people.

Only priests could enter that Sanctuary, and the High Priest himself poured the sacrificial blood there but once a year. Yet we may be sure that Simon soon learned from his father what was in the sacred and terrible seclusion beyond the gates of wild-olive wood. It was divided into two parts. In the Holy Place stood the Golden Candlestick and the Table of Showbread. On the further side of the Altar of Incense, behind a heavy double veil of rare and beautiful stuffs, was the Holy of Holies. This contained nothing, in the second Temple, but the *Ebhen Shethiyal* or Foundation Rock, on which the Mosque of Omar now rises. It covered the mouth of the pit; and the world itself, according to ancient Hebrew tradition, was founded upon it.

Simon's heart glowed and exulted. It was a great thing to be a Jew.

3

It was probably his brother who first drew his attention to certain anomalies at Jerusalem. The New Testament does not indicate which was the elder, but it does suggest that Andrew exerted no small moral influence over the impetuous Simon. He spoke less, but to the point. He was more prudent, more thoughtful, more circumspect, more observing, always peering beneath surfaces or behind appearances to find the essential truth. I think of him as darker and taller, with piercing eyes that were both gentle and alert; of Simon as heavier, more rugged, with the freckles, the wider nose and coarser mouth that commonly go with reddish sandy hair. This is imagination, not history. Yet there must have been some such contrast.

It was probably Andrew, rather than Simon, who asked their father about the building that thrust its dark ugly bulk so intrusively against the north-east corner of the Temple just outside its walls, like a blotch against its beauty. And if there was not a scowl of resentment or derision on the face of Jonas the fisherman as he told what he knew about it, he was not as well informed as a good Jew should have been after so many visits to Jerusalem. It was easy enough for the inquisitive Andrew to find out, either from him or from others, all he needed to know about the Citadel Antonia, and to pass on the information to his brother. They knew that within its gloomy and forbidding walls, on foreign and unholy ground, the upstart Pontius Pilate, proconsul of the Roman Caesar, carried on the real business of ruling Judea, while the High Priests, reduced to the ignominy of accepting their appointments from a Gentile and ungodly power, clung only to shadows and remnants of authority.

It was a long story and rather confusing. The citadel had been erected by the first King Herod. True, he had built the new Temple also, but so far as he was concerned, it was all one. Had he not raised marble shrines also to the Roman Lord of the World and his false gods, who were devils? He had rebuilt the house of Jehovah only because it pleased his vanity, or because he wished to convince his enemies, the pharisees, that he was a true Jew, or because he was superstitious, or because, according to one story, he was advised to do it by the astute Baba ben Buta, to make people forget his crimes. These were notorious enough, and so numerous that the slaughter of the innocents of Bethlehem seems to have been swallowed up in their enormity. The historian Josephus says nothing of it, and Jonas the fisherman may not have heard of it in far-away Bethsaida. But all good men had heard of the judicial murder of the two brave rabbis and their forty fellow patriots at Jericho. Everyone knew that Herod was some sort of ill omen to Israel. And yet in a way he might be a good one, too.

This Herod, Andrew discovered, was the son of the wily Idumean Antipater, who had climbed to power on the weaknesses of the High Priest Hyrcanus, plus the fortunes of war. He had placed himself at the disposal of Julius Caesar, who in turn made him Procurator of Judea. The old fox then had his son appointed Governor of Galilee, at the age of twenty-five.

Herod, like his father, was intelligent, crafty, cruel, insatiably ambitious and wholly unscrupulous, respecting nothing but power. And seeing that Rome now ruled the world, he set out to ingratiate himself with the masters of that new Babylon. The feat demanded much dexterity as the imperium passed from one contending hand to another. But Herod was both skilful and lucky. As one patron fell, he would attach himself to the successful rival with satisfactory explanations and bribes. He became the henchman of Cassius. After Philippi he gave huge gifts to Marc Antony, who accordingly made him Tetrarch of Judea. Not content with that, Herod went boldly to Rome, where he persuaded Antony and Octavius to have him crowned King of Judea, and walked between them to the Temple of Jupiter to thank the gods of Rome for the honour. Though a particular friend of Antony, he immediately won the approval of Octavius after the fall of the great lover at Actium. And by the favour of this first Augustus, as well as by certain adroit and brutal murders, he became King of the Jews in fact as well as in name.

It was not merely because he was a foreigner or even a tyrant that his subjects hated him so intensely. It was because, as the willing creature of the Lord of the world, he seemed almost the personification of that obscene blasphemy on the Tiber. The Roman eagles were particularly detestable to Jews as the symbols of the vile worship of Caesar, a puny creature of the one true Creator. Not even the magnificence of the Temple Herod had restored could obliterate this fact from the minds of devout Jews. It was true that they were proud of the building itself, and many seemed glad to have such splendour and beauty on any terms. Perhaps it did not occur to them that they were paying a high price for what must have been, on Herod's part at least, a syncretistic insult to the Most High whom he ranked with Jupiter and Astarte. But God himself had permitted this for reasons of his own. And the two rabbis who plucked the eagles off the great gate of the Temple became heroes in Israel forever, all the more so after they and their forty brave accomplices were burned to death by order of Herod. He was dying at the time in his palace at Jericho; and when life departed from his putrid body, the Jews observed the day as a *Yom Tobh, a* joyful holiday on which no mourning was permitted.

That was about when young Simon was born. Now a son of Herod, known as Herod Antipas, was ruling; a man just as corrupt as his father, and more sodden and stupid.

Yet there was an element of hope, too, in the ascendancy of the Herodian house. For the first time in Jewish history, a non-Jew had become ruler of Judea. The scriptural significance of that fact had not been overlooked, particularly among the Nationalists, who were most numerous and influential in Galilee, for it recalled a famous Messianic prediction. Simon must have heard it first from his father's lips as a lad of six or seven. In fact almost any Jewish boy could quote the striking words spoken hundreds of years earlier by the dying Jacob:

"The sceptre shall not be taken away from Judah, nor a ruler from his thigh, till he come that is to be sent, and he shall be the expectation of nations, tying his foal to the vineyard, and his ass, O my son, to the vine. He shall wash his robe in wine, and his garment in the blood of the grape. His eyes are more beautiful than wine, and his teeth whiter than milk."[1]

Puzzling as some of these expressions were, even to the most learned rabbis and doctors, it was obvious that they referred to the Messiah, the Son of the woman who, by God's promise to Eve, would tread upon the serpent's head, the prophet Moses said must be obeyed under pain of death, the Son of David, the Prince of Peace, the Anointed of God, the Holy One. There were at least four hundred and fifty-six explicit references in the Old Testament to the great Deliverer whom God would send his people in his good time.[2] All the later prophecies especially, had pointed with insistence toward One who would come to save not only Israel but all men who might be willing to receive him.

Certainly there was need of him everywhere, and especially in Palestine. For in Jewish public and private life these many years

[1] Gen 49:10-12

[2] Edersheim, *Life and Times of Jesus the Messiah,* II p.710 *et seq.*

there had been evident, under Hellenistic and other pagan influences, a rapid deterioration, an increasing moral and intellectual
confusion. Yet this very fact gave new hope to a few persons of
deep spiritual insight. Was it not in the blackest hour that one might
look for the first hint of dawn? Had it not been always when Israel
most needed help that God had stretched forth his almighty hand to
lift his people and to crush their foes? There were a handful indeed,
who insisted that the exact period of time foretold by the prophet
Daniel had elapsed, and that the Messiah must therefore have been
born. Most doctors, however, refused to take this seriously as
coming from a Jew of the diaspora to whom they would not con-
cede the name of prophet, and because the language of the
prophecy clearly implied what seemed to them incredible: the
abasement and death of the Holy One.

Andrew was keenly interested in everything he could learn
concerning the Messiah. He knew all the most famous prophecies
concerning him. The most striking of these appeared to indicate
from our perspective of the Old Testament,

(i) that he would be born of a virgin[3]

(ii) in Bethlehem of Judea[4]

(iii) when the sceptre passed from Juda[5]

(iv) after the number of years specified by Daniel;[6]

(v) he would be the One that Moses had commanded the
Israelites to hear under pain of destruction;[7]

(vi) he would establish an eternal kingdom and rule with great
power and glory, in which his people would share;[8] yet

(vii) he would be despised, misunderstood, mocked, tortured,
and shamefully put to death like a felon.[9]

Hundreds of more perplexing passages were accepted as having
some reference to Him, though interpretations differed widely.
There was a line in Zachariah, for example:

"And they weighed for my wages thirty pieces of silver."[10]

Wise rabbis took this to mean that the Messiah would hand
down thirty precepts to Israel. They also gave figurative explanations

---

[3] Is 7:7
[4] Mic 5:2. The Talmud also gives Bethlehem.
[5] Gen 49:10-12
[6] Dan 9:25-26
[7] Deut 18:18, 19
[8] Is 9:6, 7
[9] *ibid* 3; Zach 13:6; Ps 21 etc.
[10] Zach 11:12

of certain other statements by the same prophet: "They shall look upon me, whom they have pierced, and they shall mourn for him as one mourns for an only son ... and they shall say to him: What are these wounds in the midst of your hands? And he shall say, With these I was wounded in the house of them that loved me."[11] Such expressions were held almost unanimously to refer to the Messianic age to come, and the sufferings were believed to be those from which the Jewish people would be then delivered by their glorious king. Similar theories were advanced to explain the curious reference in Psalm 117 to "The stone which the builders rejected, the same is become the head of the corner."

Whether Andrew went this far in his messianic studies does not appear; probably not. The more abstruse and difficult passages were commonly left to long-bearded exegetes who enjoyed delving deeply into old words and multiplying hair-splitting distinctions. That process led some to wisdom; but most Jews, including most rabbis and doctors, were content to follow the human path of least resistance, and to stress what was so evident on page after page of the Sacred Scriptures: the glory, the power, and the triumph of the Messiah to come. It seems not to have occurred to any of them that he might have two advents. It was far easier to envisage another great warrior and ruler, successor and descendant of King David, who would drive the Roman swine from the Holy Land at the sword's point, and lay down the Law to all the lesser breeds round about, even to the far corners of the earth. Some went so far as to fancy that physical nature would partake in his triumphs. The ground would sparkle with gold and precious gems. The lush wheat would grow as tall as the trees.

From the later words and acts of Simon bar Jonas, it is plain that his conception of the Messiah, as he advanced toward manhood, was that of the vast majority of the Jewish people. Few could imagine the Holy One coming to suffer in atonement for the sins of the world, much less for the sins of Israel. Everyone knew that Moses had been punished for disobedience, that the Babylonian captivity had been the penalty for connivance with idolatry. Yet the old sense of sinfulness had yielded to a certain proud complacency, born in part, no doubt, of an awareness of very real virtues. The Jewish leaders forgot that they were a chosen people not through any special excellence of their own, but through God's favour to Abraham. This sort of smugness easily takes possession of classes

---

[11] *ibid* 12:10; 13:6.

long established in wealth and power.

The doctrine of original sin in particular had been almost wholly forgotten in Israel. True, it still stood boldly forth on the first pages of the Book of Genesis. This makes it all the more astonishing that no one preached it, and hardly any believed it. Perhaps their recent sorrows had made the Jews forget the primal tragedy which was the beginning of human history. Perhaps the vision of towering wheat-fields had little by little come to blot out of their minds the memory of the tree of knowledge, the locked garden, the flaming sword. A future woven out of hopeful dreams had become more real than a past as aching and tangible as the rocks of Judea.

It is a curious fact that this sort of idealizing is sometimes the very stuff of which materialists are made. It is because they love this world, its satisfactions and its power, that they turn away from its imperfections to an imaginary world in which they want those gratifications to be fully realized – but in the flesh, in the here and now. Only a mystery of grace could turn such mundane aspirations into a spiritual hope. Yes, Simon was very human; he was probably a typical young Jew of his time, honest, stalwart, affectionate, courageous, more than a little earthy. He probably gave less thought to the Messiah than Andrew did; and in such dreams as his more practical mind allowed him to cherish there must have been a stronger element of the personal and the selfish. The king of the Jews, if he appeared, would have need of the strong right arm, the keen eyes, the slow but steady brain, the clumsy but forthright speech of Simon bar Jonas. Humble men in Israel had risen to high places before now, without yielding to the corruption of such self-made potentates as Antipater and Herod.

Of such matters as these he and Andrew must have talked often on their journey back to Bethsaida and the shores of Galilee after the great feast at Jerusalem. It was probably Simon who did most of the talking. These were great times, and one can imagine him saying that he did not intend to be the slave of wind and water forever, like his father.

4

Simon did settle down to be a fisherman, after all. He was now a full grown man, of medium height, thick-set, powerful, with ruddy sunburned skin that emphasized, one imagines, the blue-grey of his frank but changeful eyes. Something of the sort is suggested, at least, in the earliest known representation of him in art, a bronze medallion of the early part of the second century. It shows him with a sturdy roundish head, pugnacious jaw-bones, a receding forehead such as poets and soldiers often have, and the thick bushy curly hair and beard that is likely to be dark auburn; a type not uncommon among Jews even to this day. It is interesting, too, though not historically conclusive, to learn that a mystic and stigmatic of our own time, Thérèse Neumann of Konnersreuth, 'saw' Simon, in some of her remarkable visions of 1926, without the bushy beard that artists have bestowed on him; her impression was that he had a rather sparse one. She noticed a way he had of drawing his right hand through his close-cropped hair whenever he was excited or disturbed, and of speaking vehemently, with vigorous gestures.[1] Devout though he was in his own way, he lost his temper rather easily, and like most workmen of the time, could curse and swear now and then.[2] Just a good average fisherman; and watching his lusty arms tug at the oars or hoist a heavy basket of fish to one of his knotty shoulders, one might hazard a guess that he would always be a fisherman.

He was married early to a Capharnaum girl. This seems likely from the fact that he went to live in that place, perhaps in the home of his bride's parents, or in one that they gave her for a wedding present. After a while his brother Andrew went to live with them, and the two young men continued their father's occupation on the Sea of Galilee, long after his death.

Capharnaum was much more of a place than Bethsaida. Made up of many elements, Galilean, Jewish, Greek, Roman, it was a cosmopolitan miniature of Palestinian life on the northwest shore of the sea, about two miles from where the Jordan tumbles into it. The

---

[1] *Thérèse Neumann, a Stigmatist of our Day,* by Friedrich Ritter Von Lama, Milwaukee, 1929, pp. 131, 132, 134. There is no intention to anticipate the decision as to the authenticity of these visions. They are referred to only as aids to vizualization.

[2] This seems a fair inference from Matt 26:74; Mark 14:71

air was soft, sweet, and tropical, and there were magnificent views all about: the blue waters of Galilee, sparkling away for thirteen miles to the south; the snow-capped peak of Hermon far to the north; the fertile plain of Gennesareth, chequered with farms and dotted with villages; the forests on the western horizon. Near the town bubbled a noted spring said to have its source in Egypt, since it bred fishes like those of the Nile.

If any vestige of that doomed prosperity survives, it is the black basalt foundation and door lintel of its white synagogue, supposed to have been unearthed beneath the ruins of the later village of *Tell Hum*. This hallowed edifice, solid and austere by the water's edge near the wharves and warehouses, was the spiritual if not geographical centre of hundreds of homes that went up in irregular, gleaming rows to the top of a prime slope ending in a wooded ridge half a mile away. One of those red tiled roofs sheltered the family of a good centurion, head of the Roman garrison, who had earned the affection of his Jewish neighbours by building their house of prayer. Another marked the residence of his friend Jairus, the well-to-do synagogue-ruler, and his twelve-year-old daughter. A less respected citizen, was one Levi, son of Alpheus, who served Caesar as a publican or tax-collector. Every day he could be seen sitting in the custom house near the shore, taking in the shekels and half-shekels; and people spat as they passed him by. Somewhat nearer the lake front, probably, lived Simon bar Jonas with his bride and her mother. After a while, for some reason (perhaps the death of his own parents) Andrew made his home with them.

Yet nothing can be said of the life of this little family save the most obvious conjectures that the bare facts suggest. Simon in the strength of his manhood knew something of the companionship of woman. He may have learned how inextricably two hearts and minds can become entangled through joy, through sorrow, about the tenuous life of a child. Perhaps his wife was delicate; the best opinion certainly is that she died not many years after their marriage, possibly in childbirth. But this, and all else in their brief union – the death of their baby, perhaps, and the aching questions and sad answers that bring rebellion, or faith and resignation – all this is left untold. Indeed the very existence of his wife has to be inferred from the brief Gospel reference to his mother-in-law, with whom he and Andrew were still living when the light of history first fell upon them. Simon was no longer young. Though nothing could ever

quite subdue his energetic and hopeful nature, he was often sad and
lonely, and depended more and more upon the changeful sea, and
on the comradeship of his brother and the sons of Zebedee.
Andrew had lost none of his interest in messianic studies. He
was constantly on the watch for any sign of the Holy One who had
been promised. He was keenly interested one day when he heard
that a remarkable man had begun to preach in the wastelands north
of the salty hot shores of the Dead Sea. After that no one saw him
in Capharnaum or Bethsaida for several days; while he found his
way to that ancient desert where the few remaining trees grew
gnarled and stunted among huge skull-like boulders that seemed to
have been blasted by fire from heaven; where even the wild beasts
had a starved and sickly look. When Andrew returned he was a
changed man, thinner and less of the earth than ever. Yet he was
full of enthusiasm for a prophet called John, who baptized people
with water on the bank of the lower Jordan. Andrew told Simon that
this John had suddenly appeared in the wilderness of Judea, as if
from nowhere, in that autumn of the year we call A.D. 28.[3] About
thirty years of age, he was of levitical ancestry on both sides, for his
father was the priest Zachary, and his mother Elizabeth was
descended from Aaron. He began talking to stray shepherds,
travellers, brigands, fugitives, whoever would hear, and the burden
of his preaching was, "Repent! For the kingdom of heaven is at
hand."

People listened and told others. And such was his power that
some said he was a prophet, and many went out to him from the
nearest villages across the river. Neither in speech nor in dress did
he resemble the Essenes and other ascetics who lived alone in the
deserts. He wore only a piece of camel's hair bound at the waist
with a thong of leather. He ate the food of the most wretched of the
Palestinian poor, dried powdered locusts baked into a coarse bread,
and wild honey.[4] Gaunt, emaciated, almost black from the sun, with
eyes that bored through his hearers and somehow made them feel
ashamed of themselves, he exerted an influence that spread from
hut to hut and from village to village, until people from all parts of
Judea were going out to be baptized by him and to confess their
sins. Some of the sophisticated of Jerusalem began to appear among

---

[3] It was the fifteenth year of Tiberius: Luke 3:1-3. The testimony of Josephus as to
John's mission is impressive, all the more so as he does not mention its relation to
Christ's (*Antiquities*, XVIII, 5).
[4] Matt 3:4; Mark 1:6.

the mobs that followed him; and men like Andrew, from as far away as Capharnaum in Galilee. Many seemed frightened as they heard him thunder the mighty words of the Prophet Isaiah:

A voice of one crying in the desert:
"Prepare the road for the Lord,
Make his paths straight,
Let every gully be filled up,
And every hill and knoll be brought low,
And let the crooked places be straightened out,
And the rough roads smoothed;
And all flesh shall see the salvation of God."[5]

Andrew told Peter he would have to see the grief and fervour of the crowds for himself. They were unbelievable.

"What are we to do?" they asked. "Master, what must we do?"

"Let him who possesses two coats share with him who has none," replied John. "And let him who has food do likewise."

According to Andrew, he baptized some publicans with the rest, saying, "Exact no more than what is prescribed for you." There were even Roman soldiers in the crowd, who said, "And we – what must we do?" And John warned them to avoid brutal intimidation, false accusations against civilians, discontent with their pay.[6]

A few months later Simon learned from his brother that the Baptizer had moved farther up the Jordan, to a place near the ford and village of Bethabara on the left bank. By this time many northern men were to be seen among his disciples; and Andrew bar Jonas was missing more often from his boat and from the fishing mart. He was not the only one from the sea. Another disciple was a young man named Philip, from Bethsaida. People were beginning to say, even in the remote villages of Galilee, that John must be the great prophet foretold by Moses and the others. He must be the Messiah; he must be the Christ, the Holy One of God.

Simon probably asked his brother about this, and learned that it was not true. John himself had denied it most emphatically. He was not the prophet, he declared, but his precursor. He was the one of whom Malachiah had written.

"Behold, I send my messenger before your face,
Who shall prepare the road for you."[7]

He was that voice crying in the desert, of whom Isaiah had

---

[5] Is 40:3
[6] Luke 33:11-14
[7] Mal 3:1-3

prophesied. "There is coming after me," he cried, "One mightier than I, whose sandal strap I am not worthy to stoop down and untie. I baptize you with water, but he shall baptize you with the Holy Spirit."[8]

If all this reached the ears of Simon in Galilee, it is not surprising that it finally commanded the attention of the chief priests and leading pharisees at Jerusalem. These men, always sensitive to any possible threat to their power and influence, were interested enough to send some priests, Levites and scribes all the way to the desert where the Baptizer was preaching. Some of the sceptics known as sadducees also investigated on their own account. Neither group took seriously the popular theory that John himself might be the messiah; what sort of messiah would that be? But the assurance with which he announced that the Holy One was about to appear made them curious to hear what else he would say. They were not left long in doubt. As they gazed on the half-naked prophet with contempt and derision, John steadily returned their scrutiny, and then said:

"You breed of vipers! Who has warned you to flee from the coming wrath? Produce, then, fruit worthy of repentance, and do not presume to say to yourselves, 'We have Abraham for a father.'"

So at least it was reported in Capharnaum by Andrew and by John, the son of Zebedee, who later wrote down most of the conversation. Simon could hardly fail to be astonished, perhaps a little bit pleased. What, he called the pharisees a breed of vipers! That was striking home with a vengeance at the spiritual pride that everyone knew was their worst fault. And how did the agents of the pharisees take it? First they were speechless with surprise and anger while John rushed on: "For I tell you that God is able to raise up children to Abraham out of these stones. But the axe already lies at the root of the trees; every tree, therefore, not producing good fruit shall be cut down and thrown on the fire. I indeed baptize you with water to lead you unto penance, but the one who comes after me is mightier than I; his sandals I am not worthy to carry," he repeated. "He shall baptize you in the Holy Spirit and fire. His winnowing-fan is in his hand, and he will thoroughly cleanse his threshing-floor, and gather his wheat into the granary; but he will burn up the chaff with unquenchable fire."[9]

Yes, Andrew and John reported in the fishing mart, those were

---

[8] Mark 1:7-8
[9] Matt 3:7-12

the very words of the Prophet, spoken to some of the most important men from Jerusalem.

"Who are you?" they demanded, when they had recovered from the first shock.

"I am not the Christ!"

"What then? Are you Elijah?" Everyone knew that Elijah had never died, and would return one day for a special mission.

"I am not," said John.

"Are you *The Prophet*?" Evidently they did not consider the Prophet of Moses identical with the Christ.

No.

"Who are you, so that we may give an answer to those who sent us. What do you say of yourself?"

"I am a voice of one crying in the desert: 'Make the road of the Lord level,' as the Prophet Isaiah said."

"Why then do you baptize if you are not the Christ, nor Elijah, nor the Prophet?"

"I baptize with water," John repeated once more; "but in the midst of you is standing one whom you know not – he who comes after me, whose sandal-strap I am not worthy to undo." [10]

The pharisees spurned the baptism of John[11] and went away muttering that he was mad, and possessed by a devil. Andrew probably witnessed that strange duel. It is on record, certainly, that he was present on the still more eventful day following. He could hardly wait to get back to Capharnaum to tell Simon about it. He burst into the house, exclaiming:

"We have found the Messiah! Simon, we have found the Messiah!" And he told what had occurred:

On the day after the heckling of John by the pharisees, the crowd had seen him point to a man of about his own age who was approaching him, and had heard him cry, in a voice not to be forgotten:

"Behold the Lamb of God, who takes away the sins of the world!"

The young rabbi, for his long robes of reddish brown indicated that such he was, asked to be baptized. The crowd saw John protesting and expostulating.

"I need to be baptized by you!" he said; "and yet you come to me?"

---

[10] John 1:19-27

[11] It was to this that Christ attributed their blindness: Luke 7:30

"Permit it now," said the rabbi, in a voice that everyone heard, "for so it becomes us to fulfil all righteousness."

John then took him down to the water's edge, and baptized him. Everyone felt that something tremendous was happening. Afterwards John said that as He ascended from the water, he beheld the Spirit come down from heaven in the form of a dove, and it remained upon Him.

"This is the One," he cried, "of whom I said, 'After me is coming a Man who takes rank before me, because he existed before me.' And I myself did not know him; but I came baptizing with water to this purpose – that he might be manifested to Israel ... he who sent me to baptize with water, he said to me, 'He upon whom you shall see the Spirit descending and remaining upon him, he is the one who baptizes with the Holy Spirit.' And I myself have seen, and have given my evidence, that this is the Son of God."[12]

At that moment many noticed what sounded like thunder. Some heard a distinct voice above, saying, "This is my beloved son, in whom I am well pleased."

Andrew said that the man thus pointed out as the messiah, the long-awaited Christ, was called Jesus, and had come up from Nazareth in Galilee, where he had worked with a carpenter named Joseph, apparently his father. Through his mother Mary he was a first cousin of the Baptizer; however, they had never met before.

One day not long after this, Andrew returned to tell Simon a tale even more astonishing. He and John, the son of Zebedee, were standing in conversation with the precursor when they saw Jesus gravely walking toward them. The Baptizer pointed to him and repeated his previous words: "Behold the Lamb of God! Behold him who takes away the sin of the world!" Andrew for some reason believed this, he said, and he and his companion left the Baptizer and followed Jesus. There was something about him that made it almost impossible not to do so. After he had gone a little distance from the crowd, he turned and gazed at them. He must have been terribly gaunt, for he had recently fasted forty days in the desert.

"What is it you seek?" he asked.

"Rabbi," one of them faltered, "where do you stay?"

"Come, and you shall see," he said. And turning, he strode silently on.

The two fishermen followed until they saw him stop at the place of his abode – whether in some little house in the village or in

---

[12] John 1:30-34

some wild retreat outdoors among the rocks and thistles, the Gospel does not tell us. It does say that they remained with him until four o'clock in the afternoon.[13] And what he said left them without the slightest doubt that he was the Christ.

All this Andrew told, breathlessly, to his brother Simon in Capharnaum. "We have found the messiah," he repeated. "We have found Christ!" Simon must come and see for himself without delay.

Simon may have been incredulous at first, but now he believed it to be true. Something in the wild beating of his own heart, besides the assurance of Andrew, told him that it must be true. The two set out, probably the first thing the next morning, for Bethabara, perhaps sailing down the length of the lake and leaving their boat on the southern shore while they struck across the bleak and rocky wilderness. Even so, it was a journey of three or four days at least before Simon saw the wide yellow salty lower Jordan, and further south, the cadaverous hills by the Dead Sea, like skulls picked clean by crows and vultures. Either that day or the next he arrived at the place that Andrew had told him about. And then he found himself face to face for the first time with Jesus the Christ.

What did the Lord look like to this fisherman, a few years his senior, who gazed at him with something of diffidence, hope, fear, curiosity, a tense awareness that a decisive force beyond his power to understand had come into his life? To the average Jew of his time Jesus probably looked like any other young rabbi, with a seamless woollen robe, somewhat longer than others wore, a short beard, earnest probing eyes. There could have been nothing in his appearance to suggest to the ordinary observer (unless that observer received a secret inner spiritual assurance of the fact) that here before him was infinite immensity enclosed in vulnerable human flesh, omnipotence bound with a simple girdle under a twisted turban, the eternal Word that leapt down from heaven, in the prophetic words of the Book of Wisdom, "while all things were in quiet silence, and the night was in the midst of her course," to submit to the shackles of time and place. This was obviously hidden from the many, else all Israel would immediately have recognized and accepted him, if only from motives of self-interest. Even corrupt men would have purchased gratis the gift that must be paid for with humility, sincerity and love. Plainly this did not occur.

Not a word describing our Lord has been left by any of the four evangelists. This silence in itself is a sort of description,

---

[13] John 1:35-39.

suggesting an ineffable and majestic presence which had an overpowering effect at times on both friends and foes. Yet at other moments he seemed so ordinary in his humanity that men did not hesitate to lay violent hands upon him. An old Christian tradition makes him just six feet tall. Some hints of the possible outlines of his face remain imprinted in the remarkable image on the Holy Shroud of Turin, and on the veil of Veronica in Rome; and it is a curious fact that while these naturally differ in detail when filled in by artists, the general dimensions are identical – the lean face long, powerful, beautifully chiselled and proportioned, the fine long high-bridged nose, the well-set eyes, the short square beard on a strong chin. Still, it must be significant that the saints who have been allowed to see the sacred humanity in visions have made little or no attempt at concrete description. Saint Teresa of Avila could only report that he gave her the impression of beauty beyond words, and of overpowering compassion and understanding. Yet "although I desired extremely to know the colour of his eyes, or how tall he was, so that I should be able to tell it, yet I never deserved to see it, nor was it any use for me to try to do so, lest I lose the vision altogether."[14]

All that Simon knew, as he looked into that face for the first time, was that he revered and loved this man as he had never revered and loved anybody. And before he could say anything, Jesus looked deeply into his eyes, and said:

"You are Simon the son of Jonas. You shall be called Kepha." Kepha meant "Rock"; in Latin "Petrus"; in English "Peter."

It was only years later that Simon Peter could write of "the ineffable and blissful delight"[15] of beholding the Christ. It is doubtful whether he then fully understood the significance of the moment, or the two natures of the man who was speaking to him. But he did feel in Jesus some quality he had never before encountered in any human being. It was something at once terrifying and reassuring, devastating and exalting, a scathing reproach and an infinite delight and consolation. It made one ready to forsake everything – work, pleasure, ambition, life itself – and follow this man wherever he might lead.

It may be, indeed it is likely, that Simon did not think of him at first as the Lord God, or the Son of God, the creator of all life, who had said to Moses from the burning bush, "I AM!" and had put

---

[14] *Life*, chap 19, 2
[15] Pet 1:9

words into the mouths of all his prophets. This conception of the Messiah had been lost by most of the Jews, and what remained was rather vague and often contradictory. Yet he was convinced that this was the Messiah, whatever the word might imply or connote. Here before him stood the great prophet promised by Moses. This was the deliverer of Israel of whom all the prophets had written.

Without the slightest hesitation, then, Simon Peter and his brother Andrew, with John the son of Zebedee, and Philip and Nathanael of Bethsaida, followed the Lord wherever he went. Having accomplished what he had gone to Bethabara to do, he left the desert country almost at once and walked north into the high land of Galilee. The five kept at his heels, or walked beside him, diffidently asking questions and pondering on the answers. Probably they helped themselves to corn, olives, fruit, or vegetables from fields along the way, wherever there were any, as the wilderness fell away in the distance behind them.

A few miles south of the Sea of Galilee they forded the Jordan and followed a road that skirted the southern slope of Mount Tabor until it joined the main highway running from the east through Nazareth to Acco on the Mediterranean. A constant stream of traffic was on the move there. Camel trains packed with rare and precious stuffs from Damascus, from as far as the Black Sea and India, must have passed the group of humble and earnest men as they talked along the way. Imperial chariots and the beautiful horses of sheikhs from Arabia thundered dustily by.

On the third day they could pause at a certain high place and behold an astonishing panorama. At the east rose the wooded bulk of Tabor. At the south rolled the plain of Esdraelon, often the battlefield of Israel, where Armageddon will be fought in the Last Days. At the north, beyond many villages sparkling among the hills and vales that Solomon sang of, were the hollows of the Jordan and the Sea of Galilee, and beyond them the snowy peaks of Hermon. At the west was the purple crest of Carmel where Elijah vanished in a flash of fire, and on clear days one saw a yellow line of beach and the glitter of the great sea.

In between these ancient and holy landmarks were fifteen lower hills that formed almost a circle around a sort of natural amphitheatre; and on the triangular spur of one of them, in the midst of green hills and dales some twelve hundred feet above sea-level, lay a little town of white houses with flat roofs, nestling on terraces and knolls among tall and feathery palms, the grey and silver sheen of many olive trees, the darker foliage of vineyards, figs, and orange groves, the brilliant tropical hues of flower gardens. Simon Peter knew this place as well as his companions did, and was not at all loath to visit it. There was something different about its aromatic air, the peace and well-being that seemed to enfold its people, even the dignity of the women, who were unusually straight and comely, and wore a costume and head-dress all their own.

This was Nazareth, where Jesus had lived since his boyhood.

5

It is not clear whether or not the Lord stopped in his own village on that occasion. Passing so near, he would not fail, ordinarily, to ask his followers to take some rest and refreshment at his modest home on the southern elevation, and to meet his mother. She had been invited, however, to a wedding at Cana, somewhat farther on, probably as a relative or friend; and she may already have gone, for the feast was to be held that evening. Her son, too, would have been most welcome, even if he had been a stranger, for Jewish hospitality at such festivities was open-handed, and any young rabbi in the vicinity would be sure to receive an invitation. Whether he learned of this on stopping at his house, or had previously discussed it, or knew of it without being told, he decided to attend the supper, and to take the five new disciples along. One of them – Nathanael, the Israelite without guile whom we now call Bartholomew – lived, as a matter of fact, in Cana.

All that is certain is that toward the eve of that day the six dusty pilgrims arrived in that village. It was a much smaller place about five miles north of Nazareth, probably where Keh Kenna now stands, on the main road to Capharnaum and the shore of Galilee – a walk of an hour and a half at most. As they sauntered over the hills that Wednesday afternoon they saw it rising picturesquely out of a valley chequered with orchards and fields, and already streaked with long shadows and patches of waning sunlight. Surely Galilee was the most beautiful part of Palestine. It was there that Asher had "dipped his foot in oil"; there the grapes produced the headiest and most fragrant wine; there, said a wise man, it was easier to raise a forest of trees than one child in rocky Judea. The best pomegranates in the world grew near Cana. The people, too, were typically Galilean: strictly Jewish in their religion, but somewhat more impulsive and passionate than those of the metropolis. Perhaps this was because they had "mixed blood"; for many Gentiles had settled in their country. According to the Talmud they were inclined to be quarrelsome, and cared more for honour than for money.

Simon Peter had seen Cana before, surely, for it was less than twenty miles from Capharnaum and the sea; but never under happier circumstances. As he approached the village he became aware of a vague familiar sound among the houses huddled together on the hillside. Presently he could begin to distinguish the voices of men, women, and children, mingling with the music of flutes, small harps, sackbuts perhaps, trumpets and drums, and the rhythmical clapping of hands. Suddenly around a corner from a hidden street appeared the wedding procession on its way from the house of the bride's father to that of the bridegroom.

First walked some minstrels, flushed with exertion and good red wine, blowing and strumming their best. Some servants followed, distributing nuts to children along the road, and portions of wine or oil to older persons. Then, attended on either side by bridesmaids and friends, and by "the children of the bride-chamber" came a comely Jewish girl, her long hair flowing out under a white bridal veil. In Judea she would be accompanied also by the "friends of the bridegroom" making salty remarks, the influence perhaps of such pagan festivities as Catullus describes; but not among the more austere Galileans. Some of the bride's relatives carried myrtle branches and chaplets of gaudy flowers. Others bore torches and lamps hung on poles, some of which were lighted as dusk began to creep over the hillside into the streets.

It was expected that all who saw such a procession would applaud and salute it, and praise the beauty and the goodness of the bride. In fact everybody who could walk would join the ranks of either a funeral or a wedding cortege, for the social consciousness of the Jews did not stop at caring for the poor and the outcast, but tended to make community affairs of everyone's joys and sorrows. We may be sure, then, that Jesus and the five men from the lake would first stand and applaud, and then gravely join in and follow the joyous company to the house where the bridegroom waited to conduct his lady over the threshold of their new home. Taking off their shoes or sandals at the outer door, they would then follow the other guests through a court to a covered gallery opening on various rooms, and thence into a large reception hall.

There some sort of simple marriage ritual would be spoken, perhaps by one of the rabbis from Nazareth, where the nearest synagogue was; something like, "Take her according to the Law of Moses and of Israel." Garlands were heaped upon both, and the young man then signed the *kethubah or* contract, in which he solemnly agreed to work for her, to honour, keep, and care for her "as is the manner of the men of Israel"; and of course to make the usual financial provisions for her security.

Servants were already beginning to draw water from some of the huge stone jars, holding some twenty gallons each, that Simon

Peter noticed around the edges of the gallery. Basins of it were now presented to the guests, who, as they took their appointed places, washed their hands and feet to comply with the precepts of the ancient law. They then reclined on cushioned and tapestried couches which extended from three sides of a long table. Through the open fourth side the servants came and went to light the candles and lamps, and to dispense all kinds of food, wines, and delicacies to the guests, each of whom lay on his left side, his elbow on a cushion, his head almost on the table, his bare feet away from it. A venerable old man spoke the prayer of bridal benediction, and blessed the bread and the wine. Now the banquet had begun. Over the soft music of harps and flutes, drifting from the lighted courtyard, arose a hum of conversation and of laughter. There was no clatter of knives and forks, for these were not used. Each ate with his hands, which he then wiped on a long napkin fastened to his girdle. The wine passed freely, goblets were drained and refilled.

Simon Peter and Andrew, John, Philip and Nathaniel were hungry and thirsty after their long walk when they took the couches assigned to them, some distance perhaps from the head, or at another table. They were always able, like good men everywhere, to down their share of the vintage "that makes glad the heart of man." It may be that the Master of the Feast, casting a watchful eye about from time to time, observed them with a fleeting sense of uneasiness, which courtesy made him conceal. Would the wine hold out? True, the Jews were always a temperate people, who usually mixed water with their drink. Yet they were hospitable, too, and welcomed uninvited guests to their wedding feasts. On this occasion the number may have been uncommonly large, including as it did the young rabbi from Nazareth and the five sturdy trenchermen he had brought with him.

Once the edge had been taken off their hunger, the visiting fishermen had time to look about them. There was plenty to see and hear, for no one was ever bored at a wedding feast; and at this one there was an extraordinary personage whose ways were still strange and fascinating to them. If the other guests watched him curiously and furtively, wondering about a certain distinction that was evident in him, the five workmen who had followed him from the lower Jordan, believing him to be the Messiah, could hardly keep their eyes off his noble head and grave countenance. As a rabbi he would probably be asked to recline at one end of the table with the other most honoured guests, near the bridegroom and the bride. It is not recorded that he said anything during the supper. Simon Peter, watching him closely, noticed that he frequently glanced into the adjoining rooms, where the ladies were gathered about a separate table. There was one there whose eyes from time to time met his. Simon Peter learned that she was his mother. And it is likely that on this occasion he saw this lady for the first time.

Mary was then in her late forties, but looked younger, for her lovely face had the sort of ageless serenity that nuns have; and but for the dark weeds of a widow that covered her slightly greying hair, she might have been taken for a young virgin, perhaps a sister of the bride. There was a strange story, in fact, which John most likely was the first to hear, that she was still that maiden foretold by Isaiah, even after the birth of her son. As to her appearance, as well as His, the evangelists say nothing. Artists are free, then, to imagine her as best they can. Historians, unwilling to credit the hints dropped by mystics who have seen her more or less obscurely in their visions, can at least recognize the unbroken tradition, transmitted from the earliest Christian times,[1] of a quiet majestic beauty, a completely harmonious personality, a goodness corresponding to her exemption from original sin and to her miraculous virginity. She was descended from King David, and was of levitical ancestry on both sides. Saint Luke, who had her story from her own lips and those of her divine Son, makes her seem almost angelic; indeed, she had actually seen one of the seven who stand before the throne of the Most High, and had heard him say, "Hail, Mary, full of grace! The Lord is with you!" What an experience for Simon Peter to see and hear, for the first time, a woman who had been overshadowed by the Holy Spirit, and had been clasped as a bride by the Lord of uncreated light, and of all heaven and earth!

A description of her by Saint Epiphanius in the fourth century is so definite as to suggest the possibility that tradition had handed it down to him, generation by generation, from apostolic rimes. She was not tall, he said, but a little above medium height. The fine oval of her face was slightly bronzed by the sun to something like the tint of ripe corn. Her eyes were olive coloured, the brows black and delicately arched, the hair light; the nose aquiline and perfect, the lips rosy, the hands and fingers long and slender. But the most strik-

---

[1] Saint Ignatius of Antioch, disciple of Peter, wrote of her, about 106 A.D. with profound veneration, mentioning the virgin birth as a well-known fact.

ing effect of her beauty was from within, and it was imperishable and indescribable. "She was the most lovely of women because she was the most chaste and most holy of the daughters of Eve." All Christian mystics have recognized in her the lady King Solomon praised by anticipation in his Canticle: "You are all beautiful, my love, and there is no spot in you." Saint Bernadette, who saw her at Lourdes in the nineteenth century, found her "beautiful beyond compare ... so beautiful, that when one has seen her one can no longer love anything of the earth ... so beautiful that one would wish to die in order to see her again." To the children who saw her near Fatima in Portugal in 1917 she was "a Lady all of white, more brilliant than the sun dispensing light."

Not thus glorified, of course, did she appear to Simon Peter. He saw her with the other wedding guests as one of those fine, well-balanced, vital women of few words and many deeds, who were among the glories of Israel. He assuredly discerned in her some of the qualities of that long tradition which goes back almost to him, and probably came in part from his lips. Glancing from one to the other, he must have noticed some resemblance between her and her son. What was it, then, that made him so different from everybody else? What was the quality in him that made one believe that whatever he said must be true?

As Simon Peter and his brother sipped their wine and wondered perhaps about the attraction that had caused them to follow this man, almost at once, wherever he happened to go, they became aware of a restlessness that passed through the banquet hall. There were whispered consultations among the waiters, and a hurried intervention of the Master of the Feast, who seemed rather disturbed and embarrassed as he hastily went out again. And presently the fishermen noticed that the mother of the Lord had risen, and had come to the arched doorway, where she stood looking at Him with appealing eyes. He also left the table, and approached her.

"They have no wine," she said.

Jesus replied affectionately, half in protest, in a characteristic idiom of the East:

"Woman, what is there to me and to you?"[2] Mary continued to

---

[2] The Greek original of Saint John (2:4) is "Τί ἐμοί καί σοί, γύναι?" The Vulgate gives correctly: "*Quid mihi et tibi est, mulier?*" The mistranslation of the King James version, "Woman, what have I to do with you?" implies a harsh rebuke which could not have been intended by Jesus, for Mary's next speech show that she understood he had granted her request. "Woman" in Orient was more like our

look beseechingly at him. These, perhaps, were her relatives; in any case, good people. But she made no request of him. "My time has not yet come," he added gently.

His eyes must have said something more, for she took this as an affirmative answer. Turning to the waiters, and beckoning them to approach, she presented them to her son with the words:

"Whatever he bids you do, do it."

There was something in her quiet voice and manner that made people obey without questioning. The servants looked open-mouthed at Jesus. The attention of most of the guests, in fact, including the fishermen from Capharnaum, was now riveted upon this little scene. Jesus walked, a straight and kingly figure, toward the door opening upon the gallery. Nearby stood six of the stone water pots from which the waiters had ministered to the guests before the feast. His glance swept them and returned to the faces of the servants.

"Fill the jars with water," he said.

Simon saw the men scurry about without the slightest hesitation to carry out this order. In fact they were so eager to obey that they filled the six jars to the very brims.

"Now draw off," commanded the Lord, "and bring it to the Master of the Feast."

It was a casual direction, but the looks and exclamations of those who stood near the water jars indicated that something out of the ordinary had occurred. Indeed it had. As they began to pour off the liquid from the crocks into smaller receptacles, they saw that it ran as red as rubies. It had the smell, colour, and taste of wine. And what wine! Conversation and laughter closed in upon the awkward silence as the guests began to drink it.

Some of them were still unaware of what had happened. This seems to have been true especially of the Master of the Feast, who perhaps had gone to borrow from the neighbours: for on his return he said to the Bridegroom, as they tasted the miraculous vintage together:

"Everyone sets on the good wine first, and when people have partaken freely, then the inferior; but you have reserved the good

courteous "Lady"; Priam uses it thus to Hecuba, for example, in the *Iliad*, (24, 300). The meaning of "What is there to me and to you," as Spencer literally translates it, would depend on the manner and tone of the speaker. Here obviously it carries a protest so gentle as to be really none at all. Cf. Mark 1:24, and Matt 8:29.

wine until now!"[3]

The account by Simon's friend John, the son of Zebedee, ends simply with the words, "This beginning of his miracles Jesus performed at Cana in Galilee, and manifested his glory; and his disciples believed in him." It was evidently written by a Galilean in terse and matter-of-fact Greek. But we may be sure that this was not the end of the discussion among the fishermen who had so unexpectedly become witnesses of the beginning of the Lord's public ministry. It was a staggering and almost terrifying climax to the strange adventure that had come to these simple men. One thing was certain. The Master who had shown himself able to read the mind of Nathanael at a distance, and to tell Simon Peter something of his past and his future, had now demonstrated that he wielded a power that could come only from the creator of all things.

Simon, to judge from later events, was the one who found this the most difficult to grasp, and asked the most questions. And likely enough the quicker-minded and better educated John, poet and philosopher, with deep insight into spiritual matters, was not slow to point out what was so evident to Saint Augustine four centuries later, that he who made water also made grapes, and made their juice ferment, and could easily enough change one into the other at will.

[3] John 2:1-11

6

Instead of returning to Nazareth after the wedding feast, the Lord took his mother to Capharnaum that winter, in the company of certain relatives, and established a home for her in that more cosmopolitan town. This was no disappointment, surely, to Simon Peter. To be near him, to hear his voice, to see him every day, to feel his presence – that was as near to perfect felicity as a man might hope for in this world. And there was something about the lovely face and person of Mary that purged the very air one breathed, and made the heart sing like a child's. But if the four fishermen who had seen the miracle at Cana expected to settle down without effort in their old agreeable routine, they were soon to be reminded that their lives had been radically changed by his coming. For not many days had passed when he informed them that he was going up to Jerusalem for the Passover, and that they were to accompany him.

It was early spring, and Galilee had never been more beautiful as they strode along the west bank of the crystal lake under an azure sky. The green fields, still wet with dew, were dotted with purple and gold, the red blossoms of wild mustard, the larger patches of crimson where anemones and poppy cups swayed in the north wind. Even the valley of the Jordan took on a brighter aspect at that season after the latter rain, and the half dozen drab and dusty pilgrims, as they followed its banks southward,[1] must have noticed that the oleanders by the water's edge were in bloom, and that the peach orchards on the higher ground were festive with pink. Sometimes a herd of buffaloes would stare at them across the valley. An ibex or a gazelle would gaze from a rock before disappearing in a thicket. A flock of wild ducks on their way perhaps to summer in Europe flew low over the brownish waters. It was not uncommon to see thousands of storks rising from the marshes to fly in a wide circle and then tangent off in a long line that vanished in the sunny sky.

As the spare powerful figure of Jesus swung rhythmically along the familiar road by the river, he would talk now to one, now to another, answering their diffident questions, while the rest

---

[1] Saint John does not say which route they followed. The Jordan one seems likely from the fact that he says of their return, "it was necessary for him to pass through Samaria" (4:4) as though that were unusual.

followed, listening, or closed in on either side. Sometimes he spoke to all at once. Yet it soon became apparent that while he regarded all of them with the affection of a father or of an older brother, he seemed to have a special liking for the company of Simon Peter, James and John. These latter, the sons of Zebedee, he called Boanerges, sons of thunder, doubtless because they had powerful and eloquent voices, which they rather enjoyed displaying on slight provocation, especially when moved to indignation. Very zealous they were, too, in everything pertaining to the Law; in fact, they were sometimes a little too quick to settle problems of unbelief by suggesting the simple old expedient of exterminating the offenders out of hand – a tendency that the Lord curbed with patience and quiet good humour.

It was Simon, however, who most frequently walked beside him, and as time went on, it was to Simon that he commonly looked when he wished to address them all. The others may have wondered about this. Perhaps it was because Simon was so slow of comprehension in some ways. But the Lord was infinitely patient: he seemed especially anxious that the crop-headed fisherman should understand the kingdom of God. If the others were envious, they generally managed to conceal it. When they had some special favour to ask, they would get Simon to present it.

He accepted this modestly, and made no effort to lord it over the rest. But he would have been less than human if he had not been pleased. The confidence of Jesus was like sunlight giving and strengthening life. It was a proud moment for Simon Peter when on the fourth or fifth day of the journey, after passing through flowery Jericho and climbing the steep rocky ascent that rises zigzag to the hill country of Judea, he stood once more at the turn of a road on the Mount of Olives, this time with the Holy One of Israel, and once more looked triumphantly across the Kedron valley at Jerusalem. What was to prevent the Messiah from going to the white and gilded splendour on Mount Moriah, and revealing himself to the High Priests and doctors of the Law? One manifestation of the power he had shown at Cana, and they would set on his head the crown of Israel! One burning speech, and the people would rise up and cast the Romans out.

The next morning, still full of grandiose hopes, Simon Peter was standing with the Lord near the Beautiful Gate watching the crowds of earnest pilgrims hurry through the Court of the Gentiles to make their sacrifices. One carried two doves in a cage, another a lamb, another a small goat, while still others were purchasing birds or beasts at the bazaar along one of the massive walls, or having them inspected and certified. A multitude were waiting in line before some small tables set up on the polished marble floor by itinerant money-changers. The rattle of coins sounded above the twitter of birds, the bleating of sheep, the lowing of cattle, the murmur of human voices.

Taking this all in at a glance, Jesus picked up some cords that were lying by the pigeon crates, wound them deftly into a whip and strode past wondering Simon with a terrible quiet determination toward the tables and the bazaars. Something about him made even Temple guards step hastily aside. A Christian poet of Jewish descent, a man of no small insight,[2] insists that even in anger his face was never distorted or flushed like those of other men; for it was not passion but impersonal divine justice that activated him. To the vendors of pigeons he said, curtly, "Take these things hence; and do not turn my Father's house into a market!" But when he came to the oxen and the sheep, he laid the whip of cords upon their backs, lashing at them with great swinging blows of his powerful arms and shoulders till they plunged panic-stricken in all directions among the terrified spectators and hucksters. The money changers sat paralyzed with fear as he knocked over one table after another. Coins of all nations and silver shekels of the sanctuary clattered upon the marble blocks and rolled off under the feet of the scurrying crowd.

Simon Peter had not expected anything like this. But he watched with a certain growing elation. Who else but the Messiah would dare act so boldly in this place? Who else could say in that tone of regal assurance, "My Father's house?" One of the party recalled a prophetical line from Psalm 68: "Zeal for your house consumes me," and the others nodded approval.

By this time the noise and the confusion had brought some of the chief priests and leading pharisees to the scene, and they were staring with incredulous and angry eyes at the tall man in the robes of a rabbi who was casting aside the whip of cords, and calmly turning away from the last cowering money-changer. Perhaps they learned from one of the disciples that he was Jesus of Nazareth. Some of them ventured to approach and to peer into his face.

"What miraculous proof do you show us of your right to do these things?" they demanded sarcastically.

---

[2] Fray Luis de Leon: *Los Nombres de Cristo*.

This suggests that they had heard what he had done at Cana, and were asking him for more miracles, not because they really wanted to see them, or would believe him if he complied, but because they sought a pretext to gloat over him. Knowing this, the Lord returned their scrutiny calmly, and said:

"Destroy this temple and in three days I will raise it up."

Both friends and foes would remember that seemingly irrelevant boast. Now the friends heard it with consternation, the foes with scorn.

"It took forty-six years to build this temple," retorted one of the pharisees, "and will you rear it up in three days?"

Jesus did not clarify his remark. So far as the record stands, he did not explain it even to his disciples, preferring to appeal to their faith. Peter, for one, could make very little of it. For the pharisee was right in saying that forty-six years had passed since Herod had begun the construction. And the Lord could rebuild it in three days? It was one thing to change water into wine – both liquids. Simon looked up again at the mammoth blocks of marble above him, and wondered.

Jesus did perform several miracles during that stay in Jerusalem. Whatever they were (the Gospel[3] does not specify) they were sufficient to convince many persons of the truth of his claim to be the Messiah. Before the end of the week, he was being discussed even among members of the sanhedrin, the council of the seventy elders. In fact one of them, a highly respected pharisee named Nicodemus, sought him out one night at his lodgings. John, who reported the incident with the vivacity of an eye-witness, did not take time to tell us where it occurred; in the house of one of his relatives, perhaps, for he had some in Jerusalem.[4] We are left to imagine the Lord with his half-dozen followers sitting in the *aliyah* or upper guest chamber of one of those fine upper middle-class houses on the western hill, when a servant mounted the outdoor stairway and ushered in a distinguished and heavily bearded personage. The shrill wind howled in the steep narrow streets, and the plain bronze lamp flickered like the wavering spirit of the visitor, who drew his cloak about him and glanced back to see if he had been observed.

Nicodemus, the midnight disciple, went away, as we know, without avowing his faith: a timid old man, afraid to offend the

[3] John 2:23
[4] *ibid*, 15

powerful rulers who had taken the cleansing of the Temple in such bad part. Nor was he yet quite sure what he believed. The context indicates that like most pharisees he had missed the spiritual significance of the Old Testament. Simon Peter was hardly the one to blame him, when he himself had no better understanding of some of the Lord's words. To enter the kingdom of God, a man must be spiritually reborn in Baptism. People who did not believe the Messiah were afraid of the light, and preferred to stay in darkness, because their deeds were wicked. So far so good. But to gain eternal life for those who did welcome the light, the Son of Man must be lifted up as the serpent was lifted up in the desert by Moses – what could that mean?

With this question still troubling him, Simon Peter left Jerusalem with his Master soon after the paschal feast, and instead of returning to Galilee, followed one of the good stone Roman roads westward through the hilly countryside of Judea. Wherever they stopped, in village after village, the Lord would preach in the synagogues or in the open air, and the disciples would then baptize all who accepted him. An old tradition says that he himself baptized no one but Simon Peter, who then administered the sacrament to the others. Certain it is that many converts were made.

Sometimes it seemed to Simon Peter that the souls of these people were purchased at a high price. It was oppressively hot in the highlands as summer approached, even though the nights were cool. Water was extremely scarce, for wells were to be found only in the deep valleys. People on the hills had to store rain in cisterns, and only the most charitable would give a cup of cold water. Furthermore, the disciples began to sense among these rural crowds a subtle opposition of a new sort. They noticed among them certain vaguely familiar faces, certain rabbinical tunics and wide phylacteries that evoked sour memories of Jerusalem and the Temple courts. The pharisees, alarmed by the events of the previous week, were sending spies to follow them.

These agents were in close touch with others who had been assigned to keep watch on John the Baptizer. On comparing notes, the two groups realized with concern that the disciples of Jesus were baptizing far more converts. But John was their first and more vulnerable enemy, and when he crossed the Jordan into Perea in Herod's jurisdiction, they lost no time in pointing out to the tyrant the menace that might arise from an irresponsible ascetic who was already denouncing him for unlawfully taking his brother's wife

54

Herodias. Thereupon Herod had John arrested and confined, if we may believe Josephus, in the almost inaccessible mountain fortress of Machaerus, on a cliff high above the death-struck shores of the Dead Sea. "And although he would have liked to kill him, he was afraid of the populace, because they regarded John as a prophet".[5]

Jesus learned with sorrow of John's arrest. He decided to return at once to Galilee, and not by way of the Jordan, but through Samaria. Simon Peter would probably have preferred the longer route. No orthodox Hebrew enjoyed passing through a country where food and lodging might be denied him, and theft or violence might lie in wait on every road – to say nothing of the hungry lions that infested the mountains. But it was not for him to make the decisions.

Another slight incident cast a momentary cloud on the rosy future he had been constructing for himself. The band of disciples was growing, and it may be that this was the time when the swarthy inscrutable face of Judas,[6] the son of Simon, first appeared in their midst. He was a native of the little town of Karioth, in the highlands about a day's walk south of Jerusalem on the edge of the wilderness. Nothing is recorded of the circumstances of his conversion. First perhaps he would be seen among the crowd, listening to one who said that the kingdom of God had come to Israel and that He was the promised deliverer. Next he would be asking questions, then eagerly offering his faith and loyalty. Finally he would see the eyes that probed with serene omniscience to the very depths of his mysterious soul, and hear the words, "Follow me."

Judas, too, must be limned by imagination: a spare man, let us suppose, of thirty-five or so, with searching alert and restless eyes like coals in a pale face, and a rather stern discontented mouth. It stands to reason that he must have had prepossessing qualities, to account for his acceptance by the Lord, and the absence of any resentment, at first at least, on the part of the other disciples. He could be affable and pleasing enough when he chose, though at times he was inclined to be fault-finding and peevish. Above all he was a practical fellow, who knew how to get things done, to find food, to buy cheaply, to attain ends, to save trouble – a useful type in any company. When such a man decided in any age to make a career of religion, he was almost bound to achieve some sort of distinction; and when he hailed Jesus as the long-awaited king of

---

[5] Matt 14:5-6
[6] From Ἰούδας, the Greek form of Judah

Israel, it would probably be with the vigour of one who saw an opportunity before him, and his bright enthusiasm would be re-assuring and contagious. A good business man with his feet on the earth, as they say, and no nonsense about him! That sort of man would understand also how to ingratiate himself with his brethren, once he had "got in on the ground floor", how to make the right "approach" to any "prospect" he desired to "contact" – the reality is musty, even if the terms have changed. It would be almost inevitable that sooner or later he would become the treasurer of the little band, carrying about with him the bag of coins given them in charity to buy their frugal necessities. And he would naturally expect that when Jesus finally mounted the throne of David, he would enjoy a prominent and lucrative post in the cabinet as Secretary of the Treasury, First Lord of the Exchequer, or whatever the equivalent might be in the parlance of the new regime.

Simon Peter probably had little confidence in this fellow from the first. It was natural for a Galilean to dislike a Judean on general principles. Furthermore, he had his own ideas about the organization of the messianic government, and he had some reason to hope, from the preference the Lord had shown him, that he would occupy no mean position in it. Of all the disciples, paradoxically, he was the most like Judas. They were energetic ambitious men to whom this world and its pomp, wealth, and circumstance meant much. But to one it meant everything, to the other, not quite. Like repels like, but if they are weighted in two scales, the balance may be decided by something very intangible.

7

Simon Peter was not sorry to shake the soil of Judea from his Galilean sandals; he was on his way home, and the hills became greener and less rocky, more like those he knew, as he trudged along the flagstones of the Roman road in its windings to the north down toward the plain of Samaria, while rumbling chariots powdered him with dust as teams of spirited horses hurried rich invalids to the hot sulphur baths of Tiberias, or imperial couriers to the court of Herod. He was not altogether sure that he liked this missionary life, so full of surprises and inconveniences: he would be glad to get on his boat again and feel the wind in his face. So the day passed, and at sundown they came to some high, barren hills, faced with cliffs of chalky whiteness, and there spent the night.

The next morning they reached a more friendly landscape with wide fields of grain, olive groves and wooded hills. And by noon of this second day they arrived at the intersection of several main roads on an elevation near the white-domed roofs of the village of Sychar, now Nablus. They were standing on the very parcel of land that Joseph had received from his father, and within sight of the rounded top of the tomb where the children of Israel had laid his mummy after carrying it about for forty years. By the roadside was the deep cistern that his father had dug to store rainwater. It is called Jacob's Well even to this day.

They were all tired, hungry and thirsty, for it was a very hot day about the middle of May, and they had been walking since dawn through an arid country. Even the Lord, says the Gospel, was weary. It was one of the rare occasions when he gave evidence of any such human weakness; and he sat on a large stone at the edge of the well, waiting for some of the country people to come and draw water. The narrow aperture went down some seventy-five feet and no bucket or rope was at hand.

Below on the plain of Samaria they saw miles of wheat-fields, turning saffron for the harvest. Brittle echoes here and there indicated that ancient flails were already at work, and the creaking of carts and the shouts of the harvesters came faintly through the dry air, with now and then the fragrance of roses and the unexpected song of a cuckoo. Perched high on a distant hill just ahead was the city of Samaria. A majestic avenue swept up to it, through a colonnade of monoliths between fabulous fanes and towers from which marble gods looked down on a forum of matchless beauty, and on palaces where shameful deeds were veiled behind perfumed silks and sensuous music and dancing. Herod had outdone himself in rebuilding this place. It was one of his favourite residences: and he had with him there his brother's wife Herodias and her daughter, Salome. Only big lizards now inhabit its ruins; but it was in the full noon of its pride as the eyes of Jesus rested thoughtfully and perhaps ironically upon it. Nearer at hand, on the right, towered the bulk of Mount Gerizim, on which the Samaritans with their false temple had sought to rival the true one at Jerusalem, teaching corrupted human borrowings from the revealed wisdom of Israel. This in part was why the Jews abhorred them.

While Jesus rested, his disciples, with the possible exception of John (whose account of what followed reads like that of an eye-witness) went down to the nearest village to buy some food, for the land itself was not held to be unclean. When they returned, and we may suppose that Simon Peter was among them, they were greatly astonished. For there, in the full noonday light, the Lord was conversing with a woman. It was unheard of for a rabbi to speak with one of her sex in public. Moreover, this person was plainly a Samaritan, whom no Jew would address without grave necessity; and probably a sinner. As the disciples continued to stare, they saw her turn and walk abruptly away across the fields, leaving her water-jar and rope beside the well. What could it mean?

None of them ventured to ask the Lord why he had disregarded the two conventions so dear to the pharisees. Instead, they produced the viands they had obtained in the village, and offered some to him, saying: "Rabbi, eat."

The wheat fields were rippling and glistening in the sun like a vast yellow sea. Far down in the valley the Samaritan woman was talking and gesticulating with several other persons.

"I have food to eat of which you know nothing," he said. "My food is to do the will of him who sent me, and to accomplish his work. Do you not say, 'There are four months yet, and then comes the harvest?' Look, I tell you! raise your eyes and survey the fields, for they are already white for harvesting."

It was not at the wheatfields that he was looking; the context suggests rather the woman and her friends (who by this time were on their way up the hill) and countless persons in other places and times. What had happened? Simon Peter was a man of strong curiosity. He could hardly wait to draw John aside and get from him a few particulars of the famous conversation of the fourth gospel.

"Give me a drink," Jesus had said, as the woman hauled up her bucket.

"How can you, being a Jew, ask for a drink from me, a Samaritan woman?"

"If you had known the gift of God, and who he is who is saying to you, 'Give me a drink,' you would have asked him, and he would have given you living water."

"Sir, you have nothing to draw with, and the well is deep: where then have you got the living water? Are you greater than our father Jacob, who gave us the well, and drank from it himself, as well as his sons and his cattle?"

"Everyone who drinks of this water shall thirst again; but whoever drinks of the water that I shall give him shall not thirst any more; but the water that I shall give him shall become in him a fountain of water leaping up into everlasting life."

"Sir, give me that water, so that I may not be thirsty, nor come all the way here to draw."

"Go, call your husband, and return here."

"I have no husband:'

"You have answered well, 'I have no husband,' for you have had five husbands, and the one you now have is not your husband: this you have said truly."

"I perceive, sir, that you are a prophet. Our forefathers worshipped on this mountain, while your people say the place where one ought to worship is in Jerusalem."

"Believe me, woman, the time is coming when you shall worship the Father neither on this mountain nor in Jerusalem. You worship what you do not know; we worship what we know, for salvation comes from the Jews. But the hour is coming – yes, is now here – when the true worshippers shall worship the Father in spirit and in truth, for indeed, the Father seeks for such to be his worshippers. God is a spirit; and his worshippers must worship in spirit and in truth."

"I know that messiah – he who is called Christ – is coming. He will tell us everything."

"I, who speak to you, am he!"

Already the poor creature was coming back with her paramour and some other samaritans. "Come," she had said to them, "come and see a man who told me all I ever did! Can this be the Christ?" And now the humble villagers of a despised nation were listening to

Jesus himself as he simply told them who he was and what he wanted. And some of them, at least, were probably baptized with water from the well of Jacob. It is an exaggeration to consider this incident the first step in the universalization of the gospel, for the Jews regarded the samaritans not as gentiles but as heretics, lost sheep of the house of Israel. Nevertheless, these converts had a more correct view of the ultimate mission of the messiah than his own disciples had. "We have heard him ourselves, and we know that this is truly the saviour of the world," they said. They begged him to stay with them, and he did so, teaching them for two days, somewhat to the chagrin, perhaps, of some of his followers who would need more time to adjust themselves to the idea of accepting samaritans on equal terms.

From Samaria they continued north on the main road to Nazareth, but for some reason not made clear in the gospel went by once more to Cana. They had hardly arrived there when an imperial officer came riding into the village to implore the Lord to heal his son, whom he had left desperately ill at Capharnaum. Even now the boy might be dead.

"Go," said the Master, "your son is alive and well." And the officer joyfully departed, while Jesus and the disciples continued on their way back to Nazareth.

On the following sabbath they all went to the synagogue of that place; no Jew would think of not doing so, and Jesus invariably honoured the good custom that dated from the Babylonian exile, as he did all the essentials of the Law. It was probably, like most of the Palestinian houses of worship, a simple dignified stone building, with the main entrance between two pillars at the south, and on the lintel some ornament such as the seven-branched candlestick, a bunch of grapes with vine leaves, or a flower between two paschal lambs.

Inside, a double colonnade ran the length of the building, forming two aisles, and supporting the massive rafters on which the flat roof rested. The floor was paved with slabs of white limestone, the walls solid, the windows adequate for good lighting. At the south, near the door, stood a movable ark containing the sacred rolls of the Law and the Prophets. Some steps led up to this, and before it, close to a *vilon* or curtain, hung the holy lamp which, like the one in the temple at Jerusalem, was never extinguished. The rulers of the synagogue and distinguished guests sat with their backs to the ark, facing the rest of the congregation. Women occupied a gallery at the rear.[1] In the centre of the room, where all could see and hear, was a lectern or *Bima*, a desk on a raised platform, with a chair beside it. Here the sacred scrolls were read.

On this sabbath morning Simon Peter and his brethren followed Jesus into the synagogue, we may conjecture, and took places beside him or near him on one of the benches facing the ark and the personages who sat with their backs to it. The Lord was well known there, for he had attended the service for years with his mother and his foster-father, and the utter humility of his hidden life of preparation is suggested by the fact that the people did not regard him as an extraordinary person or a distinguished guest, but merely as "the carpenter," or "the son of Joseph the carpenter" . They must have heard lately of the miracle at Cana, and it may be, therefore, that his appearance today evoked unwonted whispers and turnings of heads. It was hard to believe that a man they had known for years had turned water into wine. Yet he had done something strange in Cana; time would tell what it was. Meanwhile Jesus probably sat with his disciples among the common worshippers.

Simon Peter saw a priest, or the venerable ruler of the synagogue, go to the ark and take one of the sacred rolls of parchment from its place. Extending it with deliberate care and dignity, he turned to face toward the holy of holies at Jerusalem, and then, still standing, began to read the *Shema*, or confession of faith, from the first books of the bible. Many times since childhood had Simon Peter heard the beautiful words, but he had never tired of listening to them; sometimes Moses himself seemed almost to be there, uttering his magnificent farewell discourse to the children of Israel in the wilderness:

"Hear, O Israel, the Lord our God is one Lord. You shall love the Lord your God with your whole heart, and with your whole soul, and with your whole strength. And these words which I command you this day, shall be in your heart: and you shall tell your children, and you shall meditate upon them sitting in your house, and walking on your journey, sleeping and rising. And you shall bind them as a sign on your hand, and they shall be and shall move between your eyes. And you shall write them in the entry, and on the doors of your house."[2]

The old man paused, and turned to another place:

---

[1] This was true in Palestine; in the Alexandrian synagogues the men and women were separated by a partition about four feet high.
[2] Deut 6:4-9

"If then you obey my commandments, which I command you this day, that you love the Lord your God, and serve him with all your heart, and with all your soul, he will give to your land the early rain and the latter rain, that you may gather in your corn and your wine and your oil, and your hay out of the fields to feed your cattle, and that you may eat and be filled. Beware lest perhaps your heart be deceived, and you depart from the Lord, and serve strange gods, and adore them: and the Lord being angry shut up heaven, that the rain come not down, nor the earth yield her fruit, and you perish quickly from the excellent land, which the Lord will give you. Lay up these my words in your hearts and minds, and hang them for a sign on your hands, and place them between your eyes..."[3]

He unrolled the scroll and again continued:

"The Lord also said to Moses: Speak to the children of Israel, and then shall tell them to make to themselves fringes in the corners of their garments, putting in them ribands of blue: that when they shall see them, they may remember all the commandments of the Lord, and not follow their own thoughts and eyes going astray after divers things, but rather being mindful of the precepts of the Lord, may do them and be holy to their God. I am the Lord your God, who brought you out of the land of Egypt that I might be your God."[4]

Thus the *Torah* was read every sabbath, in 154 sections, the whole cycle being completed every three years. And when the priest had finished reading part of the Law, and perhaps also the eighteen blessings called the *Shemoneh Esreh*, it was customary for him to ask some elder or some important visitor to continue the service with a reading from the prophets. Or if none such were present, he might ask for a volunteer in the congregation. It has been conjectured that such was the case on this particular sabbath. An expectant silence followed. Then Jesus quietly arose and offered himself as the *Sheliach Tsibbur*. There was a rustle among the men, and a craning of necks in the gallery, as he walked to the Bima, and stood, tall, spare and powerful, a majestic and arresting figure, looking toward the ark.

The ruler of the synagogue now took another of the long illuminated rolls from the ark, and handed it courteously but perhaps with a questioning glance to the young rabbi. Jesus

---

[3] Deut 11:13-31
[4] Num 15:37-41

unrolled it with his customary deliberation, and on finding the place appointed for that day's lesson on the prophecy of Isaiah, seated himself before the Bima, according to custom, and commenced to read in a rich and strangely moving voice. It was a text especially appropriate for that jubilee year, one plainly recognized as prophetic of the Messiah:

"The spirit of the Lord is upon me, because the Lord hath anointed me: he has sent me to preach to the meek, to heal the contrite of heart, and to preach a release to the captives, and deliverance to them that are shut up, to proclaim the acceptable year of the Lord, and the day of vengeance of our God; to comfort all that mourn ..."

The beautiful consoling words fell on them all like music from heaven, and under their spell, and that of the voice and presence, they sat motionless and silent, hardly breathing. The hush was broken by the creaking of the parchment as the carpenter rolled it up and handed it back to the ruler of the synagogue or an attendant. Then he sat down again to make the customary discourse on the prophetical text. Every eye was upon him, every head bent to catch his words. They must all have sensed something different in him that morning.

"Today this passage of Scripture has been fulfilled in your hearing."

It was all he said, but it was enough; it was electrifying; for in effect it meant:

"I am the messiah you have been expecting."

Their first impulse was to accept it at its face value; for the gospel adds that "all bore him witness." Then, like a sudden contrary wind on the lake, a murmur of disputation swept over the audience, and contrapuntal voices of dissent began to be heard. Some one asked, "Is not this Joseph's son?" The query passed from mouth to mouth like a cold wind of doubt. Faith without roots shrivelled away before it.

Jesus did not argue or plead with them. He spoke 'like one having authority, and not as the scribes and pharisees" with their long-winded prayers and discourses, their hair-splitting distinctions. He knew already what answer their spirits had made in that moment of silence to the test and the challenge he had presented to them, and he knew what they were about to ask. They were going to request him to do some of the tricks they had heard he had performed at Cana. And because they doubted his identity, and had no intention of accepting his intrinsic authority, he did not intend to gratify their curiosity.

Simon Peter could feel the tremor of rage and wounded pride that passed over the crowd. He saw them rise to their feet almost to a man, and close in upon the Bima. Fists were clenched; garments cast into the air; teeth gnashed in rage. All was noise and confusion as they laid hands on the speaker, and dragged him through the open door and up the steep narrow street that led to the precipice at the north of the town. Nothing is said of the disciples here. Yet if they were present, as seems most likely, they must have found themselves pushed roughly to one side or crowded helplessly into a corner while the furious crowd continued on its violent way to carry out what was obviously its purpose: to cast him over the edge of the high rock where criminals were thrust to their death. Simon and the others may have taken to their heels, fearing a similar fate.

Pausing to regain their breath outside the town, miserable and ashamed, they saw Jesus walking toward them, alone, grave, safe, imperturbable. He had passed through the midst of his foes and eluded them. Whether he had become invisible, or had struck them blind, or had simply overawed them by a look – the evangelist, unlike a writer of fiction or a propagandist, does not feel obliged to tell us; he ends his narrative with the bare statement that "He went his way," and returned to Capharnaum, where he planned to preach at the synagogue on the following sabbath.

All in all this had been a bewildering and rather discouraging journey for a man like Simon Peter. The more he saw of the Lord, the more he loved him. Yet it was certainly difficult to reconcile some of his words and actions with his calm assertion and one's own inner conviction that he was the expected Holy One. By failing to perform a miracle to prove his right to cleanse the temple at Jerusalem, he had left the pharisees in possession of the field. And what had he meant by telling Nicodemus that the Son of Man must be lifted up as Moses had lifted up the serpent in the wilderness? Why had he retired from Judea before the threats of the pharisees and of the emissaries of Herod? Why had he shared the holy privileges of Israel with samaritans? And why, finally, had he allowed himself to be thrust out of his own synagogue, as if he were an impostor and blasphemer? Judas especially was curious to know the answers to these questions.

Simon Peter's loyal heart knew that the Lord would make all these matters clear in his own good time. Puzzling though they were, they could present no permanent difficulties to one who had performed such miracles as he and Andrew had seen with their own eyes. Yet small wonder if they and the sons of Zebedee were inclined to give a little more thought to the experiences that had come to them, before relinquishing a good living forever and becoming wanderers and even outcasts in a cause of which they understood so little. For if the pharisees and common worshippers in synagogues treated Jesus as they had at Nazareth, what would they do to his followers, who had none of his gifts, his charm, his power, his magnificence?

No, Simon Peter was not sorry to see the lake of Galilee lying like an irregular mirror under the blue-white of the noonday sun. A light breeze smote the surface, making one side as smooth and dark as polished steel, the other like a tapestry of glittering jewels. There were plenty of fish down there, and it certainly would seem good to lay hands on the tarry nets once more, and to feel the strong timbers beneath them, creaking under the wind.

One of the first things they heard on returning to Capharnaum was that the son of the ruler whom Jesus had consoled and dismissed had been cured of his critical illness the very same hour, as his father had learned on reaching home next day. Everyone was talking about it.

8

Every day at certain hours Simon Peter, like his father before him, used to go to the roof of his house on the hillside to offer himself to the God of Abraham, of Isaac, and of Jacob, and to ask his help in the perplexities that had come upon him. Up there against the windy sky, he always seemed nearer. There had been moments when he had almost seen him rising from the glowing sea, or descending in the flaming clouds of dawn. Today he looked for him below, in the marketplace. For there in plain sight walked his holy one, surrounded and followed by a devout and curious crowd.

It had been so ever since his return from Jerusalem. Pilgrims had brought back word of the miracles there, and of the dramatic events in the temple, and this, added to the news from Cana, had made him the only object of interest in Capharnaum. Even Levi the Publican would watch him by the hour from the door of the customs house, from under his heavy-lidded cynical eyes. People followed him about all week, wherever he went, and on the sabbath they packed the synagogue to the doors and windows; nor was there any repetition, among those cosmopolitan Jews, of the barbarous incident at Nazareth. Only the pharisees held themselves aloof from the demonstrations, and made it plain that they were not impressed, even when some enthusiasts pointed to a passage in Isaiah that seemed to prophesy the appearance of the messianic light in Galilee, despite all the prejudices of the scribes at Jerusalem.

"Land of Zabulon and land of Naphtali, toward the sea, across the Jordan, Galilee of the Gentiles: the people dwelling in darkness saw a great light, and to the dwellers in the region and shade of death, a light arose."[1]

It was in the very chapter in which the Prophet had promised the birth of a child to be called "Wonderful, Counsellor, God the Mighty, Father of the world to come, the Prince of Peace," who would sit upon the throne of David. All agreed that these words referred to the messiah. Not that the people of Capharnaum, whether Jewish, Greek or Roman, cared much about the prophets. They were inclined to be emotional, if not hysterical, and they were more interested in being diverted by a new marvel, or being restored to health, than in ancient predictions about the kingdom of

---

[1] Is 9:1,2 as summarized in Matt 4:15,16

God. The leading pharisees were not at all impressed. And strangely enough, Simon Peter and his friends also appear to have absented themselves from these demonstrations. It is not clear whether they were following some direction of the Lord, or whether they were taking time for reflection before making a final decision. At all events, they had returned to their old occupation.

It was a dangerous and exhausting life, fishing on the sea of Galilee. The capricious winds made up for the lack of tides, and the water was deep enough to swallow a thousand boats. All that is clear from the gospels is that the sons of Jonas and of Zebedee fished with nets, that they sometimes toiled all night, that on occasion they filled both boats with a single haul, and that the two sometimes worked together as a team. This is scanty enough, but it furnishes the bare outlines of a picture that can be filled in by details from what we know of such fishing at other times and places. Life is conservative in such matters. Drift-net fishing at Yarmouth, for example, has gone on with no important changes since about 500 A.D. and doubtless for many centuries before. For ages, on the coast of Spain, fishing smacks have been working together, two by two, exactly as those of Jonas and Zebedee did.

Drift-net fishing is done almost always at night, when the cool air lures the shoals of herring, mackerel or pilchards from the depths where they lurk by day – and the Sea of Galilee is two hundred feet deep in places – to the star-spangled surface. A boat at Yarmouth would be about thirty tons, seventeen feet in the beam, with seven-foot depth of hold; lugger-rigged, with a sturdy mainsail to stand the pull of a net, which can reduce the speed from eight knots an hour to one. The fishing smacks on the sea of Galilee today are much smaller and lateen-rigged. Yet on one occasion the boat of Simon Peter must have held at least twenty men. The inference is that since his time his profession has shared in the general deterioration of Palestinian life, and that we must look to Yarmouth or Brixham, or the smacks in the Bay of Biscay, for parallels.

After a good morning's sleep old Zebedee would scan the afternoon sky and the rippled surface of the sea; and if he thought there would be good fishing that night, he and his sons, and Peter and Andrew with their helpers numbering twice as many more, would go just before sundown to where the two boats lay keeled over on the yellow sand. It was the hour when the wind fell asleep, and colours changed to richer tones and varieties; while the shadows in the deep water became so clear that it was almost impossible to say which was the reality – the hills, the cliffs, the fleecy and rosy clouds above, or their images below. Sometimes one had the queer feeling that the world had been turned upside-down.

If Simon Peter used a beam net, he would take the helm and put his barque before the wind until, as she drifted into deeper water, the mainsail bellied out and strained at the rigging like a good hunting dog at the leash. Now; at a signal from Zebedee in the other boat, Andrew gave the command to "shoot" the net, which lay coiled up in readiness below, stiff with the tar and oak-bar with which it was soaked from time to time. Part of the crew handed it up, others cast it overboard while there was still light to see what they were doing. As the warp was paid out, the seizings and ropes had to be made fast at the right distances. Everything must be done methodically and at the correct moment, or the net would be twisted and the night's work spoiled.

A beam-net is shaped like a purse, bigger near the mouth, which the beam keeps open. The small end is cast out first, then the rest is "shot," and the whole hangs from the beam as the boat drives slowly forward. The front end of the beam is now slacked away from the top of the bulwark. When it is well clear of the barque and is caught by the water, it turns out at almost a right angle from the stern. The other end is then lowered, till the whole beam is level with the sea. More sail is put on. As the boat forges ahead, the two ropes fastened to the ends of the beam are paid out slowly as far as the shackles that bind them to the trawl-warp. Now the warp itself is given out steadily, and the net begins to sink toward the bottom. It is then dragged for five or six hours, held near the surface by corks, but scraping the ground where the water is shallow.

Hauling it up again is another job of an hour in good weather, and of three or more in a rough sea. The warp is pulled in and coiled away below. As the beam heaves alongside, it is hoisted and fastened. The seamen then gather in the net till only the cod or purse remains in the water. This is hoisted up by a tackle, and will be full, of course, if they have had luck. When it swings over the deck, the draw-rope is cast loose. The whole catch falls with a great shivering thump, and the slippery and writhing mass spreads out like bluish silver in the moonlight.

With a drift net, and this more likely the Palestinian fishermen preferred, the procedure is quite different. When the whole net is in the water, the crew pays out several fathoms of extra warp; then they carry the warp from the stern to the bow, and the helmsman puts her head around to the wind. The ordinary sails are taken in, and the mainmast lowered back to rest in the crutch of the mitch-board, leaving only a drift mizzen aloft to keep her head to the wind. Both boat and net now float with the current, the boat being held to leeward of the net to keep a pull on it, so that it will remain fairly straight. If the wind stiffens, more warp is paid out to lessen the strain. On the coast of Spain it is customary to use two boats in this sort of fishing, each one handling one end of the net, which is often one-hundred feet long or more; they then haul it to one place, or drag it ashore and empty it. On the coast of Cornwall the net is thrown out in a great semicircle, and the ends are gradually brought together. Methods differ with time and place, but the essentials have probably remained about the same.

Even before the fishermen of Capharnaum had their catch ashore, they would be sorting it out rapidly and skilfully in the first grey glimmer of dawn. Useless or harmful critters, such as dogfish, would be knocked on the head and tossed overboard. Then the "prime" or best and biggest would be slung on ropes. Next the "offal" would be sorted according to size or kind, and packed in various baskets. Before the sun was well up, all would be on their way to the markets at Capharnaum, or to the smoking and drying houses. In dealing with fish, time is of the essence.

It was in expectation of such a successful night that Simon Peter and his brother arranged to go out with Zebedee and his two sons one afternoon in the hot summer of 27 A.D. Before the rubied sun had vanished behind the western hills their boat was floating like a dream vessel between the sky above and the sky in the water, and as dusk began to settle down, the stiff and creaky net was cast over the quarter. It was already bellying out behind when Peter put her head to the scanty wind.

The night was keen and beautiful, with stars above and beneath, and as the dew began to fall through the darkness, the last breath of tropical heat gave place to a cool breeze. A small rag of sail kept the boat tugging at the net, her nose still to windward, following a course parallel to that of Zebedee.

Sometimes, when the wind died, the water could hardly be heard swishing at the bellied black side. The men would nap off by turns, and Andrew would spell his brother at the tiller. So for a few hours they drifted, either dragging one long net, or on this occasion, as seems more probable from the context, each with his own.

Now the stars began to pale and to flicker out in the deathlike calm that mysteriously falls in the last hour of night. Then the wind that heralds the dawn began to stir, and faint gropings of grey to streak the heavy dark of the east. The time had come for the haul. Signals were exchanged with Zebedee, the two boats put about, one made a wide semi-circle around the other, and they headed for the shore. Another gruff command in Aramaic, and the nets were hoisted dripping out of the dark water.

Both were empty. There was not even a crab in the meshes. Simon Peter probably used the language that he found rising so easily to his lips in moments of chagrin or embarrassment. They beached the boats not far from Capharnaum and went ashore, lugging the futile nets with them. Spreading them out on the beach, the tired and grumbling men began to clean them.

Cleaning nets is a long and disagreeable but essential part of the fisherman's work. A net is expensive, and its life depends upon the care it receives. Every few weeks it must be "barked" in tar, grease, oak-bar, and ochre. After each trip any broken meshes must be mended; all sand, sea-weed, barnacles and muck must be carefully scraped away. Then the whole is washed in clean water, and spread out to dry on the beach. Finally it is coiled away below decks for the next voyage.

Simon Peter and his companions were still in the midst of this chore, and the sun was beginning to mount the morning sky, when they heard an unusual sound from the direction of the city. It was that vague humming or murmur which, as it comes gradually nearer, is shattered into the harsh notes of many human voices, certainly more than could ordinarily be heard near Capharnaum at that hour. Presently a crowd swarmed over the crest of the long hill arising from the lake shore, and came toward them, milling about, gesticulating, shouting. Now they could see Jesus walking in the midst of the people, apparently expostulating or explaining to those who pressed in upon him from either side and from behind.

Plainly something unusual had occurred. The gospel does not say what it was; perhaps the Lord had miraculously saved some important person from the jaws of death when summoned by distressed relatives in the hour before the dawn: and as the news had spread from house to house through the early-waking town, grateful people had followed him, overtaking him on his way perhaps to pray in some lonely accustomed place. Their numbers were still increasing so rapidly that they seemed likely to push him into the water as he approached it.

Jesus looked calmly about. He saw the eager dark faces rising in rows above him, waiting for his words. He saw the two boats in the shallow water, their noses in the sand, and the two groups of fishermen, scrubbing their nets. Without further ado he stepped over the gunwale into the barque of Simon Peter, and asked him to push off a little from the land.

Simon Peter gave the command. As he and two or three others clambered quickly aboard, the heavy craft swung about, and slowly lumbered back into the lake. They poled her a few yards from shore, and there dropped an anchor in the calm water.

Jesus sat on the gunwale and began to address the crowd. What he said was for their ears, not ours; for none of the gospels record it, and only one, in fact, mentions that he spoke?[2] But all who have read the Sermon on the Mount and others of his discourses can well imagine the powerful effect of his words, not only on the crowd but on the dejected and tired fishermen.

When he had finished, he said to Simon Peter:

"Put out into the deep water, and let down your nets for a catch."

Simon was a fisherman, and knew that the fish did not run in shoals at that hour and that place.

"Master," he began, "we have toiled all night and caught nothing—."

Something in the face of Jesus must have stopped him. "However, at your bidding," he hastened to add, "I will lower the nets." And he spoke the necessary directions.

The mainsail fluttered up and bellied out; the bow of the boat swung around; the shore began to recede astern; and once more the tired men went through the routine of "shooting" the net. It is not clear whether Zebedee and his sons did likewise, or whether they watched from the beach. But everyone knows what befell Simon Peter on that historic occasion: how his net was so overloaded by a shoal of fishes that it broke as they hauled it over the deck, and how the boat was filled almost to sinking, until he had to signal frantically to Zebedee and his sons to come and receive the rest of the catch. Both vessels were filled to the gunwales.

Simon should have been overjoyed, and in fact he was; but his first emotion seems to have been one of terror. This has been

_____

[2] Luke 5:1-11; cf. Matt 4:18-22 and Mark 1:16-29

attributed to a superstition among the Jews, which he shared, that holy persons honoured by some special manifestation of the presence or power of God had not long to live: as the Greeks put it, "whom the gods love, die young." Peter had a natural fear of death, a strong sense of self-preservation. Perhaps this explains why he dropped on the deck before the knees of the Lord, and cried: "Leave me, Lord, for I am a sinful man!"

Jesus hastened to reassure him. "Fear not!" The words fell like manna on the fisherman's soul. "From henceforth you shall be catching men!"

Further wavering on the part of the four fishermen (if indeed they had wavered) was now clearly impossible. Love and hope had been fused in a moment into such a conviction that as soon as they beached the boats, they left them, with the nets and the gigantic mess of fish, to Zebedee and the two crews, and with hardly a farewell word or a look behind they followed the Lord along the shore back to Capharnaum. Peter and Andrew, James and John had given up vexing the sea forever; so at least they thought. Old Zebedee, speechless with astonishment, watched them vanish over the shoulder of the hill.

9

One Friday evening Simon Peter gazed thoughtfully from the top of his house across the roofs of others, dropping terrace by terrace to the shadows and reflections already intermingling on the water. He saw a dark figure rise above the bulk of the synagogue in a familiar posture, and he knew it was the chief rabbi lifting the shofar horn to his lips. As the red rim of the sun disappeared below the western hill, he heard two clear peremptory blasts, whose overlapping echoes shivered against the temples and granaries of Capharnaum. Even so the sons of Aaron had summoned the Israelites to silence and prayer in the desert. The sounds were repeated after a short pause. Then a third double note shattered the returning quiet, and everyone knew that the sabbath had begun. The minister hastened to lay down his ram's horn where he stood, lest by merely holding it he break the commandment. A hush fell over the whole community as workmen dropped their tools, housewives their brooms. All up and down the Sea of Galilee, from one town to another, the trumpets could be heard announcing the day of rest: in near Bethsaida, in Magdala across the water, even among the black basalt houses of the pagans in beautiful Tiberias, far down the shore.

Simon Peter went downstairs, and found his mother-in-law ill of a fever.

The next morning the old lady was unable to get up and go to the synagogue service. Peter and Andrew made her as comfortable as possible, perhaps leaving her in the care of some woman of the neighbourhood, and then betook them to the house of prayer. Every seat was taken, and many were standing in the aisles, for the word had got about that Jesus of Nazareth was going to preach, and the people of Capharnaum, unlike his fellow townsmen, heard him respectfully, "struck with astonishment at his teaching." They were rewarded by a striking and terrible spectacle. It was the first exorcism that Simon Peter and his companions had seen him perform.

Diabolical possession was fairly common in Palestine, as it is today in China and other missionary pagan countries where the influence of Christianity has been comparatively slight. There have been a few notable instances in the United States during the past few years, though most of the victims are probably locked up in asylums and certified by "science" to be incurably mad. It was otherwise in Judea. Everyone knew of poor wretches that haunted tombs and lonely rocks, crying out in torment through the night, falling on their faces, tearing themselves and foaming at the mouth. And it happened, on that very sabbath a man inhabited by a foul spirit found his way to one of the benches where the most respectable persons in Capharnaum sat listening in wonder to the living voice of Jesus Christ. The demon was most uncomfortable in that presence, until, finding the words of certitude and hope intolerable, he screamed through the frothing and twisted mouth, as the man fell convulsed to the floor:

"What is there to us and to you, Jesus of Nazareth? Have you come to exterminate us? I know who you are – the Holy One of God!"

"Be silent!" said Jesus, "and come out of him."

With a final convulsion of rage the foul spirit left the harassed body. It lay like a log where it had fallen among the Corinthian columns.

The effect was tremendous. "What is this?" people were saying one to another. "What an utterance! With authority and power he commands the foul spirits, and they come out!"[1]

Simon Peter found himself something of a personage in the community from that hour. For at the end of the synagogue service, the Lord accompanied him to his home, and finding his mother-in-law still in bed, and very miserable, he took her by the hand, and lifted her up as if she had been a child. And to her own astonishment and that of everyone else in the house, she felt quite normal at once, and had no trace of fever. Joyfully she went about, preparing some food and drink for her son-in-law and his guest.

This, following so close upon the exorcism, aroused so much enthusiasm throughout Capharnaum that the people could hardly wait for the sabbath sun to go down. As soon as dusk fell they flocked to the house of Simon Peter the fisherman, presenting their own infirmities or carrying sick persons on litters or mattresses. As Jesus laid his beautiful hands on them, one after another arose strong and well. Shouts of surprise and sudden laughter echoed through the cool courtyard and against the stone walls. Cripples left crutches in the garden as they strode away. Demoniacs, freed from their cruel affliction, went home praising their benefactor.

The house of Simon Peter had suddenly become a sort of public institution, something like a clinic and a shrine. Indeed, it appears that Jesus himself took up his residence there, perhaps to be

---

[1] Mark 1:23-28; Luke 4:33-37

more accessible to those who were constantly appealing to Him. Simon Peter rejoiced to see the people crowd into his courtyard, day after day, or swarm under the covered gallery and perch on the outer stairway; now he felt sure that the whole world would soon accept the Lord Jesus as the messiah. And sometimes at night he would lie awake congratulating himself on the distinction that had come to him and to his house.

One morning long before daybreak he heard the Lord arise and go quietly out into the darkness. Peter got up quickly and followed him. He summoned Andrew and one or two of the others, who appear to have been sleeping nearby, and they all trailed Jesus under the waning stars past outskirts of the town until they overtook him at a deserted spot. And there they found him praying. The gospel does not add whether he remained standing, with outstretched hands, as the Jews generally did, or prostrated himself on the ground, as on another occasion. As soon as he took notice of them, they tried to draw him back to Capharnaum, saying, "Everybody is in search of you!" Voices of disappointed early supplicants already came, perhaps, from the direction of Peter's house. Jesus said, however, "Let us go elsewhere to the neighbouring village-towns, so that I may preach there also; for I have come forth for this purpose."[2]

And with no more preparation than that, he led them off through the hills. They walked for several days through Galilee, stopping at the synagogue of each place while the Lord preached, healed, and cast out demons. Once he encountered some pharisees who demanded why his disciples plucked corn from wayside fields on the sabbath; and he informed them that he was Lord even of the sabbath. In one place they saw, rising before them, a horrible figure in rags, like a scarecrow. Simon Peter knew what that whiteness of the rotting flesh denoted. He probably felt like taking to his heels as the wretch threw himself on his knees, whining:

"If you will, you can cleanse me."

Jesus, "moved with compassion, extended his hand, touched him and said to him, 'I will; be cleansed!'"[3] And for the first time Simon Peter saw the ulcerous face of a leper resume the colour and texture of health.

The man ran away, heedless of the wishes of his benefactor, to broadcast the news of his cure. After that there were such crowds in

---

[2] Mark 1:35-39
[3] *ibid*, 2:2-4

the towns that Jesus no longer could enter them, but had to preach outside. Yet people found him even in deserted and nearly inaccessible places.

When they returned to Capharnaum after several days, the mood of welcome was almost hysterical. Simon Peter's house was overrun day and night by supplicants. The stage was set for the famous episode which drew into the open the smouldering resentment of the pharisees, and defined more clearly the issue between them and the Messiah. One warm evening the crowd was so dense that "there was no longer any room for them, not even about the door; and he spoke the word to them. And they came bringing him a paralytic, carried by four men. And being unable to get near him on account of the throng, they removed the roofing where he was, and having made an opening, lowered the cot on which the paralytic lay."

Having carried their burden up the outer stairs, the four men had loosened some of the red tiles over the covered gallery, and had let the litter descend to the very feet of the Lord, as he stood addressing the crowd below. But this was to be more than an ordinary cure. As Jesus looked across the rows of eager believing faces, he saw some scribes from Jerusalem with certain of the local pharisees, huddling together in a corner like dark birds of prey, watching and whispering, and he read their hearts. Then and there he decided to use the incident as another appeal to the ruling classes of Israel to give him the faith and love due to one who had come to keep the promise made to their ancestor Abraham: "And in your seed shall all the nations of the earth be blessed ..."[4] Instead of remarking on the disease of the man at his feet he startled them all by saying:

"Son, be of good heart, your sins are forgiven!"

The silence must have been frightening. For the challenge in the casual words was unmistakeable. Only God could forgive sins, and a man who claimed to do so by his own authority must be a God or a blasphemer. The pharisees knew that he was telling them, in effect, that he was God. They did not believe it. "Why does the man talk this way?" they were thinking. "He is blaspheming!"

Jesus regarded them patiently. "Why do you reason thus in your hearts?" he demanded. "Which is easier to say to the paralytic, 'Your sins are forgiven' or to say, 'Rise up, take up your bed, and walk?' But in order that you may know that the Son of Man possesses authority to forgive sins", here he looked down again at

---

[4] Gen 22:18

the paralytic, and spoke in a peremptory tone: "I say to you, rise up, take up your bed, and go home."

The withered limbs quivered as life began to course through them. Joy and fear were struggling on the man's face. He bent his long useless knees, rolled over, clumsily stood up. Yes, it was true; he could move every muscle and joint. Stooping again, he picked up the litter, and started for the door.[5]

It is a strange fact, but one plainly recorded, that while most of the spectators were "beside themselves with wonder", glorifying God and crying, "We have never seen anything like this!" the emissaries of the high priests and pharisees went away as incredulous as they had come, and more bitter, having been rebuked so crushingly in public. Doubtless they reported the miracle to Jerusalem, with their own interpretation of it.

Jesus, for his part, did not rest upon this victory. He wanted the love of all men, in return for his own, but first of all he wanted the love of the house of Israel. He did not intend to accept anything less than the belief and worship that belonged to him as the son of God. To elicit them from these hard hearts he must break through incrusted layers of pride, nationalism, self-righteousness, complacency, entrenched wealth and influence. And only a few days after the cure of the paralytic, Simon Peter saw him follow up his advantage in such a way as to infuriate his enemies beyond words, and to frighten even his friends.

He was walking with the disciples along the shore, followed by the usual crowd of admirers and curiosity seekers, when he saw, staring at him from the door of Caesar's custom-house, the mournful and wary eyes of Levi the Publican. Jesus paused and looked directly at him. Would he denounce him? Would he call down fire from heaven to destroy the betrayer of his people? It was a golden opportunity, from the point of view of the pharisees, and even some of his own.

To the best people in Capharnaum, and to the pharisees above all, a publican, by definition, was almost unfit to breathe. He had authority from Caesar to stop people on the way, unload their pack animals, open their saddle bags and even the letters in their pockets. He was lenient only to those from whom he might expect favours or bribes. So long as he produced revenue for Caesar, he was given considerable latitude to enrich himself at the expense of citizens who already groaned under an *ad valorem* duty of two and a half to

---

[5] Mark 2:1-12

five per cent on goods in general, and twelve and a half per cent on luxuries, to say nothing of import and export taxes, bridge and road tolls, and harbour dues.

It was bad enough for a man to be a *Gabbai*, or ordinary collector, who gathered in the ground tax (ten per cent of all grain and twenty per cent of all wine or fruit produced), or the income tax of one per cent, or the poll tax required of all men from fourteen to sixty-five and all women from twelve to sixty-five. But it was worse to be a *Mokles* or custom-house official, for the exactions of these officers were far more grievous. Repentance for a Mokles, said the rabbis, was almost impossible. And to be a Little Mokles – one who sat in the custom-house himself to prey upon his fellow Jews – this was to earn execration from all good men, and from zealots a vow of extermination.

Now Levi of Capharnaum was not only a publican, but a Little Mokles, who sat in person at the busiest intersection between the docks and the marketplace, where he could fix a stony eye upon every boat that came or went, and every person who passed. He had had an excellent view of the activities of the prophet from Nazareth these past few weeks, and doubtless had heard many of his resonant words flung by the wind from the beach or one of the neighbouring streets. And now, in a moment pregnant for him with eternal pain or joy, he saw this man stop, and felt the full force of his remarkable gaze.

"Follow me!" said Jesus. It was all he said.

Levi arose like a man waking from a troubled sleep. There, on the counting table, he left his gold, silver, and copper coins that had been piling up all day; coins of all nations, some of them with Caesar's image on them, others proclaiming that Herod was king of the Jews and friend to the Romans. At last he had seen something better than gold or Herodias, or all the marble gods of Tiberias. And as Jesus of Nazareth turned and walked along the main street, the tax collector fell in behind him with a little group of rather shabby men whom perhaps he had seen on the streets or working about the docks. Possibly he found himself by the side of Simon Peter, who in that case might be rather uncomfortable, with the eyes of all his fellow townsmen upon him. Levi cared nothing for that. He was no longer Levi, but the man we know as Saint Matthew the Evangelist.

The repercussions of this event were enormous. It is hardly to be questioned that this publican, like Zaccheus of Jericho, made amends to any he had overreached, and generous dispersal to the poor. He did another very human thing. He gave a sumptuous dinner to the Lord and his new associates. And because Levi, whatever his other faults, was not a snob, he went about town inviting all his old friends, regardless of their social or moral status. The result no doubt was rather grotesque. Among the guests were other publicans of high and low degree, and a few notorious sinners, the sort that no respectable citizen of Capharnaum associated with, and no pharisee would brush with the hem of his garment.

What would the guest of honour think of all this? For the messiah to accept such an invitation would be foreign to all Jewish preconceptions. And knowing this, an impostor of any intelligence, or the writer of a fictitious account of one, would act accordingly. But Jesus calmly went to the house of his new convert, probably with several of the disciples, and ate and drank with the other guests.

The scribes and pharisees were furious. Some of them were at the dinner, either as guests or spectators, for in Galilee it was not uncommon for those who passed to stop and look on; and they saw the whole scandalous performance. They did not venture to complain to the Lord himself. Instead, they drew Peter and his fellows aside, saying: "How is it that he eats and drinks with the publicans and sinners?"

Peter had sometimes wondered about this himself. He could not have been very happy about dining with outcasts in the sight of all his neighbours and friends, and the thought that he must now receive Levi into his own house could hardly have been a comfortable one. But before he could think of what to reply, the Lord himself said, over the heads of the banqueters so that all could hear:

"The healthy have no need of a physician, but the sick have. I did not come to call righteous people, but sinners."

The pharisees went away unconvinced. It soon became evident that they were trying to make use of the followers of John the Baptizer, by inciting them to complain against those of Jesus, who did not keep the rabbinical fasts so strictly. He remarked that the groomsmen would have time to fast after the bridegroom had been taken away from them?[6]

---

[6] Matt 9:9-15; Mark 2:13-20; Luke 5:27-35

10

The conflict was unmistakable when Simon Peter accompanied the Lord to the holy city for the second time. The gospel says nothing of this journey except that "there was a Jewish festival, and Jesus went up to Jerusalem."[1] Yet it leaves no doubt as to why he went and what he did. He began by curing a man, at the angel's pool near the Sheep Gate, of a paralysis he had had for thirty-eight years. It was on a sabbath, and the scribes and pharisees lost no time in reminding him of the fact.

"My Father is working till now," he replied, "and I also work." The quiet implication stung them so sharply that they "wanted all the more to kill him, for the reason that he not only broke the sabbath but also called God his own father, making himself equal to God."[2]

The still more vigorous words in which he replied to their murderous unbelief shocked them just as today they shock those most in need of them. They had every reason to know, from his miracles, that he came from God, and therefore must be credited when he said he was the son of God. As the custodians and interpreters of the scriptures, they had no excuse for not understanding the prophecies of his coming. Yet even as they glowered at him, he loved these stubborn creatures of his. He loved them enough to be surgical with the pride and hypocrisy that kept them from seeing or acknowledging who he was. And the words he now addressed to them, though merciful and appealing, were also frank and vigorous:

"He who does not honour the Son does not honour the Father who sent him. Indeed, indeed, I say to you, that he who listens to my word and believes him who sent me, possesses eternal life ...

Indeed, indeed, I say to you that the hour is coming – yes, is now here – when the dead shall hear the voice of the son of God, and they who hear it shall live. For as the Father possesses life in himself, so he gave the Son also the possession of life in himself; and he gave him authority to execute judgment because he is the Son of Man. Wonder not at this; for the hour is coming when all who are in the tombs shall hear his voice, and shall come forth those who have done good to a resurrection of life and those who have done evil to a resurrection of judgment ...

The evidence that I have is greater than that of John: for the

---

[1] John 5:1
[2] *ibid* 5:18

works which the Father has given me to accomplish, the very works which I am doing give evidence about me that the Father has sent me.

The Father also who sent me has himself given evidence about me. You have neither listened to his voice at any lime, nor had regard for his image; and you have not his word abiding in you; because you do not believe the one whom he himself sent.

You search the scriptures, because you think that in them you have eternal life; and it is they that give evidence about me. Yet you are not willing to come to me that you may have life.

I do not receive honour from men. On the contrary I know you, that you have not the love of God in yourselves. I have come in my Father's name, yet you do not receive me; if another shall come in his own name, him you will receive! How can you believe, receiving honour as you do from one another, while the honour which comes from the only God you do not seek? Do not imagine that I will accuse you to the Father; there is one who accuses you – Moses, on whom you have set your hope. For if you believed Moses, you would believe me, for he wrote about me. But if you do not believe his writings; how are you to believe my statements?"[3]

All who heard this virile but dispassionate utterance knew exactly what he meant. No one there was ignorant or depraved enough to pretend that he was a kind, impractical, itinerant teacher, a gentle moralist and nature lover, a rustic poet and philosopher to be mentioned with Socrates, Buddha, or Lao-Tzsi. Here was a magnificent human, a man in his early thirties, proclaiming himself to be omnipotent, omniscient, author of life itself, sole judge of the living and dead. Either he was God, as he said, or he must be dismissed as a lunatic or an impostor.

Yet it was impossible for any sane and just mind to regard Jesus of Nazareth as a madman. His words were lucid, majestic, full of truth, wisdom, magnanimity; they moved men as learned as Nicodemus, and inspired great throngs irresistibly to action. All that he did or said had the quality of supreme greatness. This presented a dilemma to his enemies: great and sane men do not commonly assert that they are God. The greater a man is, the less likely he is to boast of unusual gifts and powers. The only possible exception would be a man who really was the incarnate God.

It was no easier to prove him an impostor. Charlatans are always looking for something for themselves, and it does not take a wise observer long to discern what it is. It may be money, power,

---

[3] John 5:19-47. The reference is to Deuteronomy 18:15,18.

women, the gratification of mere vanity; but it can not long be concealed. Quacks are also likely to make alliances, however secret, with powerful persons who may help them attain their ends; they are easily bought. Yet this man seemed to go out of his way to offend all the potentates who might, for their own good reasons and his worldly advantage, make common cause with him. His wants were those of the humblest of the poor. He repudiated flattery and lip-service. He asked for nothing but faith. Even his bitterest enemies have acknowledged his goodness.

Why did the responsible leaders of Israel brush aside the evidence, refusing even to weigh it seriously? This must have created no small difficulty for Peter, who had been taught from childhood to revere them. Naturally he accepted the Lord's explanation that the temple rulers did not believe him because they really did not believe in God the Father and his prophet Moses, whose names were always on their lips. In effect then, if not professedly, they were atheists. And how could men with their advantages have fallen into such an abyss of spiritual darkness?

Simon Peter probably never found the complete answer to this question, for it led back to that mystery called the problem of evil. But it may be that during this second missionary visit to Jerusalem he learned enough about the background of his Master's enemies to make them seem viable, if not understandable. His curious brother, Andrew, would not be slow in making inquiries and putting two and two together. John, the son of Zebedee, who had the perceptions of a poet and philosopher, was related to some of the most influential families in the city, who were well acquainted with the high priests.[4] Judas Iscariot was a Judean, and the sort of man who made it his business to be informed about everything in the practical world. From one source or another, Simon Peter began to get a clearer idea of what motivated the little bureaucratic pyramid which extended down from the temple rulers through the ranks of two powerful groups, the pharisees and the sadducees.

The pharisees were originally the *Chasidim* or pious men who followed Esdras in destroying pagan and idolatrous influences after the Babylonian exile. They supported the Maccabees in restoring the kingdom of Israel after five hundred years, and in casting the false gods out of the temple on that glorious Feast of Light, 25 December 164 B.C. They won the veneration of the Jewish people by shedding their blood freely during the persecution by Antiochus.

---

[4] John 18:15

It was then that they became known as pharisees, "those set apart." The Maccabean War left them with even greater influence. And though their quarrel with the Asmodean house (the Maccabees) brought on the Roman occupation, it entrenched them with such power that they were now virtually identified with official Judaism, and the recognized teaching authority of Israel. Much good, too, they had done. They had been right in their insistence that the Jewish people observe the Law strictly, and keep aloof from idolators and other degrading influences. The presence in their ranks of such devout and sincere men as Hillel, Gamaliel, Nicodemus, and Saul of Tarsus still reminded Israel of the noble pharisaic traditions of former times.

For some decades it had been apparent, however, that an evil yeast was at work corrupting the leaven of this pious brotherhood. It was not accidental, perhaps, that they owed so much to the passions of war and dissension. The peculiar temptation of the good, the great, and the successful is always the primal one of pride. At the very moment when these heroes were taking into their hands the future of the Jewish people (and to a great extent, of all men) they were beginning to turn their gaze from the vision of the Lord God and his infinite perfections to the contemplation of themselves. This is a sort of idolatry; and like all idolatry it isolates the offender from the supreme spiritual reality. Thus the pharisees lost the gift of faith. Faith, the certainty of truth not seen, was the essence of the ancient religion of Abel and Noah. Faith in the unseen omnipotent God, faith in his promise to make all nations blessed in the messiah, the seed of Abraham – this had been the strength of Abraham himself, of Jacob, Joseph, Moses, all the mighty prophets, judges, kings, and martyrs of the chosen people. The name of God, to be sure, was still constantly on the lips of the pharisees. But he was no longer in their hearts. Even so good a man as Nicodemus had suffered from their spiritual obtuseness; hence the question Jesus had asked him: "Are you a master in Israel and do not know these things?"

Having lost the precious kernel of supernatural belief, they had become materialists. But in clinging to the outer husks of it, they had incurred the additional guilt of a hypocritical and empty formalism. Having lost faith, they neglected important "good works" and overstressed minor ones, especially such external and ostentatious obligations as fasting, ceremonial washings, avoidance of "unclean" persons and places, and so on to the point of fanaticism. These they gradually reduced to a deterministic system in which God, being but a name to them, was like a mere book-keeper or accountant, bound to give each person his reward in strict mathematical proportion to his works. "The famous pharisee of the gospel did not ask favours from God; he made up the balance sheet of his own actions."[5] It was more shocking to eat with unwashed hands, or to heal on the sabbath, than to lie or oppress the poor. The ceremonies which meant only that the messiah was coming blotted out a true understanding of who and what he would be. Commentaries on the Torah and the Prophets were studied to the neglect of the holy books themselves and the divine commands they contained.

Thus the pharisees led a large part of the Jewish people into a forgetfulness of the mission for which they had been chosen. They were not merely to keep the Law themselves, but by good example to prepare all nations for the coming of the Christ. "Behold, I have given you to be the light of the Gentiles, that you may be my salvation even to the farthest part of the earth."[6] Jonah was punished by God for refusing to carry out this apostolate in regard to the Ninevites?[7] The same negligence of their high calling explains why so many Jews were blind to its culmination in the appearance of Christ. The chief guilt for this, as his words indicate, belonged to the pharisees. Instead of dispensing the light given to them, they hugged it to their own breasts, despising the nations they should have taught, and building about themselves and a large number of their fellow Jews the spiritual ghetto of racism and false nationalism. It was of them that Ezekiel had prophesied: "Woe to the shepherds of Israel that fed themselves: should not the flocks be fed by the shepherds? ... My sheep have wandered in every mountain, and in every high hill, and my flocks were scattered upon the face of the earth, and there was none that sought them, there was none, I say, that sought them ... Therefore, you shepherds, hear the word of the Lord ... behold, I myself come upon the shepherds, I will require my flock at their hand."[8]

Having such guilt to conceal – and it was such that when fully hatched, not nineteen centuries of exile and misery would suffice to

---

[5] Giordani, *St Paul, Apostle and Martyr*, New York (Macmillan) 1946.
[6] Is 49:6
[7] 4 Kings 14:25. See also St Gregory the Great, *Moralia*, Job 5:12:13 and St Bernard, *Sermon* 14.
[8] Ezek 34:2, 7, 10

expiate it without repentance – the pharisees had become, before the advent of Christ, a secret society (fraternity or *Chebher*) of about six thousand members, scattered throughout Palestine, especially in the provinces. Members were admitted in a formal initiation ceremony, and were ranged in four degrees "marking an ascending scale of levitical purity or separation from all that was profane."[9] Secrecy and dispersion gave them an influence far out of proportion to their numbers. And the attitude of the messiah toward them leaves no doubt that this was a baleful power. It is not necessary to suppose that they had been inoculated with the poison generated in the Orphic and Eleusinian mysteries, as their ancestors had been by the contagions of Beelphezor and Baal. What they had done was to reduce Judaism, in their ranks, to a sort of worship of themselves under the pretext of exalting the Jewish people. But this is the beginning of atheism. Concealed within all such collective self-worship in the city of man is the primal tempter who said "Eat of the fruit of this tree and you shall be as gods." Humanitarianism, father of heresy and socialism, is often satanism in disguise.

Behind these Hebrew puritans were the sadducees. Fewer in numbers, and strong chiefly in Jerusalem, they had no such definite organization, but were rather a class of philosophical sceptics who had reacted under the influence of Greek speculation against false rigidity and exclusiveness. They were rationalists who denied the resurrection of the dead and the immortality of the soul. Yet they defended the ancient dogma of free will against the determinism of the pharisees; and on this subject, and similar ones, the two groups had many long and bitter public disputes. Extremes have a way of meeting, however, and both being essentially materialists, secularists, pragmatists, compromisers, children of this world, the two groups managed to work in close harmony when common interests were at stake. Thus the sadducees, when in office, would conform outwardly to the dogmas and rituals of the pharisees. And in political and economic affairs, both parties were guided and dominated by a small oligarchy which was also a plutocracy.

Through their control of the high-priesthood (which they owed not to Israel but to the Romans) a few interlinking wealthy families dominated all Jewish life, and levied tribute on almost every Jew in the world. They received a percentage on each transaction of the money changers in the temple. And these financiers not only exacted their ten to twelve per cent for replacing the coins of all nations

---

[9] Edersheim, *op. cit.*, I, 311 *et seq.*

with silver shekels of the sanctuary, but charged foreign Jews for currency to pay expenses while in Jerusalem. They received commissions for handling gifts sent to the Temple by generous Israelites of Alexandria or Antioch. They probably carried on various other money-lending enterprises besides.

Finally, the high priests and their relatives were the secret owners of the bazaars called the temple market, probably in the Court of the Gentiles. It was there that people usually bought animals to sacrifice, paid for a meat and drink offering at prices fixed monthly by tariff and for counterfoils or tokens with which to procure the complement of sacrifice, and gave a fee to the commissar or *mumchen* ("one approved") who inspected and certified the beasts or birds. Every transaction increased the wealth of the corrupt luxurious minority. It is to them, and not to the Jewish people as such, that the four Evangelists generally refer when they write of the "Jews".

The head of this parasitic clan, this official totalitarian Judaism, was Ananos the son of Seth, better known to us as Annas. This old sadducee was the very one whom Simon Peter had seen, on his first visit to Jerusalem at the age of twelve, arrayed in violet and purple and double-dyed scarlet, the mitre of Aaron on his head, the gold tablet on his forehead. He had bought the high priesthood from Quirinius, and had regarded it from the start as a financial opportunity. Cold, cunning, daring, resourceful, implacable, he had managed, in seven years, to build up the bureaucracy which now controlled all civil as well as ecclesiastical affairs. He and his sons, with the families allied to them by marriage or interest, bribed and corrupted judges, intimidated the sanhedrin or council of seventy elders, and quietly collaborated with Pilate and other Roman officials while pretending to denounce them in public. After seven years of such "service", Annas had made himself so unpopular that he deemed it prudent to retire. Five of his sons succeeded him in turn; then one of his grandsons. The present high priest, the pharisee Caiaphas, was his son-in-law. But these were only appearances. Annas still held the reins of power behind the scenes, and not only "advised" Caiaphas from some informal and unofficial eminence, but presided as *Nasi* or prince over the sanhedrin. He was the uncrowned king of the Jews.

The people heartily detested this old racketeer and his henchmen. A rabbi complained that "they themselves are high priests, their sons treasurers, and their servants beat the people with sticks." The Talmud tells of a curse put upon them by a noted rabbi of Jerusalem, Abba Shaul; and contemptuously imputes to them a special sin of "whispering", which apparently means something like "hissing like vipers." The contemporary Josephus mentions Annas, junior, as "a great hoarder of money" who robbed the common priests of their revenues by violence or intimidation. About three years before the fall of Jerusalem the long-suffering citizens arose in wrath and destroyed the bazaars of the sons of Annas, as they called the temple market – but too late; unfortunately, to avert the promised doom.[10]

Annas cared nothing for that. He was interested but in himself, envisaged in the power that money gave him. He honoured with his hate only what threatened that power. And he formed his opinion of Jesus of Nazareth from that point of view alone. As soon as he saw him and heard him, he knew that if he accepted him as the messiah, he would have to confess himself to be a robber and oppressor of the poor, a hypocritical servant of God; he would have to surrender his stolen wealth and ease. Too depraved for this, he conceived a deadly hatred for the holy one as he watched him cross the porch of Solomon. Annas had always been evil. Now he was satanic.

The venom of his hate pursued the Christ even after he left Jerusalem one spring day to return to Galilee. Wherever he went with his friends, the spies of Annas were watching, listening, whispering. They complained when the disciples plucked a few ears of corn one sabbath. They were waiting in a country synagogue on another sabbath, to see what the Lord would do, "in hope of finding a charge to bring against him." When he gave them an unanswerable reply, and cured the withered hand of a paralytic, they had no recourse but to become "filled with senseless rage," and "they discussed among themselves what they could do to Jesus."[11] Levi, the reformed publican, recorded that after this incident "the pharisees went out and consulted together as to how they should destroy him."[12] They were ready now to make use of any weapon. They even conspired secretly with the Herodians, an extreme and corrupt faction of the sadducees whom they professed publicly to abhor,[13] against him whom their ancestor Jacob had called "the desire of the everlasting hills."

---

[10] Edersheim, *op. cit.*, I, 367-372
[11] Luke 6:1-11.
[12] Matt 12:14
[13] Mark 3:6

11

As the conspiracy against him developed, Jesus left the Galilean hills, and went down to the inland sea. Yet this journey was not at all like a flight; it was more like a royal progress. For pilgrims returning from Jerusalem had carried everywhere the news of his defiance of the pharisees and of his miracles, and the accumulative effect was now evident in the growing crowds that cluttered the roads and camped in the fields. They were coming from all parts of Galilee, from the highlands of Judea, from the ten cities of Decapolis, from Idumea far to the south beyond the Dead Sea, from Transjordania and Syria, even from the Phoenician villages near Tyre and Sidon on the shore of the Mediterranean.[1] Whenever it pleased him to do so, he would heal the sick and expel demons. But for some reason that Peter could not fathom, he now desired to be alone; and when they came in sight of the blue flashing water of Galilee, he told them to get him a boat.

Likely enough this was near Capharnaum, and the vessel may well have been the one of Peter and Andrew, which had lain keeled over so many days on the beach with her nets and halyards baking in the sun. Jesus and his chief disciples went on board and put out into the deep, leaving the huge crowd grumbling behind them on the shore. They followed a southerly course along the west bank past Bethsaida and past the dark radiance of Tiberias, where Herod perhaps at that very moment was being steamed in the vapours from a sulphur spring of a hundred and forty-three degrees, as he sought in vain to feel young and clean again. So far as is known, Jesus never entered that place, avoided by Jews because it was built over an old cemetery. Somewhere below it they beached the boat and went ashore.

From the wooded lake-front he took a road that went sharply up the slope to the southwest, winding in and out among the hills and skirting the southern incline of Mount Tabor, until he and his followers arrived near a smaller hill known today, from its odd shape, as the Horns of Hittin;[2] it has been compared also to a saddle. It was not as high as Tabor, some nine miles to the northwest, but it was more accessible, and on the top was a small

---

[1] Matt 4:25; Luke 6:17
[2] This is the traditional site visited by pilgrims for centuries. Objections have been made in favour of a hill north of Capharnaum.

flat plateau from which arose an eminence commanding a view of the Sea of Galilee, Mount Galaad, and a large part of the northern hill country up to snowy-capped Hermon. On this level eminence, as dusk began to steal up out of the vales, Jesus left his followers and went to the peak above to spend the night, as often he did, in solitary prayer.

Peter and the others meanwhile would be making a fire and partaking of some supper. And while they were still discussing the events of the day, they would be joined by others of the disciples, now numbering several dozens, who had followed them in boats or over land, by pre-arrangement. The succeeding events suggest something of the sort unless we are to assume that the gospel narrative is telescoped here, and that more than one night was spent on the mountainside. The crowds that followed the Christ in his journeys were most persistent, and often beat their way to where he was through fields, swamps, or woods that seemed impenetrable. Others continued to arrive through the night, as the disciples huddled by the embers of their fire, thinking of the lonely one far above. Hearing the foxes cry in the fields below or the wolves howl on a nearby hill, they must have felt like their ancestors of long ago waiting for Moses to return from the mists of Mount Sinai.

Early on a fresh spring morning they saw him coming down to face the still growing crowd. When he had almost reached the flat place where the disciples were, he stopped, and announced that he intended to choose twelve apostles from their number, one for each of the sons and tribes of Israel.

Simon Peter had good reason to expect that he would be one of these. Yet he probably waited with no slight anxiety while the grave commanding eyes swept along the row of faces until they rested upon his own, and the voice of Jesus uttered his name:

"Cephas!"

Joy darkened the freckled face of the fisherman. He could hardly have expected to be mentioned before John, the son of Zebedee! Yet here he was, the first on the list. He lumbered heavily up the incline and waited, while the Lord called out the other eleven names: those of Peter's brother Andrew, John and James the sons of Zebedee, Philip of Bethsaida and Thomas the Twin; Bartholomew of Cana and Levi (Matthew) the ex-publican of Capharnaum, James the Less, the son of Alpheus, who was the Lord's cousin and probably bore a resemblance to him; holy and conscientious Simon the Canaanite; Jude Thaddeus the brother of James the Less; and

Judas Iscariot. The initial powers committed to these men were to heal the sick and to cast out devils. It was plain, too, that they had been selected for definite offices above those of the other disciples, in a hierarchical order. In the three lists of the synoptics, Peter always appears first, with Andrew and the sons of Zebedee following; Philip fifth, and Judas last.

From various hints in the gospels it is possible to make some sort of guess as to what may have passed through Simon Peter's mind in those golden moments. Convinced that Jesus was the messiah, he had every reason to believe that his own position, not only as a member of the government in embryo but as its first and ranking cabinet officer, was secure. He saw a long, peaceful, prosperous and happy life extending before him. He was hardy more than forty, and in the prime of his manhood; he might marry again and beget children; he might conceivably become the founder, under the messiah of course, of a new dynasty. Was not King David a shepherd lad? And Moses of plebeian origin? Naturally, once in power, he would love all good men, and put the quietus on his enemies and God's, who would be more or less identical. He would enjoy the applause of his contemporaries and of posterity. He would have wealth, power, ease, pleasure; a beautiful mansion, perhaps, on the shore of Lake Gennesareth, near enough to Capharnaum. And of course he would continue to heal the sick, drive out devils, judge between his fellow-citizens, and prophesy, for their edification. Finally, after a full and glorious life, well rewarded for his virtue by God and man, he would go to dwell with his father Abraham, who had earned him all this, in imperishable felicity.

Peter's reverie, if we may presume thus to imagine it, was broken by a familiar sound, the sound of a great mass of human beings approaching over the shoulder of the next hill, the thumping of tired feet and the murmuring of relieved voices. A large part of the crowd they had left near Capharnaum had found out where they had gone and had successfully followed them over hill and dale, over stream and pasture, to this remote place; and they began swarming up the incline to the little plateau, crying the name of Jesus and begging him to speak once more to them, to heal their infirmities, to give them the hope of his kingdom for their dark future.

It was all happening as in a dream or a play; the mob was entering at exactly the right moment, and Peter was not sorry to have so many witnesses to the opening of his public career. Jesus meanwhile was taking all this in with a sweeping compassionate glance. He decided to speak to them, and going a little way up the mountain, until he found a rock or a ledge which would serve as a pulpit, he turned and looked about once more. He saw the larks rise overhead, and pigeons fluttering back and forth over the oleanders and wild oaks that broke the dusky green of many olive trees, the streaks of blue iris, warm cyclamen, scarlet poppies and anemones. Nature had taken particular pains on this radiant spring day to decorate her amphitheatre. It was full of human beings, waiting patiently for the voice that was about to rise on the keen and fragrant air. The eyes of Jesus rested for a moment on all his various creatures. Then, abruptly uttering the sublime Beatitudes, he began the sermon on the Mount.

What thoughts passed through the head of Simon Peter as he listened to the words that would send lusty men into deserts and monasteries, draw lovely girls into grilled cells, bring sinners to their knees with tears, and give martyrs the strength to die? If the heavenly discourse so moves us now from the printed page, what must it have inspired in a listener? A reverie like an ineffable music weaving a world of dreams; a trance like that high prayer in which truth and beauty and goodness are seen, heard, and felt rather than understood.

"Do not be anxious about your life, what you shall eat or what you shall drink, nor about your body, what you shall wear ... Look at the birds of the sky, how they neither sow nor reap nor gather into barns; yet your heavenly Father feeds them ... And why should you worry about clothing? Observe the field-lilies, how they grow; they neither toil nor spin; yet I tell you that even Solomon in all his magnificence was not arrayed like one of them. But if God so clothes the grass of the field, which exists today and is thrown into the oven tomorrow, will he not much rather clothe you, O you of little faith? Do not therefore worry, saying, 'What shall we eat? or what shall we drink? or what shall we wear?' for the heathen seek after all these things; and your heavenly Father knows that you need them all. But seek first the kingdom of God and his holiness, and all these things shall be given to you besides. Do not then be anxious about tomorrow, for tomorrow will take care of itself ...

Ask, and it shall be given to you; seek, and you shall find; knock, and it shall be opened to you ...

Whatever therefore you wish men to do to you, do also yourselves to them; for this is the law and the prophets ...

Enter through the narrow gate; for wide is the gate and broad the road that leads to destruction, and many there are who enter through it. How narrow the gate, and confined the road leading to Life! and few there are that find it ... .

Not everyone who says to me, 'Lord! Lord!', shall enter the kingdom of heaven, but only he who does the will of my Father who is in heaven. Many will say to me in that day, 'Lord, Lord, did we not prophesy in your name, and cast out demons in your name, and do many miracles in your name? And then I will declare to them, 'I never knew you; depart from me, you workers of iniquity!' ...[3]

But I say to you who listen: Love your enemies, be generous to those who hate you, bless those who curse you, and pray for those who ill-treat you. And to him who strikes you on one cheek offer the other also; and if anyone takes your cloak, do not prevent him from taking your coat as well. Give to everyone who asks of you; and from one who takes your property do not ask it again. And as you wish men should do to you, do so yourselves to them. And if you love those who love you, what thanks to you? For even sinners love those who love them. And if you benefit those who benefit you, what thanks to you? For even sinners do this. And if you lend to those from whom you hope to receive in return, what thanks to you? For even sinners lend to sinners, in order that they may receive an equivalent in return. But, rather, love your enemies, and do them good, and lend, expecting nothing in return; and your reward shall be great, and you shall be sons of the Most High; for he is kind to the ungrateful and the wicked. Be compassionate, therefore, as your Father is compassionate.

Judge not, and you shall not be judged. Condemn not, and you shall not be condemned. Forgive, and you shall be forgiven. Give, and it shall be given to you; good measure – pressed down, shaken together and overflowing – they will give into your bosom. For with the same measure you measure with, it shall be measured out to you in return ... .

And why do you observe the mote in your brother's eye, but do not notice the beam in your own eye? ... You hypocrite! first remove the beam from your own eye, and then you will see clearly to remove the mote that is in your brother's eye.

For there is no good tree that produces bad fruit, nor again a decayed tree that produces good fruit; for every tree is known by its own fruit. For people do not gather figs from thorn bushes, nor pluck a bunch of grapes from a bramble bush. The good man

---

[3] Matt 6:25-34; 7:7-8, 12, 13-14, 21-23

produces good out of the good treasure of his heart; and the bad man produces evil out of his evil treasure; for out of the abundance of the heart his mouth speaks.

But why do you call me 'Lord, Lord,' and yet do not practice what I say? Everyone who comes to me, and listens to my words, and puts them into practice – I will show you whom he is like. He is like a man building a house, who dug, and kept deepening, and laid a foundation upon rock. And when a flood came, the torrent broke upon that house, and could not shake it; for it had been well built. But he who listens and does not practice is like a man building a house upon the ground without a foundation; against which the torrent broke, and at once it fell; and the wreck of that house was utter." [4]

The great voice died away; and for a few moments there was such a silence over all the assembly as follows a music almost too exquisite to hear. Then. the crowd began to shuffle, to break into groups, to fill the vale with the murmur of a thousand conversations. They trampled the lilies and startled the birds, perhaps, as they went off in search of something to eat or drink. But they did not go far. When Jesus and the apostles finally descended from the mount, they were still waiting, and many of them followed him back to Capharnaum.

Simon Peter was never quite the same after that experience. For a long time he could hear in his soul the mighty strophes of the Beatitudes, destroying and creating a world:

"Blessed are the poor in spirit, for theirs is the kingdom of heaven. Blessed are the meek, for they shall inherit the earth. Blessed are the mourners, for they shall be comforted. Blessed are they who hunger and thirst after righteousness, for they shall be filled. Blessed are the merciful, for they shall obtain mercy. Blessed are the pure in heart, for they shall see God. Blessed are the peacemakers, for they shall be called the children of God. Blessed are they who suffer persecution for the sake of righteousness, for theirs is the kingdom of heaven. Blessed are you when men revile you and persecute you, and say everything evil against you falsely, for my sake. Be glad and rejoice, because your reward will be abundant in heaven; for so they persecuted the prophets who were before you ...

But woe to you who are rich! for you have received your consolation. Woe to you who are filled! for you shall go hungry. Woe to you who laugh now! For you shall mourn and weep. Woe to you when all men speak well of you! for in this way their

---

[4] Luke 6:27-49

forefathers used to treat the false prophets!"[5]

Yet as Peter began to turn over the sermon in his slow mind and to think of what various parts meant, he had to admit that a great deal of it went against the grain. It was not his nature to love those who hated him, to bless those who cursed him, and to offer his other cheek to one who struck him a blow. The notion of giving without return, of living from day to day with no thought of future savings or security, struck at the very foundations of the future he had been imagining. Why should anyone rejoice under persecution? Why should the scribes, pharisees, and Romans be allowed to stand in the way of the holy one of Israel and his friends when their time came? Many such questions must have occurred to Simon Peter when he tried to analyze what the Lord had said.

His friend John, who was more intuitive and more studious, probably understood better.

"There is one fact Simon, that would make it all true."

"What's that?"

"The fact of death."

Death was something that Simon Peter did not like to think about. He preferred to put such morbid ideas out of his mind as much as possible, and to think of life, health, and the future. Yet parts of the Sermon continued to haunt him with uneasy whispers. Not that he doubted the Lord – oh, no! He knew that Jesus must be right, because he was the messiah. Still, He certainly could go out of his way at times to utter hard sayings! Peter's distress seems inferable from some of the questions he asked the Lord during the following months. "Lord, how often shall my brother wrong me, and I forgive him?" he asked one day. "As many as seven times?"[6] The rabbis said three times, and Peter may have felt magnanimous in extending the number. "Seventy times seven," replied Jesus, as his eyes read the guileless mind before him, "and from the heart." Another day, still months later, he said impulsively, "See, we have left all and followed you. What then shall we have?"[7] What do we get out of it? He was angry with James and John because they aspired to sit on either hand of the Messiah.[8] But Jesus answered all his questions patiently, knowing that they were not the crafty ones

---

[5] Matthew begins with the Beatitudes as here given (5:3-12). Luke summarizes them more briefly and adds the "woes" (6:20-26). Mark and John do not quote any of the sermon.

[6] Matt 18:21-22

[7] ibid, 19:27-28

[8] ibid, 20:24

of the pharisees, but the honest ones of a man who loved and
believed.

On returning to Capharnaum, he remained there with his
friends, apparently, until Pentecost. Then they strolled through the
Galilean countryside until August. And during that third journey
Peter saw something that answered most of his questions.

They were walking one hot summer day along the high rolling
hills between Endor and Shunen, on one of the six roads leading to the
walled city of Nain. They had passed an ancient cemetery on a
hillside, and were already within sight of the town, when they heard
the wailing of flutes and the quavering voices of women; and
presently they saw, filing out of the principal gate, a familiar
spectacle, recognizable even at a distance. It was a procession of
many persons, headed by women in dark weeds, paid mourners, who
in shrill cadences to the accompaniment of timbrels and flutes were
keening the old heart-breaking laments of Israel. Following these (and
they went first, according to the *Midrash*, because woman brought
death into the world) walked a funeral orator; after him came a group
of barefoot persons who took turns carrying the wicker bier on which
lay the dead. Behind them were friends and relatives, and a very large
part of the community, some of whom also lined both sides of the
road shouting their sympathy amid sobs and prayers.

Usually such a demonstration had the right of way, and Simon
Peter would have stepped aside to watch it pass, while adding a
word of commiseration on his own account. But he noticed that the
Lord remained in the middle of the road, as if waiting for the dead,
until the cortege was forced to halt; and now he could see that the
form laid out on the bier was that of a young man, his face
uncovered and chalky-white in the glaring sunshine, his dark hair
glistening with burial ointments among the myrtles strewn about
him. The weeping woman near him was his mother, a widow, with
no other children.

As the voices faded to silence and the flutes were still, Jesus
stepped up to this poor woman and said, compassionately:

"Weep not."

He then touched the stretcher and said, this time in a different
tone:

"Young man, I say to you, arise!"

Simon Peter saw the dead youth stir and open his eyes.
Presently he sat up on the bier and began to mutter.

"And he gave him to his mother," amid exclamations of fear

and joy, as the people, realizing what had occurred, commenced to glorify God, and to cry, "A great prophet has arisen among us! God has visited his people!"[9]

Simon Peter knew the Scriptures well enough to remember that Elijah (Elias) and Elisha (Eliseus) also had raised dead persons to life. But there was a striking difference. Those men had done so by appealing to the higher power of Almighty God. Jesus had simply spoken like one having authority in himself to create or restore life. "I say to you, arise!"

This may well have been the very moment when Simon Peter became aware of what it might mean to be the messiah. It was not merely to be the son of David, a chosen one of God, a great king. Words written by the Psalmist centuries before, and often heard without understanding, now flooded his mind with revealing light:

"The Lord said to my Lord: Sit you at my right hand, until I make your enemies your footstool ... From the womb before the daystar have I begotten you!"[10]

Simon Peter knew at last that he was walking with the master of life and the lord of death; and the questions and doubts of his literal and carnal mind yielded to a fierce and joyous certainty. Yet it was hard to put it into words.

[9] Luke 7:11-17
[10] Ps 110

12

Like everyone else, including Shakespeare, Simon Peter sometimes had an odd awareness of life as a drama planned by a
consummate playwright who might allow the actors to improvise
within the limits of their free-will, but deftly directed the passionate
movement of each scene to its appointed close, while the
protagonist moved gigantically and irresistibly toward the final
climax, and the lesser characters were drawn into the vortex of his
stride. Sometimes, as in the second act of a masterly play, there was
a noticeable heightening of emotion and action. Simon Peter would
not have been surprised, after what he had seen lately, if the stars
began falling in showers, like figs from a tree in a strong wind, or
the sickly sun curdled into hot blood. These were days such as the
prophet had spoken of in a passage he was fond of quoting, when
young men would see visions and old men would dream dreams.[1]
This change in the mood, this more pulsing tempo, seemed
connected somehow with the fate of John the Baptizer. It began
about the time when he sent two messengers from his dungeon, far
above the rocky coast of the Dead Sea (or wherever it was) to ask
Jesus to confirm his identity as the messiah; and he did so, adding
some high praise of John, as "a prophet, and much more than a
prophet," and as great as any born of women. From then on it was
noticeable that Jesus talked more about individual death, and the
consummation of this world. It was during his next long rather
obscure journey that the sinner supposed to be Mary of Magdala
found him in the house of Simon the pharisee, and wiping his feet
with her hair, anointed him as if for his burial.[2] In the beautiful
Lake Sermon, preached from a boat there was an accent, for the
first time, on the end of all things and the last judgment. This ran
like a new motif through the parables of the sower, the cockle, the
mustard seed, the leaven, the treasure trove. The kingdom of heaven
was like a fisherman's net, from which the good and bad fish would
be separated in the end; the cockle would be plucked from the
wheat and burned; heaven, and not this earth, was the home of the
kingdom and the place to store riches. This could not have been
entirely clear to Simon Peter, especially when the Lord explained
that he spoke in parables so that the undeserving would not profit

---

[1] Joel 2:28
[2] So at least he said on a similar occasion. Matt 26:12; Mark 14:8

by the instruction.

Yet there was always something to remind him that faith goes on where reason stops. Jesus calmed a raging storm on the lake, when they were all terrified, by merely commanding the winds to be still. He exorcised the fierce demoniac in the land of the Gerasenes, whom no man had been able to tame or even to keep chained among the tombs; and Peter saw the fearful spectacle of the thousand devil-ridden swine thundering down a rocky declivity to perish in the churning waters, like damned souls plunging into hell. Only Peter, James and John were allowed to witness the raising of the daughter of Jairus from the dead – that unforgettable climax to a journey which ended with the Lord's sorrowful farewell to unbelieving Nazareth. Levi Matthew noticed a brooding sadness in him as they made their way through the villages of Galilee back to Capharnaum. "And observing the crowds he felt compassion for them, because they were harassed and scattered like sheep that have no shepherd." He looked at the little group of his followers and said, "The harvest is plentiful, but the labourers are few. Pray, therefore, the master of the harvest to send out labourers unto his harvest."[3]

From Peter's house, early in the winter, he sent the twelve on their first missionary journey without him. First he gave them careful instructions as to how to proceed – instructions that are followed by many monks and missionaries to this day. Then he dispatched them, two by two, with his blessing, and they went forth into a hostile world, as he said, 'like lambs in the midst of wolves.'

Simon Peter may have gone either with his brother Andrew or with his best friend John. Following the Lord's command they set out barefoot, possibly wearing sandals but no shoes, taking only the clothes they had on their backs, with no staff to ward off stray dogs or wild beasts, and no money in their girdles, not even a copper denarius. They avoided the towns of Samaria and pagan places such as Tiberias, going rather to "the lost sheep of the house of Israel," for it was the Lord's purpose to reveal himself to his own people. When they came to a village in Judea or Galilee, they lived on whatever alms were given them, for, as he had said, "the workman is entitled to his maintenance." On entering such a place, they would inquire where they could find some devout Hebrew, who loved God and honoured the prophets, and making their way to his house, they would salute it, and invoke the peace of Christ upon it, saying, "The

---

[3] Matt 9:38; cf also Luke:10:2-3

kingdom of heaven is at hand!" If there were any sick, they would heal them.

Through the good offices of the master of the house, they would then go to other homes, or speak in the marketplace or the open fields. Frequently they cast out diseases and devils. But if the house they appealed to was unworthy – inhabited by those who did not desire to hear the Word of God or did not deserve to hear it, they would feel their peace return to them. And as they left that place, they would shake its dust from their feet, as a testimony against it before heaven. In this manner, on occasion, they would appeal against a whole town or city, if none would receive them. And they had the promise of Jesus himself that it would be "more endurable for the land of Sodom and Gomorrha, in the day of judgment, than for that town."[4]

This journey was a revelation to Simon Peter in many ways. It was not merely that he discovered in himself new powers against sickness and diabolical possession and the malice of men; these had been promised him, and he was not much surprised. But he learned something else about the nature of the Lord's teaching. It was a way of life: and the living of it explained and clarified the unsearchable wisdom of its theory. The winter rains fell, and sometimes he was soaked through; but it did not seem to harm him. On some days he was hungry, but never for long; someone always gave him bread or wine when he really needed it. He had less of the world's goods and paraphernalia than ever before, yet never in all his life had he been so happy and contented. No house, no ship, no extra clothes, no money to change, nothing but his own body and soul, and the poor bedraggled rags that hung upon him: yet he needed nothing; he was absolutely carefree, and best of all, there was a quiet something that sang constantly in his soul. It was the joy that infused a person and satisfied his whole being beyond words when the loving eyes of Jesus Christ rested upon him. Now at last Peter knew what the Lord had meant when he told them to be like the birds of the air and the lilies of the field. Now he began to understand the Sermon on the Mount. He could hardly wait to get back to Capharnaum to report all this to the Lord Jesus. And the other eleven did likewise.

It was spring again, and the hills of Galilee were festive with colour, as if to join in their elation. But soon, on the very heels of mirth, as usual, came pilfering sorrow. For John the Baptizer, as they

---

[4] Matt 10:15. For the instructions see Matt 10:5-42; Mark 6:7-11; Luke 9:1-5. St Matthew's lengthy ones of may perhaps include those of later journeys, "telescoped".

heard, had been murdered in his dungeon. Herod had had him decapitated to gratify a whim of his paramour Herodias, and the still bleeding head of the Precursor had been presented to her on a golden dish.

This event marked the beginning of a new and more urgent phase in the tragedy (humanly speaking) that the messiah and his friends were enacting. He was deeply moved, for John was his cousin and had laid down his life for him. The apostles, too, must have been greatly depressed, knowing as they did why John had been apprehended, and how well his death fitted the motif they had lately remarked in the messianic discourses. Nor was the connection lost upon the tyrant as he sought forgetfulness in the arms of his mistress or the dances of her daughter Salome among the gardens of Machaerus or Samaria. Fear revealed to him what love had told the disciples, and he who could not yield to faith became so obsessed by superstition that he began to imagine that Jesus was John the Baptizer arisen from the dead; and once he sent him an invitation to visit him, doubtless to satisfy his curiosity, and perhaps to entertain him with a few miracles.

Jesus meanwhile, on hearing the sad news, said, "Come apart into a desert spot and rest a little." And going into a boat, probably Simon Peter's, he and the apostles escaped from the growing crowds at Capharnaum, and having crossed the Sea of Galilee, approached the eastern shore at a place seldom troubled by human voices or footsteps; the nearest town was Bethsaida Julius. But lo and behold, as they put into a cove, they saw before them a crowd of some five thousand, gazing across the waters and shouting a cheerful welcome. They stood elbow to elbow on the sand and wholly filled a wide grassy vale that formed a sort of natural amphitheatre between the water's edge and the green hillside.

Somehow these people had guessed or noticed where the Lord was going, and had come on foot, beating their way through fields and wastelands, from many towns and villages at the north end of the sea. Nor was their number so incredible considering the hordes that had followed Jesus on his last journey through Galilee. Even women had begun to appear among those who camped out in the meadows to hear him. Some of these – Mary of Magdala, Joanna the wife of Herod's steward Chusa, and Suzanna, were persons of means, from which they contributed to the bag of coins that Judas Iscariot, as treasurer, carried in his girdle to feed the poor.[5] The wonder was

---

[5] Luke 8:3

how so many people managed to subsist on so little. It reminded one of the children of Israel, a moving city of more than a million persons, living for forty years in the desert. And today more than ever; for there was no village near where they could purchase food.

Jesus might still have escaped in Simon Peter's barque. But as he looked at the tired faces, "he pitied them"[6]... He had compassion on them, because they were like sheep without a shepherd.[7] And going ashore, he healed some sick persons, "and he began to teach them many things."

It goes without saying that the hours passed quickly and delightfully; and as he continued to speak, he seemed not to have noticed that the sun was far down the western sky, and shining across the lake in their faces. Finally the twelve, after many whispered words and nudges, ventured to interrupt him, and to suggest that he dismiss the hungry people while there was yet time for them to find something to eat at Bethsaida or some of the less remote villages.

"There is no need of their going away," said Jesus. "Give them something to eat yourselves."[8]

During another startled and embarrassed pause the disciples took stock, and they found that Judas Iscariot had only some two hundred denarii or pennies in his leathern bag. One of the twelve asked the Lord whether they should spend the entire sum for bread at the next town. Practical Philip, estimating the number of people, retorted that two hundred pennies would not buy enough to give a tiny morsel to each.

"How many loaves have you?" asked Jesus.

"There is a lad here," said Andrew, well-informed as usual, "who has five barley-loaves and two fishes; but what are these among so many?"[9]

They all saw the point: one loaf per thousand would not be very satisfactory. But Jesus seemed quite unconcerned about the mathematical or economic aspects of the situation.

"Make the people sit down," he said. The twelve hurried about like Aaron and his Levites in the wilderness, dividing the crowd into companies of hundreds and fifties,[10] who sat on the grass in orderly ranks, expectantly facing the Lord.

---

[6] Matt 14:14
[7] Mark 6:34
[8] Matt 14:16
[9] John 6:9
[10] Mark 6:40

Peter saw him take each of the five loaves, hold it before him, and bless it, looking up to heaven. Then he broke it into fragments, which he handed to the apostles who stood about him. They in turn began to pass them out to the nearest ranks of spectators.

This went on for a long while. Time after time the twelve went forth clutching armfuls of bread, and returned for more. The two fishes likewise were blessed, broken into pieces, and distributed.

All four of the evangelists, including two eye-witnesses, record the essentials of this remarkable scene. All agree that there was enough to satisfy the five thousand guests; and that when the Lord commanded them to gather up the fragments that were left over, twelve baskets were filled.

"This is certainly the prophet who was to come into the world!" The cry passed from one mouth to another as the sated people began to realize the implications of what had occurred. They were all on their feet now, gesticulating and shouting at the top of their lungs, hailing the messiah, the son of David, the Christ, the Holy One, the king of Israel.

"Crown him king," cried a voice. "Crown him king!" cried hundreds and thousands. And paying not the slightest attention to his remonstrances, they began to close in upon him. It was plainly their intention to lift him to their shoulders, to set some improvised coronet upon his head, and to carry him in triumph to Capharnaum – perhaps even to Jerusalem.

Two of the apostles, we may be sure, entered heartily into the spirit of this outburst. To Simon Peter and to Judas it must have augured the realization of the hopes on which they had staked all they had or might expect to have. Both wanted Jesus to be king. Differing in the unselfishness of their love, they were at one in feeling, at that moment, that they had made no mistake in casting their lot with him who stood so majestically silent, sadly regarding the thousands who praised him with hysterical joy. Judas saw himself seated in the treasury on Mount Moriah, clothed in purple and fine linen; and the coin that passed through his fingers was not silver, much less copper, but purest gold. Simon Peter could feel on his finger something like a seal ring, sparkling with gems, as he presided over the elders of Zion, dispensing wisdom to all men and no small share of glory to himself.

These fantasies were dispelled by a peremptory command from the king of Israel himself. The details are not given. But he, "perceiving that they were about to come and forcibly seize him in order to make him king, retired again into the mountain by himself alone."[11] How he escaped from so large a mob – whether he awed them by the authority of his negation, or passed invisibly through their midst – is not stated. He did go to a high place nearby to pray; and before doing so, ordered the twelve to go aboard their boat and to cross the sea. They obeyed reluctantly. Pushing their way through the clamouring crowd, they climbed aboard and shoved off into the gathering dusk.

With Peter at the helm no doubt, and Andrew, James and John hoisting the sails, the stout little vessel containing the entire apostolic college nosed out into the deep water between clouds of fiery crimson and gold, both above and below. They would have been happier if the Lord had come with them, and they tarried near the shore to the last moment, hoping that he would appear after the crowd had dispersed. But when darkness scattered the last voices far up and down the shore, and there was no sign of him, they obediently put on more sail and departed. For some reason they had not been so much impressed by the miracle itself as by the popular demonstration. "They did not understand about the loaves, but their hearts were benumbed."[12] This strange observation by Simon Peter's disciple, incidentally, is one of many that support the integrity of the gospel story, for it would hardly have occurred to a romancer or an impostor. At all events, there they were, the twelve apostles, each thinking his own thoughts as they seemed almost to float in the air between the wind and the water. After a while Simon Peter put her head about and steered for Capharnaum.

The lights of the nine lake cities were beginning to dance on the purpling water and to mingle with the reflected stars. The tropical night enfolded all things in its soft embrace. Through the pure trembling air came the distant vibrations of harps and flutes and human voices. Even time grew drowsy, and one after another the tired men fell asleep.

Simon Peter became aware of something like a cold hand on his cheek. The wind had freshened and veered to the north, and they were in for one of those capricious blows that can make the sea of Galilee as rough and dangerous as the Mediterranean. He called to his companions. Andrew and the sons of Zebedee began to reef. By this time it was clear that there was no sense in trying to tack against the wind, for it was more like a gale than a gust. Even after

---

[11] John 6:15
[12] Mark 6:52

the last rag of sail had been taken off, the heavy craft was being tossed about like a cork in a southerly direction far out of her course. There was nothing to do but man the three sets of oars that were there for such an emergency; and taking turns at these, the brawniest of the twelve barely managed to keep her head to windward and to hold their own in the churning middle of the wild lake.

Thus for hours, it seemed, the fishermen tugged, and choked, and sweated without making much progress, while Judas Iscariot and the other landlubbers huddled in the hold and fervently wished they were ashore, even among the wolves on the hills. We have the word of one of the stout oarsmen, John the son of Zebedee, that they had gone only about four miles at three o'clock in the morning with the north wind still in their teeth, when they were all startled by a sound that shrieked over the howling of the wind and the moaning of the water. It was the voice of one of their number, crying: "A ghost! I see a ghost!"

They were then in the middle of the lake; yet they all distinctly saw what appeared to be the figure of a man walking on the tops of the huge waves and about to pass near them. As they gazed in terror, a familiar voice came out of the darkness from this phosphorescent figure: "Take courage, it is I; be not afraid!"

Simon Peter was the first to recognize him. "It is the Lord!" He felt a wild joy and fearlessness surge through his wet form. "Lord, if it is you," he cried, "bid me come to you upon the water!"

"Come!" said Jesus, holding out his hands.

"Peter accordingly went down out of the boat and walked upon the water," continues the eye-witness narrative of Matthew. "But seeing the violence of the wind he became afraid, and beginning to sink, he cried out: "'Lord, save me!' Immediately Jesus, extending his hand, seized him, and said to him, 'O you weakling in faith! Why did you doubt?' And when they had come up into the boat the wind lulled; and those who were in the boat came and worshipped him, saying, 'Truly you are God's Son!'"[13]

The storm subsided. The morning star looked serenely on the calm lake, and by sunrise they had landed at Capharnaum.

---

[13] All the evangelists tell of the storm and of the appearance of Jesus on the water, but only Saint Matthew relates Peter's adventure: 14:28-32

13

They had not been long ashore and the day was not far spent when people discovered who they were and who was with them; and, as many witnesses were now returning on foot or by boat with news of the miracle of the loaves and of his mysterious disappearance; the whole community began to seethe with excitement. Simon Peter saw the usual mobs assembling on the beach and about his house. They were seeking Jesus, yet they seemed greatly surprised when they found him.

"Rabbi, when did you come here?" they demanded. Then, as on the day before, they hailed him as Son of God and King of Israel.

Although this was precisely what he wanted them to believe and to say, Simon Peter noticed that He received it with marked coldness.

"Indeed, indeed I say to you, you seek me not because you have seen miracles, but because you ate of the loaves and were filled!" he said. "Labour not for the food that perishes, but for the food that endures to eternal life, which the Son of Man will give you; for him has God the Father sealed."

With this, apparently, he turned and walked away. It was as confusing to the apostles as it was to the multitude. Had they not called him the Son of God? Had they not made their belief plain? What was the everlasting food he was going to give them? They were all puzzled, not knowing the test he was about to apply to this "faith" of theirs. But they still clamoured after him as he passed along the shore to the white synagogue with the pot of manna carved on its door lintel, and they packed it almost to the roof in their eagerness to hear him explain his cryptic statement. The twelve, with some of their fellow disciples, pushed their way in behind him, and stood together as near to him as possible.

They noticed, close by among the townspeople, some strangers, evidently pharisees and sadducees from Jerusalem. They saw the Lord turn when he reached the Bima, and quizzically regard the long rows of dark faces and gleaming eyes that filled the dim synagogue. He said nothing, but waited. They began to grow restless, and some of them, speaking for the rest, asked questions.

"What must we do in order to perform the works of God?"

"This is the work of God," replied Jesus, "that you believe in him whom he sent."

There was another pause, and then several voices demanded:

"What proof, then, do you show so that we may see it and believe you? What miracle will you work? Our forefathers ate the manna in the desert, as it is written, 'He gave them bread out of heaven to eat.'"

This was what he had been waiting for. They too had noticed the device over the door. "Indeed, indeed, I say to you," he answered deliberately, "it was not Moses who gave you the bread from heaven; but it is my Father who gives you the true bread from heaven. For the bread of God is that which comes down from heaven, and gives life to the world."

"Lord, always give us this bread!" they cried.

It was then that he threw down the challenge.

"I am the bread of life," He said.

The men from Jerusalem were whispering together. Others who knew people in Nazareth were asking one another, "Is not this Jesus the son of Joseph, whose father and mother we know? How can he now say, 'I came down from heaven'?"

Simon Peter strained to catch the next words. He knew that the Lord could explain this, as he had so often explained other parables. If he was thinking of his doctrine as a figurative spiritual food, or if he was referring to bread as a symbol of his teachings, this would be the right moment to make it clear. But Jesus said:

"Do not grumble among yourselves. No one is able to come to me unless the Father who sent me draws him: and I will raise him up at the last day ...

"I am the bread of life," he repeated. "Your forefathers ate the manna in the desert, and they died. This is the bread which descends from heaven, in order that if anyone eats of it he may not die. I am the living bread which came down from heaven. If anyone eats of this bread, he shall live forever; and moreover, the bread which I will give is my flesh for the life of the world."

Simon Peter hardly dared look at his companions. Men all about them were wrangling, and several were demanding loudly:

"How is this man able to give his flesh to eat?"

There was pleading, perhaps, but no relenting in the voice of Jesus as he continued. On the contrary, he fortified the challenge:

"Indeed, indeed, I say to you, unless you eat of the flesh of the Son of Man and drink his blood, you have no life in yourselves. He who eats my flesh and drinks my blood possesses life everlasting, and I will raise him up at the last day. For my flesh is real food, and my blood is real drink. He who eats my flesh and drinks my blood abides in me and I in him. As the living father sent me, and I live because of the father, so he who eats me, he too shall live because of me. This is the bread that came down from heaven – not such as your fathers ate and died. He who eats of this bread shall live forever."

What an experience for a man like Simon Peter to hear these words flung at him, solemnly and deliberately, by one he loved and revered! They left his mind reeling and staggering, as it were, on some remote borderland of reason, where invisible powers battered him and tried to cast him down among the mad wretches that howled at midnight among the deserted tombs. Nor was he the only one who found them incomprehensible, for now he would hear some of his fellow disciples saying to one another:

"This is a hard doctrine; who can listen to it?"

Hard indeed it was. It was hard because it was so obviously meant to be taken literally. "Indeed, I say ... My flesh is real food ... My blood is real drink." It must have been plain from the words, from his voice, and from his look of deadly earnest, that he wished them to understand that he intended to give them his flesh to eat and his blood to drink. He could easily have reassured them by suggesting a figurative or symbolical interpretation. On the contrary, he cried:

'Does this scandalize you? What then, if you behold the Son of Man ascending to where he was before? It is the Spirit that imparts life; the flesh can give no help whatever. The words I have spoken to you are spirit and life.

"There are some of you, however, who do not believe."

He turned toward the dismayed group of apostles and disciples, for as the gospel explains, "He knew in the beginning who the unbelievers were, and who his future betrayer was," and he looked directly at Judas Iscariot.

"For this reason," he added significantly, "I have told you that no one can come to me unless it be granted him by the Father."

The implications of that moment are plain enough now. The terrible silence was pregnant with the torments of martyrs, the rising and crashing of empires, the thunder of wars and crusades, the boring and beating of a thousand heresies against the City of God, the fate of millions of human souls for eternal good or ill, the decisive onslaught of Christ and Antichrist in the last days. The speech of the messiah fell across the shadows of centuries to come, separating believers from unbelievers, the children of light from the children of darkness. And by some secret anticipatory decree it fell between two of the twelve who stood regarding him among the rest. This apparently was the very moment when Judas Iscariot said in his heart, "I do not understand this: therefore I will not believe and I will not serve!" Simon Peter, equally perplexed and tormented because he loved deeply, felt as he had the night before when death had beset him, and there had been no hope but to clasp his outstretched hand.

The separation of spirits did not stop there. Some of 'the Jews' and Galileans were already shoving through the crowd and stamping their way out, with exclamations of disgust. Worse still, the closely packed group of disciples began to separate, and a considerable number, including some who had seemed most fanatical in their devotion, followed the unbelievers, repeating disgustedly, "This is a hard saying; who can listen to it?" And "they walked no more with him."

Even the twelve were wavering now. The stony silence of Judas Iscariot had broken their ranks invisibly, and a restlessness came over them all. Yet Jesus offered not a syllable of explanation. He made no appeal, no promise. Instead, He presented the issue to them coldly, with the simple question:

"Do you also wish to go away?"

There was another silence as deep as eternity. It was broken by the trembling voice of Simon Peter.

"Lord, to whom should we go?" he stammered. "You have the words of eternal life; and we ourselves steadfastly believe that you are the Holy One of God!"[1]

This is the climax of that remarkable scene. But the anti-climax that follows is even more startling, and must have some profound significance. The eye-witness account of John records no answer by Jesus to Peter, not the slightest word of thanks, approval or gratitude for what must have required a supreme effort of the will under an excruciating and plausible temptation. Instead of noticing what the fisherman had blurted out, he looked down the row of frightened faces accusingly, and as his eyes rested once more on those of Judas, he said scathingly:

"Did I not choose you, the twelve? Yet one of you is a devil!"[2]

The conclusion is almost inevitable that Simon Peter's con-

---

[1] So Spencer, from the Greek, p. 279 – the Vulgate and some mss. have "the Christ, the Son of God."
[2] John 6:25-70

fession was not all that Jesus desired. It began with a half-despairing question, and it ended with a term, "the Holy One of God," which still suggested hesitation or wavering, since it might include all degrees of messianic expectation. This theory finds support in a question that the Lord flung at him not long after the scene in the synagogue: "Are you, too, even yet without comprehension?" It is confirmed further by the events of the following weeks.

After his repudiation by the people of Capharnaum, Jesus left the scene of so many of his miracles, and led the twelve, with the few remaining disciples, across the Galilean hills and down to the Great Sea, where it sparkled out to meet the western sky. Nothing is said in the sketchy account of this sixth and most northerly journey as to what route they took: whether they followed the main road to Acco, and thence went up the Mediterranean coast, or whether they traced the Jordan almost to its source, and then descended to the coastal plain. It is clear, however, that they passed through many villages of Phoenicia until they arrived almost at the walls of Tyre, perched on its rocky isle two thousand feet above the blue waters.

It does not appear that Jesus and his friends entered the wicked city; but after preaching nearby, and healing the blind, the deaf, and the dumb, he returned to Galilee, and made another tour through the cities of Decapolis, where he repeated the multiplication of the loaves and fishes for a crowd of four thousand. They then crossed the sea in a boat to Magdala, where they were overtaken by some spies of the pharisees, who complained because the disciples ate with unwashed hands. "You hypocrites!" replied Jesus. "Isaiah prophesied admirably of you when he said, 'This people honours me with their lips, but their heart is far from me: but in vain do they worship me, teaching as doctrines the precepts of men.'[3] With that he crossed the water again to Bethsaida, and warning the apostles against "the leaven of the pharisees, which is hypocrisy," he led them ashore and up the narrowing banks of the higher Jordan past the Waters of Merom.

After a few days' walk they found themselves in one of the loveliest parts of Palestine, among rounded hillsides dotted with straggling sheep, and rolling meadows where the morning dew was like a blanket of diamonds on the rich grass. They were at the southern slope of Mount Hermon, which swept to its snowy eminence eight thousand feet above. Near at hand was the city of

---

[3] Is 29:13, in Matt 15:8, 9.

Caesarea-Philippi, rebuilt by Herod and Philip the Tetrarchs in honour of Augustus. The cold Grecian beauty of its columns, porticoes, frescoes, and archways rose out of the greenery of the hills with an almost painful perfection against the cobalt blue of the summer sky.

Jesus and his apostles passed by all this serene magnificence, however, and proceeded to a wild and sheltered nook not far away, where one of the sources of the Jordan leaps from a cave like a flash of quicksilver across an orange-tinted rock to a deep chasm below. Long ago Greek colonists had set this incomparable spot apart for the worship of Pan, whose shrine they had built in the grotto whence sprang the sacred river. The statue of the god had already fallen to decay. But the partridge and woodcock still fluttered between the almonds and olives and the immemorial oaks; and looking across the fresh and verdant expanse, one had a superb view of the Jordan Valley and the Galilean hills with the mist and sunlight on them.

It was in that beautiful corner of his creation that the Lord Jesus completed the mysterious work he had begun in the soul of Simon Peter in the synagogue at Capharnaum. One day they found him praying alone within sound of the high and delicate song of the silver water as it started on its long meandering to the Dead Sea. As they approached he turned suddenly, and confronted them with an unexpected question:

"Who do men say the Son of Man is?"

They stammered and gave various answers.

"Some say John the Baptizer," said one.

"Others, Elijah.

Others, Jeremiah, or one of the prophets."

Jesus looked along the row of puzzled faces.

"But you," He insisted, "who do you say that I am?"

It was Simon Peter, of course, who blurted out the mighty truth that had been crystallizing in his mind since the day at Capharnaum:

"You are the Christ, the Son of the living God!"

There was no hesitation or stammering this time, no confusion in thought or in speech. Simon Peter meant that God himself, the Creator of the universe, had become incarnate, and stood before them in the person of Jesus Christ, the promised saviour of Israel and of the world. He was the Lord God who had spoken to Moses from the burning bush: and as he had said, "I AM" to Moses, so he could say, "I AM" to all the world.

"Blessed are you, Simon bar-Jonas!" He said, "because flesh and blood have not revealed this to you, but my Father who is in heaven. And I also tell you that you are a rock, and upon this rock I will build my Church, and the gates of hell shall not overpower it. And I will give to you the keys of the kingdom of heaven; and whatever you shall bind on earth shall be bound in heaven, and whatever you shall unbind on earth shall be unbound in heaven."[4]

Peter still had no idea what the Lord had meant when he said that people must eat his flesh and drink his blood. But he knew that as the Son of God he could not speak falsehood, and that time would throw a revealing light upon that statement. Now he knew also that the Lord was perpetuating the house of Israel in some special way that implied sovereignty over all human consciences, and a breath-taking pre-eminence of glory for him. Time would explain this too. His heart glowed and exulted. He probably did not even notice the cold sceptical eyes of Judas Iscariot, who, as he compared this little travel-worn band under the oaks with the splendour of the high priests at Jerusalem, must have felt, even more than he had at Capharnaum, that he had made a great mistake.

---

[4] Matt 6:13-20

14

Peter should have been thoroughly aware by this time of what so many mystics have discovered about association with Jesus Christ in this world. Jesus had promised to make him a fisher of men; and there were times when he himself, in dealing with the souls he had chosen seemed like an expert fisherman, now letting out the line to permit the victim to feel the relief of rushing freely through the cool spiritual waters; now drawing it in firmly, steadily, inexorably, but with no harm done, for in this instance the victim, in the phrase of Saint Thérèse of Lisieux, was a victim of love. In the life of the soul here there is always a mysterious ebb and flow, a systole and diastole of consolation and sorrow. And this contrast is most necessary. For man can stand only so much anguish. Yet it is in misery and abasement, not joy and prosperity, that he finds himself and God.

This is why the children of Israel, as one of the greatest teachers of mystical theology has remarked, were humbled by the Lord and taught to know themselves in poor working clothes, after laying aside their festive attire. This is why Moses was abased before he was exalted. This is why Job was left naked and wretched on a dunghill before the Most High came down to reveal his wisdom to him, as never in the days of his prosperity.[1]

Now the Christ, even while on earth, dealt with the soul of Simon Peter precisely as he had with his special friends under the Old Law. And he gave him a disagreeable reminder of this on the way back to Galilee from his hour of grandeur at Banias. Walking through the heavy fragrant fields of August, they had come to a little village in the north country; and Jesus, in the course of a sermon to the people who assembled about him, remarked that he was going back to Jerusalem "to endure many sufferings and be rejected by the ancients, chief priests, and scribes, and be put to death, and after three days rise again." And "he made this statement openly."[2]

This must have been like a sudden dash of icy water to a man still glowing from the distinction recently conferred on Peter. The phrase about rising again meant nothing to him, and he hardly noticed it, for his attention had been caught by the word "death."

---

[1] Saint John of the Cross, *The Dark Night of the Soul,* Book 1 Chapter 12, *passim.*
[2] Mark 8:30-32

But that was more than enough; and his whole being, as usual, recoiled from the impact of any suggestion of crawling worms and whitened tombstones. He could hardly wait for the Lord to finish speaking to draw him aside from the rustic crowd and to chide him.

"Mercy on you, Lord!" he said earnestly in his ear. 'This shall never happen to you!"

It took no small assurance to offer not merely advice but direction to one whom he had recently acknowledged to be the Son of the living God; and that Peter felt free to do so speaks volumes for the childlike case and confidence which the love of Jesus communicated to his friends. Ordinarily their well-meant blunders were corrected with patience and gentleness. But on this occasion, apparently, it was necessary to teach the fisherman a sharper lesson. Perhaps he had been a little too self-important since he had been promised the keys of the kingdom. Perhaps, too, he was more to blame for remonstrating with his Lord, now that he had a clearer idea of who he was. He was certainly still far from cured of that soul-sickness which, to quote St John of the Cross again, makes fallen men "measure God by themselves and not themselves by God." This probably explains the sudden severity of Jesus as he said:

"Go behind me, you Satan! You are a stumbling-block to me; for your thoughts are not on divine things, but on human things!"[3]

Peter had nothing to say. He was humbled to the dust. The only other apostle who had ever been rebuked so scathingly was Judas Iscariot. And to leave no doubt as to the meaning of the lesson, the Lord added:

"If any one desires to come after me, let him deny himself, and take up his cross daily, and follow me. For whoever wishes to save his life shall lose it; but whoever loses his life for my sake, he shall save it. For what benefit would it be to a man if he were to gain the whole world, and lose or forfeit his own soul? For whoever is ashamed of me and of my words, of him the Son of Man will be ashamed, when he comes in his glory and the glory of the Father and of the holy angels."

It is probable that in accepting this with all the humility he was capable of, Peter still found it difficult. "Take up his cross daily," was beyond him. But his sanguine heart must have leapt up again at the reference to "his glory and the glory of the Father and of the holy angels." Glory was something that he understood better than pain or humiliation. And perhaps the Lord felt that he had had

[3] Matt 16:22:23

enough of the divine therapy for the present, for he concluded with a more consoling thought:

"But I tell you truly, there are some of those standing here who shall in no wise taste of death until they see the kingdom of God."[4]

With this he left the village where the discussion had occurred, and, followed by the twelve and the larger company of disciples, continued on his way westward. Leaving the rocky gorge of the upper Jordan, they entered the wild downs that extended toward the mountains of Naphtali and the Great Sea. It was on this plain, near the waters of Merom or Huleh, that Joshua had fought for the third time with the kings of the heathen, and routing them utterly, had burned their chariots. Now the green of the meadows was broken only by straggling sheep, by cultivated fields of corn or millet, or by wild beds of scarlet flowers under the drying sycamores. Even the soil was different there; it was no longer the grey limestone dust of the north they were walking on, but the dark basalt rock formation of Bashan. As they threaded their way southwest they saw on their left the crystal waters of Merom, half tans, half fen, a jungle of reeds and willows. Now and then a startled flock of wild fowl would rise through the pearly mist. It was nothing unusual to see a herd of gazelles bound over the crest of a hill.

Thus for about a week they pressed on down the green hills and meadows to the Plain of Gennesareth, then up again into the highlands of Galilee, past Nazareth and Cana, and finally, it would seem, in a wide parabola to the south and east, until, on the eighth day after Peter's humiliation, they found themselves at the bottom of a verdant and bulky mountain. It was probably woody Tabor, though this, too, has been disputed. Wherever it was, Jesus commanded most of his following to remain and wait for him, while he ascended to one of the higher places to pray. And indicating that Peter, John, and the elder James should accompany him, he proceeded up the incline.

What Peter saw there with the other fishermen was literally enough to raise him from the vale of misery in which he had been walking, to the very gates of heaven. Of the three factual accounts of the transfiguration in the synoptic gospels, one, that of Mark, probably came from him. The most complete, however, is that of Luke:

"Now it was about eight days after these words that he took with him Peter, John and James, and ascended the mountain to pray. And it came to pass that while he prayed, the appearance of

---

[4] Luke 9:27

his countenance became altered, and his clothing white and dazzling. And behold, two men were talking with him; and they were Moses and Elijah, who, appearing in glory, spoke of his decease, which he was about to accomplish in Jerusalem.

Now Peter and his companions were heavy with sleep; but becoming fully awake they saw his glory, and the two men who were standing with him. And as they were parting from him, Peter said to Jesus, 'Master, it is delightful for us to be here! So let us erect three tents – one for you, one for Moses, and one for Elijah'; but he knew not what he said.[5] As he spoke thus, however, a cloud came and overshadowed them; and they were awestruck as those entered into the cloud. Then a voice came out of the cloud, saying, 'This is my son, my chosen one; hear him!' And with the utterance of that voice Jesus was found alone."[6]

None of the three evangelists mentions the place of this sublime episode, or the hour of the day; hence artists have added details to suit their own conceptions. Teresa Neumann, the stigmatic of Konnersreuth, "saw" it all in an ecstatic vision she had on the Feast of the Transfiguration (6 August) in 1926; and she offers some interesting and plausible particulars. She saw Jesus on a flat and rocky eminence at the hour of sunset, wearing his reddish-brown robe, with a cloth like a mantle across his shoulders; and he prayed standing, after the Jewish custom. Peter, James, and John had been sitting on the rock, a few feet away, but they had all fallen asleep. Suddenly she saw the Lord raise himself about half a metre from the ground, and remain suspended in air, while his whole drab garment became peculiarly and utterly white. His face, too, became luminous, but not blinding, for she continued to see his eyes and all his features plainly, as he remained looking upwards. Now there was a thick cloud under his feet. At his right, on another cloud, appeared a man with a splendid long beard, in a garment of many folds, like a mantle. On the left stood another with a shorter beard, and a robe that was girdled about him; he also wore a mantle. They spoke with Jesus.

At this point the three fishermen awoke from their deep slumber. The oldest, apparently Peter with his close-cropped hair and beard, said something in Aramaic that she did not understand. John, a younger man with no beard, sat at his left. Toward the front was James, who looked older than John. Suddenly all three seemed

---

[5] He was too frightened, adds Mark 9:6
[6] Luke 9:28-36

"filled with fear" and fell forward on their faces. A great cloud obscured the three figures above, of Christ, Moses, and Elijah. Then she heard "a clear strong voice", but could not understand what it said. Presently Jesus stood there as before in his reddish-brown garments. He went down to where the three frightened apostles cowered on the rock, and taking Peter by the right arm, said something to him. Then all the vision disappeared.[7]

The light that Peter was allowed to see shining from within the person of his divine Lord and bathing him and his robes in splendour was evidently that uncreated light that so many mystics have found impossible to describe. "Oh Jesús mio," cried Saint Teresa, "who could make understood the majesty in which you show yourself?" and she called it "the light that never sets, and has no night."[8] It was in that clean spiritual glory, of which our blazing sun is but a dim and impure reflection, that the fisherman of Galilee was permitted a glimpse of his master's divinity. This was his reward for the confession of faith near the waters of Banias, for the humility with which he had accepted the rebuke in the north country.

It is plain, too, that his new faith was being confirmed and fortified to prepare it for the new assaults that were to be made upon it. Sooner or later he would be obliged to take literally the Lord's predictions of his ignominious death, and the shock of disillusionment would be severe. Not only that, but from then on his footsteps would be directed down a path very different from the glorious one he had been expecting. Saint Thomas Aquinas suggests that no man could follow such a Via Dolorosa without losing heart unless he had some notion of an end worth the trouble, and that the Lord was offering him a glimpse of the everlasting joy which would follow his sorrows and persecutions.[9]

It was also necessary for him, as Saint Leo the Great noticed, to understand the two natures of Christ, the divine and the human. Most of the disruptive movements called heresies had their origin, he said, in a failure to acknowledge one or the other; an error from which the first head of the divine Church must surely be saved.[10] This observation loses none of its force when the conduct of Peter at the Transfiguration is recalled. By proposing to venerate the

[7] Angerer, A., *Das Phanomen von Konnersreuth,* Walsassen, 1927, quoted in von Lama, *op. cit.* I, pp. 131-2
[8] *Book of Life*, Chap 28
[9] S.Th. III d.45 a.1
[10] *Sermons* 32 and 51

Christ along with Moses and Elijah, as Mohammed later ranked him among the prophets, and smug professors honour him with Socrates and Confucius, this clumsy man was stumbling into the very pitfall of syncretism. It was to shatter this embryonic adventure in "comparative religions" or "interfaith" levelling that the mighty voice of the Father of Lights thundered out of the cloud, "This is my Son!" No wonder the three fishermen fell on their faces in terror!

Yet Peter had come so near to seeing heaven that he never forgot it. More than thirty years later, as an old man, tried in the faith and about to die, he wrote of it to some of his disciples; and the recollection moved him to eloquence and poetry of no mean order:

"We were not following artfully invented fables when we made known to you the power and the return of our Lord Jesus Christ. On the contrary, we were eyewitnesses of his majesty. For he received from God the Father honour and glory when a voice such as this was borne to him from the majestic glory, "This is my beloved Son, in whom I am well pleased: And we ourselves heard this voice borne down out of heaven when we were with him on the holy mountain. Moreover, we have the still firmer word of prophecy; to which you do well to give attention, as to a lamp shining in a gloomy place, until the day dawns, and the Morning Star arises in your hearts."[11]

Early on the morrow of this experience the three fishermen followed their Lord, with a new sense of awe, down the mountainside to rejoin the seventy or more disciples. They found them standing together like sheep hemmed in and surrounded by a large and noisy crowd from various villages, who were imploring or berating them. Evidently something unusual had occurred, and Peter was not much surprised when he saw the inevitable scribes and pharisees from Jerusalem. Distinguished by their wide phylacteries, self-important air and long beards, they strutted about, questioning and cross-examining the obsequious onlookers.

As Jesus approached this scene, many recognized him, and in a few moments his name was on all tongues. The whole mob, in fact, began to turn toward him; and Peter now noticed that some seemed astonished to find him there, while others showed signs of fear. Then he saw a middle-aged man break from the thickest part of the multitude and cast himself at the Lord's feet, saying:

---

[11] 2 Pet 1:16-20

"Master, I have brought to you my son, who is possessed by a dumb spirit; and wherever it seizes him, it flings him down, and he foams and grinds his teeth; and he is wasting away. And I asked your disciples to expel it, but they had not the power."

"O you unbelieving generation," said the Lord, perhaps looking reproachfully at the disciples, who stood humbled and crestfallen before their enemies from Jerusalem and the Galilean crowd. "How long shall I be with you? How long shall I bear with you? Bring him to me."

Three or four men lugged the boy to where he stood. On seeing him the poor lad fell to the earth and rolled about, foaming at the mouth and grinding his teeth with horrible grimaces.

"How long a time is it since this has befallen him?" asked the Lord.

"From childhood," said the distraught father, "and it has often thrown him into the fire and into the water in order to kill him. However, if you can do anything, have pity on us and help us!"

"If you can! Why, all things are possible to him who believes."

"I do believe!" cried the man. "Help my unbelief!"

Jesus then said, "You dumb and deaf spirit, I command you, come out of him, and never enter him again!"

With a violent shriek and a last terrible convulsion, the boy fell back and remained as motionless as a stone.

"He is dead!" said some of the crowd. "The boy is dead!"

When Jesus took his hand, however, he opened his eyes and stood up.

This was a rather depressing experience for Peter, in a way, after the ineffable delight of his vision on the mountain; but there was worse to follow. For when they had left the crowd, and were on the way north, Jesus told them again that he was soon going to Jerusalem to die. "The Son of Man shall be delivered into the hands of men," he said, "and they will put him to death; and having been put to death he shall rise again after three days."[12]

Mark's account, derived probably from Peter, adds that "they did not know what this meant, and they were afraid to question him." Peter had no wish to be called satan again, yet he was unable to accept such a prophecy literally. It simply did not make sense to him, any more than it did to a pagan like Euripides,[13] that a deity should allow his creatures to injure him. Once he had found it

[12] Mark 9:32; also Luke 9:45
[13] In *The Bacchae*.

difficult to grasp how the messiah could be God. Now, having seen him in his glorious divinity, he was finding it a bit of an effort to believe in his complete humanity. Even when he felt the touch of his hand and saw the dust on his sandaled feet beside his own, he found it impossible to think of him as dying or dead.

Perhaps the Lord was putting them through another of those perplexing tests of his. Peter was confident that when they reached Jerusalem, it would be plain enough who was God and who was man. If only the high priests and pharisees had had a glimpse of that transfiguration on the mountain, and of Moses and Elijah honouring the Christ! Well, the messiah could do anything he wished: that was plain enough now. And Peter was determined, without being aware perhaps that he was pitting his puny will against the eternal, that he should not die, but should live and be glorious. So thinking, as they returned by a roundabout way to avoid the crowds, he came to a high place near Arbela, and saw the summer sunshine on the roofs of Capharnaum and the waters of Galilee.

15

Capharnaum gave them a cold reception this time. Here where the shouts of adulation had shivered from the water to the stars, here where the crowd had swarmed so thickly that a cripple had had to be hoisted through a roof, they heard only grumbled insults and saw sour and suspicious faces. "Impostor!" "Seducer!" "Eat his flesh, indeed!" "Beelzebub!" "Samaritan!" The scribes and pharisees had done their work well.

Though Peter knew the reason, he found it hard to believe that these people could have changed so much in a short time. How well the Lord had understood them when he had shaken off their flattery with the remark that it was only because they had been filled! The summer that began with the multiplication of the loaves and fishes was not yet over; the wheat that had been breaking the ground on that wild day in the synagogue was not yet gathered into the barns. Yet in this very town where all had been "beside themselves with wonder," he was walking through streets almost deserted save by his own rather bedraggled-looking friends, including the former publican Levi and a few of the rabble.

Instead of a welcoming multitude, several of the twelve found waiting for them at the corner near the Custom House some individuals with beady eyes and hatchet faces, agents of the treasury at the temple in Jerusalem, who wanted to speak on official business to some responsible person among them. The other apostles seem to have pointed out Simon Peter. Perhaps they had already begun to have certain doubts and suspicions about the man who carried the bag. At any rate, it was to the fisherman, according to Matthew's account, that the tax collectors addressed themselves.

"Does not your master pay the half-shekel?" they demanded. The sons of Annas were efficient in matters of this sort. They had probably investigated at Nazareth and had concluded that Jesus had not paid the annual tribute that year or the year before. Now they had a new weapon against him. They could not impugn his honesty or his sanity, but they could say he was "unpatriotic," or something of that sort. It was an old trick, but it usually worked. Every adult Jew was on the list. "Does not your master pay the half-shekel?"

"Yes," said Peter without the slightest hesitation. "Of course he does."

Perhaps he wished to save his Lord from suspicion or

annoyance. Hasty and awkward as usual, he had forgotten that the messiah was not under any obligation to contribute to the upkeep of his father's house. He had put him on record as being liable for the tribute. Matthew the ex-publican would hardly have made such a blunder; but his account of this incident is so discreet that we are left to imagine his sophisticated half-smile and the almost imperceptible lowering of his eyelashes as he listened; and perhaps the cold contempt on the dark brooding face of Judas.

Peter went home with the depressed feeling, half of shame and half of truculence, of a man who has made a wholly unnecessary blunder. It is not clear whether he intended to tell the Lord what had happened, or to maintain a discreet silence, hoping that no one else would speak of the matter. Before he had an opportunity to open his mouth, however, Jesus greeted him:

"What is your opinion, Simon? From whom do earthly kings take tolls or taxes? from their own sons, or from other people?"

Peter saw that the fat was in the fire. "From other people," he replied sheepishly.

"Then the sons are free." In other words why should the son of God have to pay the temple tribute? "However, in order that we may not scandalize them, go to the sea and cast in a hook, and take the fish that first comes up, and on opening its mouth you shall find a shekel. Take that, and give it to them for me and for yourself."[1]

The rest is left untold. But the inference is that Peter got out some of his old fishing tackle and carried out these orders to the letter, while the other eleven looked on from one of the wharves of Capharnaum, greatly enjoying his embarrassment as men do under such circumstances, and waited to see what would happen. The success of the cast, for he had lost none of his boyhood skill, seems to be taken for granted by Matthew, who forgets to mention it as he rushes on to tell the sequel, one of the most unexpected and most touching of the messianic discourses.

It must have been on the way back from the waterfront to the house that the eleven became involved in their celebrated dispute over the positions they would occupy when the Lord established his regime. Probably it began with some mention of the keys of the kingdom, and the power to bind and loose, that had been bestowed on Peter the Rock at Banias. Certainly none of them ever questioned his position as their leader, and their concern on this occasion was probably over who should be second in command.

---

[1] Matt 17:25-27

The only one of his brethren with any semblance of an official post was Judas, whose ambitious character allows us to suppose that he would not have been at all backward in urging his own claim. Nor would the sons of Zebedee, who, encouraged perhaps by the preference shown them at various times, had a keen awareness of their qualifications for distinctive places in the messianic government. Very human were these apostles, like a small cross--section of our common nature: as if to warn pharisaical minds of later days (not all Jews, either) against disdaining the Church for the faults of its members. The voices of these vigorous men clashed angrily as they strode along. But when they came to Peter's house, they stopped bickering, knowing that if the Lord heard them, he would disapprove.

As they were about to separate they heard his voice calling them, and went to where he was sitting.

"What were you discussing on the way?" he inquired.

There was no need of an answer. He knew.

"If anyone wishes to be first," he said, with a glance perhaps at Peter, who by this time had wound up his tackle and had come to show the shekel or stater he had found in the fish's mouth, "he shall be last of all, and servant of all."[2]

Possibly, the face of Peter revealed how little he relished the thought of being servant to Matthew the ex-publican, or to Judas Iscariot, or even to the sons of Zebedee; and how far he was from suspecting that a long line of his successors would sign themselves, in deference to that moment, "Servant of the servants of God." But Jesus knew this, and he had not finished the instruction. Just then he saw a small child passing the door or romping through the courtyard of the house. According to an old Christian tradition he was a boy with golden hair, who later became Peter's disciple, succeeded him as Bishop of Antioch, and gave his life for Christ in one of the Roman arenas, devoured by lions – Ignatius, "the wheat of God." Whether this is so or not, Jesus called him, set him in the midst of the twelve, and putting his arms around him, said to them:

"Indeed I tell you, unless you turn back and become like the little children, you shall by no means enter the kingdom of heaven. Whoever, therefore, humbles himself as this little child, he is the greatest in the kingdom of heaven. And whoever receives one such little child in my name receives me; but whoever occasions the ruin of one of these little ones who believe in me, it were well for him

[2] Mark 9:35

that a great millstone[3] were hung around his neck, and he were drowned in the depths of the sea! ... See that you despise not one of these little ones; for I tell you that in heaven their angels always behold the face of my father who is in heaven."[4]

This was the beginning of the striking homily to the apostles alone, in which Jesus extended to all (including Judas) the powers of binding and unbinding, of forgiving sin or not forgiving it, that he had given to Peter at Banias. He insisted on the importance of communal prayer, on the authority of his Church, on the preference for death to the slightest compromise on his divine teachings, on the certain reality of the punishment of hell, "where their worm dies not, and the fire is not quenched"; again and again on the fundamentals of utter humility and love. It was in answer to Peter's question that he told the parable of the unmerciful steward, and insisted on forgiveness, seven times seventy, and from the heart. And again he may have glanced with grave appeal at Judas Iscariot as he went on:

"It must be that scandals come, but woe to that man by whom the scandal comes! ... It is not the will of your Father who is in heaven that one of these little ones should perish ... If the salt loses its saltiness, with what will you season it? Have salt in yourselves, and have peace with one another!"

The twelve listened in silence. No one likes to think of the flames of hell, and it was terrifying to hear from the lips of the Son of God, the lips that denied mercy to no repentant sinner, whether harlot, thief, or murderer, and cried out so often with an almost heart-breaking urgency, "Come to me, all you who labour and are heavy-laden, and I will give you rest!" the solemn assurance that eternal punishment was as much a reality as eternal bliss. It was a scene never to be forgotten: the startled face of Judas, the wondering eyes of the child, the majestic mien of Jesus. There was nothing here of the epicene and ineffectual Christ of sickly art, puling fiction, and flabby preaching. The twelve men went away knowing that they had heard the voice which had spoken to Abraham and to Moses and would reverberate one day over the charred embers of the visible world.

This stern reminder was by way of preparation, perhaps, for another momentous journey. It was not long afterward that Jesus re-

---

[3] Literally, in the Greek, "an ass's millstone," meaning a large one turned by a beast of burden.
[4] Matt 18:1

ceived a cordial and seemingly pious invitation from some of his own relatives to accompany them to the Feast of Tabernacles in Jerusalem on the fifteenth of Tizri, in late September or early October. They professed concern that so few thus far (and those mainly in Capharnaum and other parts of Galilee) had seen his miracles. They wanted him recognized by more important people in the metropolis. "Manifest thyself to the world!" they urged.

Knowing that it was not love and faith, but a subtle sort of malice proceeding from envy and scepticism, he replied:

"My time is not yet arrived, but your time is always ready. The world cannot hate you; but it hates me, because I give evidence regarding it that its doings are evil."

After they had gone, however, he informed the twelve and the disciples that he intended to go to the Feast privately; and one warm day in September they all set out, with as little preparation as ever, along the less common route through Samaria, the relatives probably having taken the longer and safer way by Jericho. So far as we know Jesus never again set foot in the house of Simon Peter. It was the last time he honoured Capharnaum with his presence.

They slowly climbed the thirty-eight, steep, dangerous miles to Arbela. This probably took two days; on the third they would reach the main road that ran south through Sichem and Samaria to the Holy City; and following this, they stopped at a certain high places not mentioned in the gospels, where Jesus solemnly dispatched seventy of his disciples to scatter through the country of the samaritans and to prepare for his preaching there, with instructions very similar to those he had given the previous year to the twelve. Then Simon Peter saw him turn toward the north-east, where perhaps they had a last view of a splash of sunlight on the highest tower and pillars of Capharnaum, rising to its rocky bluff out of the sea, with Bethsaida and Chorazin smugly sprawling nearby; and he heard him say something that must have fallen on his heart, native as he was to those places, like the voice that came to Jeremiah on the burning wind:

"Woe to you, Chorazin! Woe to you, Bethsaida! For if the miracles done in you had been done in Tyre and Sidon, they would have repented long ago sitting in sackcloth and ashes. It shall be more endurable, however, for Tyre and Sidon in the judgment than for you! And you, Capharnaum, shall you be exalted as high as heaven? You shall be brought down even to hell.[5]

---

[5] Luke 10:13-15

124

It is a terrible thing, as one of Peter's colleagues said, to fall into the hands of the living God. Nothing at all remains of Capharnaum except the foundation stones of the white synagogue in which he first promised the Mass and the Eucharist to men, and was spurned. Even this is conjecture, for it is not certain where the city was. Chorazin is mentioned nowhere else in the Bible. Nothing is known of it but its doom.

The remainder of this journey is rather obscure. The evangelists were not writing history or biography as such, but occasional pieces hastily prepared when some teaching of the Lord was challenged. What is most evident here is a change of mood. The sorrow of Peter's farewell to his own city was yielding to a joy that seemed to colour the events of several days or weeks. It was a happy hour when the seventy disciples rejoined their Master not far from Samaria (Sebaste, as Herod now called it) with the news of the success of their mission.

"Lord, even the demons are subject to us in your name!"

"I was looking on and saw Satan falling from heaven like a lightning flash," he replied. Then, becoming "enraptured with joy in the Holy Spirit," he went on, "Blessed are the eyes which see the things which you see![6] ... Come to me, all you who labour and are heavy-laden, and I will give you rest. Take my yoke upon you, and learn of me, for I am gentle and humble of heart; and you shall find rest for your souls. For my yoke is easy, and my burden light."[7] A divine sermon it must have been, including the parable of the good samaritan, with which he silenced an owlish doctor of the Law who tried to entangle him in casuistry.

Having left the Samaritan plain and ascended the Judean hills, they arrived, not long after, at Bethany, about an hour's walk from Jerusalem. It was then, as now, a little village sprawling on a hillside, with nothing much to see in it. But there was a home such as Jesus loved in one of the square white houses with rounded domed roofs, and he stopped with his followers to visit it. Very little is known of its inmates, considering the renown that was to be theirs. They seem to have belonged to a middle class family of some importance, for they were well known in Jerusalem, and had many friends there.[8] Above all, they must have been good people, simple, sincere, and affectionate, for John remarks that "Jesus had a deep

---

[6] Luke 10:21-24
[7] Matt 11:29-30
[8] John 11:18-19

friendship" for them.[9]

Lazarus was a grave, studious, thoughtful man, whom grief had given a bent for spiritual things – grief perhaps over the loss of his parents, and the early wildness of his younger sister. For Mary was probably the repentant sinner who had washed the feet of Jesus with her tears in the house of Simon the pharisee. Her gratitude was in proportion to his mercy in expelling seven devils from a body which art and tradition have represented as extremely beautiful, with an aura of golden hair. Sorrow for a wasted youth in the jolly set of Magdala or Capharnaum had shown her the difference between what men call love and what she saw in the healing eyes of Christ. Now she wanted only to sit at his feet and learn more about the eternal life he promised. Thus she became the prototype of the mystic and contemplative, while her sister Martha will always stand for the more active life which also has its place in the world, even though, as she was gently reminded on this occasion, it be a secondary one. She had always been good: she was one of those capable, industrious women who were generally the wives and mothers of Israel; and it was probably from her busy hands that Peter and his companions received the fragrant bread she had baked and the red wine she had made from the grapes that grew on the hillside behind the house.

Many pilgrims on their way to the Feast passed that sedate and orderly home surrounded by its gardens, fields, and barns, without suspecting the domestic scene which would be remembered until the end of the world. For Jesus did not join the stream of caravans and pedestrians. He was still resolved to go secretly to the Feast, and not to make his appearance until it was well under way. It may have been at night, therefore, that he took leave of Lazarus and his sisters, and accompanied by the twelve, went over and down the Mount of Olives, crossed the Kedron Valley, and entered the Holy City through the Gate of Damascus.

It was easy to escape notice that evening. The Feast of Tabernacles was in full rhythm, and there had never been a merrier one. All week, with feverish good humour, immense crowds had been commemorating the forty years in the desert and anticipating the messianic glory to come. On the streets, in the marketplace, throughout the Court of the Gentiles they had made tents out of boughs, thatching them with leaves; and in them for a full week they slept, ate, and revelled. Peter followed his Lord among these

[9] *ibid* 11:5

booths from one stone terrace to another, up a narrow twisted street through the soft light of a thousand tapers. They threaded their way among children gambolling in the flickering shadows, youths and maidens dancing on the flagstones to the clapping of hands and the strumming of zithers, late vendors still hawking their wares, old men feebly chanting the most joyous and consoling of the psalms.

"Our feet were standing in your courts, O Jerusalem, Jerusalem, which is built as a city, which is compact together. For thither the tribes went up, the tribes of the Lord: testimony of Israel, to give praise to the name of the Lord. For there are set up the seats of judgment, seats upon the house of David ... Let peace be in your strength, and plenty in your towers! ..."

Never mind tonight if the palace of the Herods sits high on the hill where David sang those words! On this Jewish Thanksgiving Day everyone has plenty to eat and to drink, for the harvest has been rich and the new wine is good. God's people are rejoicing together now, as in old times they shared one another's sorrows. One might easily think, to hear the laughter and the song, that their ancient hope had been realized, and that the Holy One, the Son of David who was also to be the Son of God, walked among his people.

So indeed he did, but only Peter and a few others were aware of it. Yet the secret was too tremendous to be kept; the restless birds that flew among the smoky tapers knew it, and the very stones seemed to murmur under each passing sandal, "He is here! He is here!" In fact there was a general expectancy of his coming in Jerusalem that night and the next day, to heighten the emotional currents and cross currents with which the old city pulsated.

Most alert of all, as the gospel of John makes plain, were Annas and his lieutenants. "The Jews were looking for Jesus at the festival, and kept asking, 'Where can he be?'" And among the crowds of merrymakers, some were saying, "He is a good man!" while others, closer to temple headquarters, were scoffing, "Not he! On the contrary, he is misleading the populace!" What the sons of Annas really thought about freedom of speech is suggested in the comment added by the evangelist: "No one, however, spoke openly about him for fear of the Jews."

Jesus and his friends meanwhile had taken up quarters either in some friendly house in the city, possibly the one Nicodemus had visited, or had returned to the Mount of Olives to sleep there under the autumn stars in the shelter of the olive trees, or in an old farmhouse placed at their disposal, as some have conjectured, in the garden of Gethsemane, halfway up the slope. It is certain that they spent at least one night in that seclusion.[10] The triple hill was not then as scrubby and barren as it is today. It was green and fragrant with pines, palms, and myrtles interspersed with the silvery grey of many olive groves, some of which had been there in David's time. Peter and his fellows might have slept comfortably on the long grass among the stones, while their Master prayed alone farther up the hill; for the first rains of October had not begun, and the air was still dry and warm enough when the wind was southerly. Or they could watch the brilliant stars through the lacy foliage, wondering drowsily what might befall on the morrow, until they fell asleep.

---

[10] John 8:12

16

When the feast was half over and the revelry at its height, Jesus quietly appeared on one of the porches of the Temple, and sitting where all could see him, he began to teach. The effect was sensational. It was like the sun suddenly appearing out of dark clouds, and flooding the world with light.

Something like that was sensed immediately by the thousands who were trooping through the marble courts – devout Jews from all parts of the world, violent and fickle Jews of the streets of Jerusalem, a sprinkling of scribes, pharisees and other adherents of the temple oligarchy, and of course the twelve apostles and other disciples. And something of the sort must have been the deliberate intention of the speaker. From what happened it is clear that Jesus wished to reveal the mystery of his person as clearly as possible both to friends and foes. He was giving the latter another chance to believe him on the only terms acceptable to a God – his own. He was making it plain to his followers that although he was love itself, his primary purpose in this manifestation of himself was truth. Before love could work in the hearts of men, truth and justice must make a way for it. We can love only what we know. A love mingled with error or compromise would be polluted at the source. He would have none of it.

What he said in that opening discourse was so true, so beautiful, and so powerful that his very enemies were stared into a grudging admiration. "How has this Man a knowledge of letters, since he has never learned?" the pharisees were asking one another. And Jesus, knowing this, answered them over the heads of the shuffling and perspiring mob:

"My doctrine is not mine, but his who sent me. If anyone desires to do his will, he shall know, as regards the doctrine, whether it is from God, or whether I speak for myself ... Did not Moses give you the Law? Yet none of you observes the Law. Why do you want to kill me?"

"You have a demon!" screamed a voice, and the Jerusalem populace took up the cry: "You have a demon! Who wants to kill you?"

Yet the bolt had hit its mark, and had divided the unruly mass under the very eyes of those who usually directed its emotions. They were saying, "Is not this the man they are seeking to kill? Yet there he is speaking in public, and they say nothing to him! Can it be that the authorities have come to recognize that this man is the Christ?" But some of the opposition still resisted his influence, retorting, "However, we know this person's origin; but when the Christ comes, none will know his origin."

It was amazing to Peter how quickly Jesus knew what they were murmuring down there, and how promptly he replied, "You not only know me, but you know my origin; and I have not come of myself; but he who sent me is true, whom you know not. I know him, because I am from him, and he sent me."

This silenced them. All over the court a mumble of approving voices arose. Left to himself, the average Jew, even of the temple entourage, was probably inclined to accept this overpowering personality. "This is certainly the prophet!" said some. "This is the Christ!" cried others. All about the place men were demanding of one another, "When the Christ does come, will he work more miracles than this man has worked?" Peter and Andrew, standing near one of the pillars with the sons of Zebedee and the rest, heard this with exultation. The question seemed unanswerable. A little more, and the moment would be ripe to conclude that scene which had been interrupted after the miracles of the loaves: the crowning of the king of the Jews, right here in the temple.

Annas and the pharisees were resourceful men, however. And having rejected the opportunity that the messiah had offered them, they now sent to arrest him. Their officers came back empty-handed, saying, "No man ever spoke like this one!" Annas or one of his creatures sneered in reply, "Are you too led astray? Has a single one of the rulers or of the pharisees believed in him? But this rabble, ignorant of the Law, are a cursed lot!" Nevertheless Annas saw that without the help of that blind emotional proletariat which he despised, he could do nothing against such an adversary. And he promptly sent emissaries among them to silence the most vociferous with plausible arguments. "What!" they would say. "Does the Christ come out of Galilee? Has not the scripture said that the Christ comes of the race of David, and from Bethlehem, the village where David was?" It is likely enough that Annas, with his resources of information, had already learned where Jesus had been born and whose descendant he was. But having decided not to acknowledge him, he used against him the very facts that should have counted in his favour. While waiting for results from this strategy, he neglected no other weapon; hurriedly he convoked the sanhedrin.

Among all the political time-servers now unworthily filling the chairs of mighty elders of Israel who had died for truth, only one dared raise a voice against the false leadership. And as Nicodemus was still the timid rich old merchant who had visited the Lord so stealthily on a gusty spring night two years before, he did not go so far as to uphold him as the Christ, or even as the probable Christ, but offered an oblique defence on merely legalistic grounds.

"Does our Law condemn the man, unless it first hears what he has to say, and ascertains what he is doing?" he asked.

Nicodemus knew that they had heard what Jesus had to say, and had ascertained what miracles he had performed. Nineteen centuries later he might have been seen in the first banquet seats, boasting that the divine Church was not out of harmony with the Declaration of Independence or the United States Constitution, and receiving medals for promoting tolerance and brotherhood. But having been born when he was, his only reward was the contempt of more intelligent, courageous and evil men, who saw that the issue was not the rights of free speech or fair trial but the deity of Jesus Christ, and silenced him with the same sophistry they had used against the mob:

"Are you, too, from Galilee? Search and see that no prophet arises from Galilee!"

Yet the protest of Nicodemus may not have been wholly in-effectual. The sanhedrin adjourned without taking action. And "every man went to his own house; but Jesus went to the Mount of Olives."[1]

Peter must have been emotionally exhausted that evening as he fell asleep, with his master and his friends, on the green hillside east of the Kedron valley. But it was soon morning, and time to renew the struggle; and while the haze still hung over-the-hollow of the Dead Sea in the east, and the early light was rising like a climbing angel on the white and rosy glory of the temple to the west, they bestirred themselves, and followed after the pilgrims who, having spent the night on the lower slope, were returning to the temple.

A vast crowd was assembled when they arrived, and the high priests and pharisees were already on the ground, prepared to renew the struggle. But none of them ventured to interfere with Jesus as he walked across the Porch of Solomon; and Peter saw him sit down where he had been the day before, and begin to talk.

This was the day when his enemies dragged before him the woman taken in adultery, hoping to place him on the horns of a

---

[1] John 7:14; 8:2

dilemma before the public. If he condemned her to be stoned according to the ancient Law, he would be discredited for seeming to repudiate his own gospel of mercy and forgiveness. If he let her go free, the Jewish people could be persuaded that this sabbath breaker was against the whole Mosaic law.

Peter watched anxiously to see what he would do. And when he heard him destroy the dilemma with the quiet words, "Let him who is without sin cast the first stone," and saw him dismiss the poor wretch with the injunction to "go, and sin no more,"[2] his jubilation can be imagined. But the battle was not yet over. And after the woman and her accusers had departed, he saw the Lord rise, and walk over to the treasury building, where, perhaps, there was a larger crowd. The temple rulers and chief pharisees followed with the little group of Jesus' friends; and all heard distinctly the remarkable challenge he presented:

"I am the Light of the world," he said. "He who follows me shall never walk in darkness, but shall have the Light of Life."

This was plain enough for anybody, and no sanhedrinist could possibly be in doubt as to what he had to say. Meanwhile, however, the most determined group of Annas's henchmen, smug doctors of the Law, leading pharisees with wide phylacteries and well combed and perfumed beards, had recovered sufficiently to shove their way to the forefront of the mob, and had begun to bait him again. They did this all the rest of the day, until he told them plainly why they could not accept him on his own terms. He had said it before, but he repeated it with emphasis:

"You judge according to the flesh ... You neither know me nor my Father. If you knew me you would know my Father also ... I am from above. You are of this world; I am not of this world. I therefore told you that you shall die in your sins; for unless you believe that I am he, you shall die in your sins."

Peter saw one of the pharisees step forward as if he desired to pluck out the speaker's heart.

"Who are you?" he snarled.

Jesus had often told them. "Even the same that I said to you from the beginning," he repeated serenely and patiently... "When you have lifted up the Son of Man, then you shall know that I AM."[3]

It was plain now that he had met his enemies on their own

---

[2] *ibid*, 8:3-11
[3] John 8:12-28

ground and had reduced them to angry silence. In fact it began to look as if Jewish public opinion, smothering the protests of the bureaucrats, would accept him wholeheartedly and crown him king. This seemed almost a certainty after he touched the eyes of a man born blind, on the sabbath of that week, and restored his sight. The poor Jew whose first visual image in this world was the compassionate face of Jesus Christ fell on his knees and adored him as God. All through the city people were saying that only the Christ could have done such a thing. The temple rulers, still grumbling about the sabbath, had little more to say when Jesus answered them with the Good Shepherd discourse, insisting on a simple and united faith in him and in his Church.

"I came into this world for judgment," he said, "that those who do not see may see, and that those who see may become blind."

"Are we also blind?" demanded the pharisees.

"If you were blind you would have no sin; but now you say 'We see'; your sin remains ... Indeed, indeed, I say to you, he who does not enter the sheepfold by the door, but climbs in another way, that man is a thief and a robber; but he who enters the door is shepherd of the sheep ... I am the door... I am the good shepherd. The good shepherd lays down his life for his sheep . ... I know mine, and my own know me ... and other sheep I have which are not of this fold; these also must I bring, and they will hear my voice, and there shall be one flock and one shepherd."

Jerusalem was in an uproar that night. Excited people went about reporting what he had said and what the scribes and pharisees had said. And though some still sneered, "He has a demon, and is mad; why do you listen to him?" most Jews were giving them the obvious retort: "These are not the utterances of a demoniac. Can a demon open the eyes of the blind?"[4] If this was the popular opinion, what must have been the satisfaction of Simon Peter as he and his friends reviewed the events of the day! They had seen a Jerusalem mob following the shepherd about like docile sheep.

It was highly instructive to them, however, to watch how he tested the faith of these enthusiastic converts on the following day. He did it with an observation that, like a little key, unlocked their hearts and let in the light.

"If you continue steadfast in my word," he said, "you will really be my disciples, and shall know the truth, and the truth shall make you free."

[4] John 9:1; 10:21

He had delicately touched the weakness that these people shared with the pharisees: the pride of race, amounting almost to self-worship, which had blotted out the remembrance of original sin, and with it the true image of the God who reveals himself only to the humble. This became evident at once in their prompt and angry reply:

"We are the descendants of Abraham, and have never yet been in slavery to anyone; what do you mean by saying, 'You shall be set free'?"

"Indeed, indeed, I say to you, that everyone who commits sin is a slave of sin. Now the slave does not remain in the house permanently; but the son remains permanently. If then the son sets you free, you shall be free in reality. I am aware that you are descendants of Abraham; yet you are seeking to murder me, because my word has no place in you. I declare what I have seen with my Father, yet you do what you have heard from your father."

"Our father is Abraham!" The words thundered and echoed against the temple walls.

"If you are the children of Abraham, do the deeds of Abraham. But now you seek to murder me, a man who has declared to you the truth which I heard from God. This Abraham did not do. You do the deeds of your father," he repeated with greater emphasis.

"We were not born of fornication. We have one father, God!"

"If God were your father;" he said deliberately, "you would love me; for from God I proceeded and have come; for I have not come of myself, but he sent me. Why do you not comprehend my language? Because you cannot give ear to my word. You are of your father the devil, and it is your will to carry out the desires of your father. He was a manslayer from the beginning, and stands not in the truth, because truth is not in him. When he speaks falsehood, he speaks according to his own nature, for he is a liar, and the father of such!"

Each word now was like the lash of a mighty whip, driving them on to complete self-revelation.

"Because it is I, however, who speak the truth, you do not believe me. Who among you can convict me of sin? If I speak the truth, why do you not believe me? He who is of God listens to the words of God. You do not listen to them for this reason that you are not of God."

Now it was out in the open; and anger prodded them into proving that all he had said of them was true.

"Were we not right," they hissed, "in saying that you are a

134

samaritan, and have a demon?"

"I have not a demon; on the contrary, I honour my Father, while you dishonour him. I do not, however, seek my own glory; there is one who seeks it and judges. Indeed, indeed, I say to you, if a man lives by my word, he shall never see death."

"Now we know you have a demon! Abraham died, and the prophets as well; yet you say, 'If a man keeps my word, he shall never taste of death: Are you greater than our father Abraham who died? The prophets also died. Who do you claim to be?"

They had had no conception of who he really was, then, when they had acclaimed him yesterday as the messiah? Jesus again told them why:

"If I should glorify myself, my glory would be nothing. It is my Father who glorifies me, of whom you say that he is your God; yet you have not known him; but I know him; and if I were to say that I do not know Him, I should be like you, a liar; but I know him, and keep his word. Your father Abraham rejoiced, that he was to see my day; and he saw it, and was glad."

"You are not yet fifty years old," they jeered, "and have you seen Abraham?"

His reply fell with a crushing effect as that strange drama approached its climax:

"Indeed, indeed, I say to you, before Abraham was born, I AM."

They picked up stones to cast at him. At heart they had been murderers all along. But "Jesus became hidden and went out of the Temple." Thus ends the masterly reporting of John.[5]

In repudiating the lip-service of these false converts, Jesus had given his bated enemies an advantage which they were not slow to grasp. Very early next morning they were waiting for him; and having exhausted all other weapons, the temple rulers stooped to borrow one from the rabble. They called him a demoniac to his face. He had expelled devils and healed diseases, they taunted, by the power of Beelzebub, prince of devils. Their repudiation of him was now complete. In calling God Satan, they had made their definitive choice.

This is suggested by the terrible discourse that followed. He seemed to regard them almost as lost souls, who had deliberately chosen their own damnation: "... If Satan casts out Satan, he is divided against himself; how then shall his kingdom endure? And if

[5] John 8:31-59

I cast out demons by the agency of Beelzebub, by whose agency do your own disciples cast them out? They therefore shall be your judges! But if I by the spirit of God cast out demons, then the kingdom of God has overtaken you!... He who is not with me is against me, and he who does not gather with me scatters. Therefore, I tell you, every sin and blasphemy shall be forgiven him; but whoever speaks against the Holy Spirit, it shall not be forgiven him, either in this world or in the world to come ...

"You breed of vipers! How can you utter what is good when you yourselves are wicked? For out of the abundance of the heart the mouth speaks...'

Some of them had the temerity then to demand a sign of him. And Peter heard him say, with mordant irony:

"A wicked and adulterous generation demands a sign! No sign, however, shall be given it but the sign of the prophet Jonah. For as 'Jonah was three days and three nights in the sea-monster's belly,' so shall the Son of Man be three days and three nights in the heart of the earth ..." He compared them to demoniacs from whom a foul spirit had been expelled, only to return with seven others more wicked than himself; "and the final condition of that man becomes worse than the first. So too shall it be with this wicked generation."[6]

Some of this was as obscure to Peter as it was to the other listeners; but just then, as the Lord paused, a well-to-do pharisee came forward and invited him to breakfast. To their surprise, perhaps, he accepted, and the context indicates that the twelve also went along, and heard the stinging rebuke he administered to his host for wondering why he had not washed his hands. The pharisees, he said, were like hidden tombs. Loving prominent seats in the synagogue and salutations in the marketplace, they were full of extortion and wickedness, and disregarded justice and the love of God. "Woe to you!" he said; and when a smug scribe interrupted with, "Master, in saying these things you insult us as well!" He retorted, "And woe to you, doctors of the Law! for you load men with unsupportable burdens, while you yourselves do not touch these burdens with one of your fingers; you did not enter yourselves, and those who were entering you prevented." The words went reverberating on their way down the centuries, over the unhonoured graves of Wolseys and Talleyrands who would not be Jews, seeking in vain a resting place in books of etiquette or in Newman's definition of a gentleman as "one who gives no pain."

[6] Matt 12:24-45

The host and his professorial guests were shaking with suppressed rage. Clearly, it was time to be going. Jesus and the twelve departed from a house where it was plain they were no longer welcome?[7]

A tremendous crowd was waiting outside: they were "countless," according to the evangelist, and "they trod upon one another." Yet Jesus paid no attention to them. Instead, he addressed himself to the apostles, evidently wishing to stress the point of the morning's experience while it was fresh in their minds.

"Beware of the leaven of the pharisees, which is hypocrisy;" he said ... "And to you who are my friends, I say, be not afraid of those who kill the body and after that have nothing that they can do. But I will warn you whom to fear: fear the one who, after killing, has power to cast into Gehenna; yes, I tell you, fear him! Are not five sparrows sold for two cents? Yet not one of them is forgotten in the sight of God. But even the hairs of your head are all numbered. Fear not: you are of more value than many sparrows. I say to you, moreover, every one who acknowledges me before men, the Son of Man will also acknowledge before the angels of God; but whoever disowns me in the presence of men shall be disowned in the presence of the angels of God. And whoever speaks a word against the Son of Man," he repeated, "shall be forgiven; but he who blasphemes against the Holy Spirit shall not be forgiven. And when they bring you before the synagogues and the magistrates and authorities, do not be anxious how or what to say; for the Holy Spirit will teach you in that very hour what you ought to say."

He talked for a long time, stressing again much that he had said in the sermon on the Mount, particularly as regarded detachment from material concerns, the need of trust that God would feed and clothe them as he did the birds, and constant watchfulness for his coming.

Peter interrupted at this point. He had no wish to die. The idea of being dragged before synagogues and magistrates did not appeal much to him. And truth to say, some parts of the sermon on the Mount were still a little beyond him.

"Lord, are you addressing this parable to us, or to all as well?"[8]

The answer was a pointed instruction for the head of the apostolic college in person: "Who, now, is the faithful and prudent servant, whom his master will place over his domestics to give

---

[7] Luke 11:37-39
[8] Luke 12:41

them their allowance of food at the proper time? I tell you truly, he will place him over all his possessions ..." But the evil servant, "who knew his master's will, and did not prepare for him, nor acted in accordance with his will, shall be flogged with many stripes ... And of every one to whom much has been given much will be required ... I came to cast fire upon the earth; and what do I desire but that it were kindled already? ... Do you suppose that I came to bestow peace upon the earth? No, I tell you, but on the contrary, division! ..."

While Peter was struggling inwardly to make these thoughts his own, the Lord turned serenely toward the crowd, which was becoming restless and surly, and said clearly:

"You hypocrites! You know how to read the appearance of the earth and the sky; then how is it you do not read the present time? ... Unless you repent, you shall perish as well."[9]

This was his farewell to the fickle Jerusalem mob as he departed with the twelve for another journey through Galilee, and possibly Samaria. But eight weeks later he returned for the Feast of Lights on 25 December, commemorating the purging of the temple in 67 B.C. by Judas Maccabeus.

The Feast of the Dedication, as it was more commonly called, was likewise joyous in mood; every house was brilliantly lit, and the people went daily to the temple and the synagogues, singing the Hallel and bearing palms and branches of trees.

The enemies of Jesus were waiting for him, however, on the Porch of Solomon.

"How long are you going to keep us in suspense?" they sneered. "If you are the Christ, tell us so plainly."

"I did tell you," he replied, "yet you do not believe. The works which I do in my Father's name, these give evidence about me. But as for you, you do not believe because you are none of my sheep... I and the Father are one."

They took up stones again with murderous intent, and sought to arrest him, but once more "he passed out of their hands," and left the city. Ascending the Mount of Olives and passing Bethany, he went down the road toward Jericho, but turned off and crossed the Jordan to the wild and desolate country near Bethania where John the Baptizer had first preached. It was terrifically hot there, even in January; and as the twelve looked wonderingly at the seared rocks among which the Jordan tumbled into the Dead Sea, they must have

---

[9] Luke 12:42-59; 13:1-5

found it hard to believe that this had once been the green, beautiful, well-watered land of Lot before God rained fire upon wicked Sodom, and obliterated even the site of it under the briny waters at the bottom of that monstrous world.

Another incredible fact was that the pharisees followed them even among those scorched rocks and that stifling haze. They continued to spy on their enemy when he went north through the towns of Perea in Herod's jurisdiction. Hearing him relate the parables of the prodigal son, the unjust steward, the great supper, the lost sheep, and many others, they were not at all pleased to learn that they were going to be cast out, and replaced in Israel by publicans, sinners, and gentiles from afar. They openly mocked him when he said, "You cannot serve God and mammon;" for, as Saint Luke adds, "they were fond of money." He replied with the parable of Dives and Lazarus, with its crushing and prophetic conclusion: "If they will not listen to Moses and the prophets, neither would they believe were one to rise from the dead." Finally they approached him with a curious bit of advice: He had better leave Perea, for Herod intended to kill him. Their intent may have been to get him to return to Judea, where they themselves had plans for him.

"Go, tell that fox," he said, "behold I will cast out demons and perform cures today and tomorrow, and the third day I shall end my course. I must go on, however, today and tomorrow, and the day following; for it cannot be that a prophet should perish outside Jerusalem!"

The suggestion of a return to Jerusalem fell unpleasantly on the ears of Peter and his companions. They all knew what narrow escapes the Lord had had during the last two visits there, and although they still doubted that he would die, they were inclined to let well enough alone. While they were discussing the matter, however, they were overtaken by a messenger from Martha and Mary in Bethany, perhaps one of their servants, who having ridden day and night to find them, presented a tablet on which these words were written into the wax:

"Lord, he whom you love is sick."

Peter, who knew His affection for Lazarus, noticed that he did not seem greatly concerned. "This illness is not unto death," he remarked, "but for the sake of God's glory, so that the Son of God may be glorified." And he remained in the village where they happened to be.

Two days later he said, suddenly, "Let us return to Judea."

There was a chorus of protest. "Rabbi," said one of them, unnamed, "the Jews were just now attempting to stone you, and are you going there again?"

Peter watched him earnestly. "Are there not twelve hours in the day?" said Jesus. "If anyone walks in the day he does not stumble, because he sees the light of this world; but if he walks in the night, he stumbles because the light is not with him." Then he told them bluntly that Lazarus was dead. "And for your sakes I am glad that I was not there, that you may believe. However, let us go to him."

They looked at one another in dismay. Thomas the twin was the first to speak.

"Let us go too", he said with gloomy determination, "that we may die with him."[10]

They set out for the ford and the Jericho road.

---

[10] John 11:1-16

17

The raising of Lazarus shook the Jewish world like an earthquake.

Peter was happier than he had been since the Transfiguration. From the moment when he saw the dead man stagger forth from the cave, the damp cerements falling from his pale and startled face, he seemed to be walking on music, riding on a veritable crescendo of triumph that could have only one outcome. Even some of the spies from Jerusalem had gone away from that scene declaring their belief in Jesus. Who could reject him now?

A crafty yellow-faced old man in the temple could have given him the answer. For Annas was reasoning from different premises. And the moment he heard the bad news from Bethany only two hours after the event, he called an emergency meeting of the Great Council of the Elders of Sion, and as their president or Nasi placed the situation before them in no uncertain light. Jesus had raised a man from the dead under circumstances too notorious to deny, before witnesses too numerous to doubt, including their own.

"What are we about?" said Annas or one of his sons. "For this man is working many miracles. If we let him go on like this, everybody will believe in him, and the Romans will come and take away both our place and our nation."[1]

"Our place and our nation." It was the place they were thinking about. But such men are always clever in masking their interests behind some wider cause that will enlist the idealism of those they need to use. And by this adroit appeal to Jewish nationalism Annas contrived, before the end of the meeting, to persuade most of the sanhedrin leaders that Jesus must be put to death – not at present, of course, for he was too popular, but at the first good opportunity, when the miracle was forgotten. It might be necessary to do something about Lazarus, too, for his existence would always be a reminder of that unfortunate episode. Apparently some of the Elders – Nicodemus, perhaps, or Joseph of Arimathea – offered some mild objections. But Caiaphas, resplendent in his high priest's robes, cowed them with a violent and arrogant speech:

"You know nothing whatever! Nor do you reflect that it is expedient for you that one man should die for the people, and not let the whole nation perish!"

---

[1] John 11:47

This was a strange remark for him to make. It did not escape the notice of thoughtful John the fisherman that "he did not say this of himself, but as he was high priest of that year, he prophesied that Jesus was to die for the nation."[2] Blindly he was offering the lamb of God to the Father for them all. In pronouncing the last passionate prophecy of official Judaism, the high priesthood was decreeing, with the death sentence on the Messiah, its own suicide. And from that day to this the word "expedient" has kept something of the pharisaical aroma of self-righteous Caiaphas.

The subject of this discussion meanwhile was taking his departure from Bethany, perhaps to escape from the admiring crowds, perhaps to avoid his enemies for the time being, and was leading his apostles to the little town of Ephrem, an oasis in the desert a few miles distant. Then after a short retirement they returned to Galilee by way of Samaria. There may be truth in the conjecture that he had arranged to meet a large number of his disciples, including his mother and many women from Capharnaum, Nazareth, and other places, so that they might accompany him to Jerusalem for the coming Passover. This is passed over lightly in the gospels. Yet no ordinary preparations were being made; and there was something formidable about the little army of men and women who proceeded down the well-beaten road along the bank of the Jordan. The term may be anachronistic, but it was like a crusade.

Peter, judging from the context of the gospel he inspired,[3] set out on that last journey to Jerusalem with the highest hopes; and it must be admitted that despite all he had seen and heard, they were worldly ones. Apparently nothing, after the restoring of Lazarus, could convince him and the sons of Zebedee that the Lord was speaking literally of his coming persecution and death; the average Jewish mind could not imagine that the messiah would submit to anything of the sort.

Even the sobering incidents and discourses along the way had no effect on their optimism. They had hardly left the Sea of Galilee when they saw, rising up like wraiths out of a field, the horrible shapes of ten lepers, who came toward them hobbling on limbs that were twisted and warped and whining from white ulcerous faces bandaged with foul rags, "Jesus, Master, have pity on us!" All ten were healed and ran joyfully away. Only one, a samaritan, returned to give thanks; and the Lord's sadness over the ingratitude of the

[2] John 11:45-53
[3] Mark 10:1-45

rest had something in it almost too significant, too prophetic. Later he insisted on the indissolubility of marriage to some pharisees who laid a trap for him along the way. When the disciples prevented some children from approaching him, he rebuked them, and welcomed the little ones with an austere and touching affection. It was on this journey too, that the rich and virtuous convert went away sorrowful, because he could not relinquish his possessions, while Jesus, loving him, looked after him with regret. All of this made very slight impression, apparently, on the twelve. For their hearts were set on the glory they expected to find waiting for them in the holy city. They actually resented it when they heard the Lord explaining how difficult it was for rich men to enter the kingdom of God.

"Then who can be saved?" they demanded.

"Things that are impossible with man are possible with God," he replied gravely.

Then it was that Peter made the outburst of which he would one day be ashamed. "See!" he blurted out, speaking for all, "we have left all and followed you. What then shall we have?"

Jesus answered patiently, "Indeed, I tell you that in the regeneration, when the Son of Man shall sit upon the throne of his glory, you who have followed me, shall yourselves sit upon twelve thrones, judging the twelve tribes of Israel. And everyone who has forsaken houses, or brothers, or sisters, or father, or mother, or wife, or lands, for my name's sake, shall receive a hundred-fold, and inherit life everlasting.

"But many that are first shall be last," he added significantly, "and the last first."

It is doubtful whether Peter noticed these last words of warning. The thought of a throne was more appealing. Yet none of them had been completely reassured by his answer. There is a suggestion in the gospel that they all remained a bit disgruntled and perplexed as they trooped after him along the yellow Jordan. "Jesus was walking in the lead; and they were struck with wonder and awe, and his followers were afraid."[4]

James and John, the sons of Zebedee, had dropped behind the rest to talk over their prospects with their mother Salome. An ambitious and determined lady, she felt perhaps that her sons had not advanced their claims as forcibly as became two of the earliest adherents of the king of Israel. Deciding to take the matter into her own hands, she hurried on with them to where Jesus walked, alone

---

[4] Mark 10:32

and majestic, at the head of the procession.

"What do you wish?" he inquired.

"Command that these two sons of mine may sit, one at your right and one at your left in your kingdom."

"You do not know what you ask! Are you able to drink the cup which I am about to drink?"

"We are able!" said the Boanerges in unison.

"You shall, indeed, drink my cup," he replied, "but to sit at my right and my left is not mine to grant except to those for whom it has been prepared by my Father."

This conversation did nothing to increase the popularity of the two fishermen with their fellow apostles. Peter had been listening to it with growing indignation. He had good reason to hope that he would occupy the coveted seat at the right hand of the Lord in the day of his glory. James the Less, as his cousin, might at least expect to be considered for the place on the left. Andrew had been the first of all to follow him. Thomas had been willing to risk his life for him. Matthew was a man of no small experience in the world. Judas, as treasurer, was one who knew his own worth, and was never shy about speaking his mind. The result was what might have been expected of human nature. As soon as Salome rejoined the women in the rear, her two barrel-chested sons found themselves surrounded by ten angry brethren who left them in no doubt as to what they thought of the performance they had just witnessed. They were so obstreperous, in fact, that the Lord turned about and gave them the instruction for which he had allowed the little scene to develop:

"You know that the princes of the heathen lord it over them, and the great ones domineer over them. Not so shall it be among you! On the contrary, whoever desires to become great among you, shall be your servant, and whoever wishes to be first among you, shall be your slave; just as the Son of Man came not to be served, but to serve, and to give his life a ransom for many."[5]

This seemed to be aimed especially at Simon Peter. But it did not long repress the ardent hope in his soul as they advanced toward the holy city. The welcome at Jericho, if nothing else, would have put it out of his mind. For that pagan and worldly city, having heard of the raising of Lazarus, turned out for Jesus now as it had on other occasions for Cleopatra and Herod. The heat was sweltering. Yet the crowd was so dense when Jesus walked through the principal street that blind Bartimaeus had to cry out to him from a distance,

[5] Matt 20:25-28

144

"Jesus, son of David, have pity on me!" and little Zaccheus, the publican, had to climb a sycamore tree to get a glimpse of him, and to learn of his unexpected good fortune.

It was easy to forget, in that triumphant hour, a remark that would have crushed them with sorrow if they had been able to foresee its fulfilment. Jesus had told them, on the way to the tropical city, that to accomplish all the prophets had written he would be ridiculed, spat upon, scourged and put to death.[6] Yet "the meaning of this utterance was hidden from them, and they failed to comprehend what was said."[7]

The festive atmosphere of the Jericho road, too, must have contributed to the illusion. Hundreds of pilgrims passed them on their way to the feast, and they knew that other thousands were converging joyously from all directions on the city of David. The whole countryside hummed with expectation, with a sense of deliverance and victory. When they arrived at Bethany on the Friday before the Passover, a cheerful moon, about two-thirds full, was shedding its radiance on the compact house of Lazarus and his sisters as they came forth to welcome the Lord to whom they owed so much.

On the next day, the sabbath, their hosts took them to dine at the house of a well-to-do neighbour called Simon the Leper. The reason is obscure. One theory is that he was their father; another, that his house had the largest guest chamber in town; or he may have been cured of his leprosy by the Lord himself, and wished to show his gratitude. However this may be, it was his residence that furnished the setting for the memorable second anointing of Jesus by the sinner he had saved.

Mary Magdalen was one of the three persons who probably took literally his predictions of his death. And seeing the comparatively little honour that was paid him as he reclined among the other guests, she ran to her house nearby to fetch a large alabaster vial containing about a pound of rare nard, brought from India long ago by Persian merchants, and stored away half-forgotten, perhaps, since her conversion. Indifferent to the curious eyes of the banqueters and of the inevitable pharisees from Jerusalem, she made her way through the crowd to where he was. Then, breaking the neck of the vial, she poured some of the oil on his head and the rest on his feet, which she then wiped with her beautiful hair.

As the choice perfume spread through the house, Judas

---

[6] Luke 18:31-34
[7] *ibid*, 34

Iscariot, as a man of business, was naturally the first to sniff, to appraise the value of the nard, and to protest indignantly:

"Why was not this oil sold for 300 denarii, and given to the poor?"[8]

He was not the only one who objected to her extravagance. The gospel makes it plain that others also "grumbled at her"[9] and one of them may well have been Peter, who, however slight his acquaintance with Persian nard, knew that a labourer toiled all day for one denarius, and that the vial therefore contained enough to support a poor family for almost a year. Yet Jesus knew something more. He knew that Judas Iscariot was the spiritual father of all unborn humanitarians who would deplore large and sumptuous churches in God's honour on the identical ground that the money should be given to the needy. He knew that such persons would often be found enriching themselves while they reduced to slavery the masses for whom they professed such tender concern; just as Judas Iscariot had spoken "not because he cared about the poor, but because he was a thief, and being keeper of the purse carried away what was put in it."[10] But all that He said was:

"Let her alone. Why do you trouble her? She has done a noble deed to me. For you have the poor with you always, and whenever you will, you may do good to them; but you have not me always. She has done what she could: she has anointed my body beforehand for the burial. And indeed, I tell you, wherever the gospel shall be proclaimed in the whole world, this, too, which she has done, shall be told as a memorial of her."[11]

To Judas Iscariot this public rebuke, gentle though it was, seems to have been the last straw. He had secretly rejected Jesus as Lord God in the synagogue at Capharnaum. He had grown afraid when John the Baptizer had been killed. He had despised Jesus for not allowing himself to be crowned king, and ever since had been only a half-hearted servant, while discontent and self-pity gnawed at his frustrated heart. Now, feeling publicly humiliated, he began to experience something more like an active hatred for the man he had once loved and almost adored. This hatred taught him, as love revealed to Mary Magdalen and to the Lord's mother, that he would die. And there was a certain relief in the thought for the apostle who

---

[8] John 12:5
[9] Mark 14:3-9
[10] John 12:6
[11] Mark 4:6-9

could no longer endure the tranquil questioning of his eyes.

Peter accepted the rebuke amiably. It would take more than that to dampen his enthusiasm for this particular trip to Jerusalem. He had probably forgotten all about the incident when they left Bethany early next day to join the continual stream of pilgrims on their way over the Mount of Olives to the holy city. It was a bright Sunday morning in spring. The first harvest was being gathered in after the latter rains. Birds sang in the blue sky; flowers seemed to rise up out of the dew to greet them. A host of pilgrims from Bethany and nearby villages had gathered behind them, singing psalms and clapping their hands. As they crossed the top of Olivet, they saw the temple gleaming wondrously in the morning sunshine. This was the day Peter had been waiting for.

Before descending the western slope, the procession paused while the Lord sent two disciples, probably Peter and John, to Bethphage just under the city walls across the Kedron valley.

"Go into the village opposite you," he said, "and immediately you will find an ass tied, and a colt with her: untie them, and bring them to me. And if anyone says anything to you, you shall reply that the Lord has need of them, and he will send them at once."[12] He did this to fulfil the prophecy of Isaiah: "Say to the daughter of Sion, 'Behold, your king comes to you meek, and riding upon an ass, and a colt, the, foal of a beast of burden.'"[13]

The two hastened to obey, and all happened as he had said. They found the colt with her mother, and brought back both; throwing their mantles over the foal to make an impromptu saddle for the Lord. But even before they reached the place where he was waiting, they heard shouts and laughter from the city; for the news of his coming had already spread from Bethphage, and people were crowding from the Damascus Gate and running down the road toward the Kedron Brook. On the way they stopped to pluck palms and the branches of trees. These they waved as they advanced; and Peter could now hear them shouting fragments of messianic prophecies and psalms:

"Hosanna to the son of David! Blessed is he who comes in the name of the Lord! Hosanna in the heights of Heaven!"[14]

Jesus mounted the colt, and with two of his apostles guiding her – probably Peter on one side, John on the other, and James

---

[12] Matt 21:2-4
[13] Is 62:11
[14] Zach 9:9; Ps 117 [118]:25, 26

leading the ass – he turned his face toward the holy city. By this time the pilgrims behind him had taken up the joyful paeans; and those from the city, as he approached, spread palms and leafy branches on the road before him as they turned and led the way triumphantly back. Jerusalem was lost to view for a few moments as the road dipped behind a shoulder of the hill. Presently, as they reached the top of a declivity above the Kedron valley, they saw it again in all its magnificence.

Then it was that Jesus wept. It was not the white glory of the temple and the palaces on the western hill that he saw now, but the Tenth Legion camping on the very spot where he paused; on the right and left of him the battering rams and mounds; the four trenches around the Castle Antonia; the dead bodies falling from the walls, the unburied corpses in the streets, the children eating dung, the silence of death falling, the despairing priests leaping into the flames. As the tears coursed down his cheeks and beard, he said:

"If you had but known, at least in this your day, what is for your peace! but now it is hidden from your eyes. For the days shall come upon you when your enemies shall cast up an embankment about you and encircle you and hem you in on every side, and lay you level with the ground, and your children who are in you, and shall not leave in you one stone upon another; because you did not recognize the time of you visitation."[15]

There was no time for Peter and the other enthusiasts to inquire into the meaning of this. The two crowds were already pressing in upon them, seeking to touch the garments of the holy one; the palms and branches crackled beneath their feet, the shouts and music seemed to bear them deliriously on through the gate, and thousands of hands seemed to push or pull them thence to Mount Moriah and the Temple of Sion. All about them thunderous voices were singing:

"Blessed is He who comes as king in the name of the Lord! Let there be peace in heaven, and glory in its heights!"[16]

Some of the pharisees forced their way to his side and said: "Master, rebuke your disciples!"

Jesus answered, "I tell you that if they were to hold their peace, the stones would cry aloud!"

So he was willing to be king at last! He was entering the city of David in triumph. The pharisees had shrunk away, fearing the hysterical crowd. The whole being of Simon Peter sang for joy.

[15] Luke 19:41-44
[16] Ps 117 [118]:26 in Luke 19:38

18

It was a bit disconcerting after all this to see the mood of Palm Sunday gradually wither before a spirit of conflict more harsh and unyielding, if possible, than that of last year. On Monday, to be sure, the whole city still sang the praises of the messiah. "All the common people were struck with admiration at his teaching,"[1] and "hung upon him, listening."[2] Some heard a voice above, like thunder, glorifying him.[3] The blind, the sick, and the lame approached him in the temple, and went away healed, thanking God. Most touching was the spontaneous tribute of a large group of Jewish children, who marched past him singing snatches of psalms and prophecies they had heard their elders shouting the previous afternoon: "Hosannah to the Son of David! Hosannah to the Son of David!"

Even some of the temple priests and members of the sanhedrin believed in him that day. It was significant, however, that they kept this to themselves for fear of excommunication, "for they loved the approval of men more than the approval of God"[4] – significant, because it indicated that the real powers of Jerusalem, the sons of Annas, were silent not because they had seen the light, but because they were afraid of being lynched by the populace. Only once that day did they disclose their real feelings, when they complained to Jesus because he allowed the children to hail him as the messiah.

"To be sure," he replied. "Have you never read, 'Out of the mouths of babes and sucklings you have brought forth perfect praise?'"[5]

They recognized the psalm, but he was not deceived by their silence. He knew what he had to expect from these men. One of his first acts on Monday morning was to curse a barren fig tree that he saw on the way from Bethany to the temple. Peter noticed the next day what had happened to its new leaves and left-over buds. "Rabbi, look!" he cried. "The fig tree you cursed is withered!"[6] Jesus then told them that with true faith they could move a mountain; but

---

[1] Mark 11:18
[2] Luke 19:48
[3] John 12:28
[4] ibid 12:43
[5] Ps 8 [9]:3
[6] Mark 11:12-17

when they prayed they must forgive their enemies as they hoped to be forgiven. It was evident as the day went on, however, that he expected no such faith, no such prayer, from the scribes and pharisees. When they reached the temple, Peter saw him once more cast out the money-changers and vendors, and overthrow their tables and chairs, exclaiming, "Is it not written, 'My house shall be called a house of prayer for all the nations'? You, however, have turned it into a den of robbers!" The atmosphere was more and more like that of a battle in which no quarter is asked or given.

When he returned to the temple early Tuesday morning, his enemies had recovered somewhat from their drubbing of the two previous days, and were preparing, though with due regard for their necks, to wrestle again with him for their pomp and wealth, and for the souls of the thousands of Jews already swarming through Solomon's Portico to acclaim him. Peter had thought that the victory was won. Yet now he saw pharisees, Herodians, and sadducees advance one after another in what was plainly an organized plan to attack him, to lay traps for him, to discredit him with the people by all means fair or foul. He saw the Lord parry each thrust and hurl them reeling back: the pharisees, who demanded his authority, and whom he silenced with the question about John the Baptizer which exposed their hypocrisy; the Herodians, to whom he returned the coin with the advice to render unto Caesar the things that were Caesar's, and to God the things that were God's; the sadducees, who tried to make his teaching of the resurrection ridiculous by a far-fetched example, and were answered so decisively that even one of the scribes cried, "Master, you have spoken admirably!"[7]

Having called them hypocrites to their faces, he proceeded to overwhelm them with the great parables so obviously aimed at them: that of the wicked servants who killed their master's men, and were themselves dispossessed and destroyed; that of the two sons, with its moral that repentant publicans and harlots would enter heaven before the high priests, scribes and the pharisees; and that of the king's son whose unworthy marriage guests were slain, and their city burned. They had rejected the cornerstone of Psalm 117; yet "every one who falls upon that stone shall be broken, but upon whomsoever it shall fall, it shall grind him to dust!" That was the moment when the scribes and chief priests wanted most to lay hands on him, had it not been for the people: "for they knew that he had

---

[7] Mark 12:31

told this parable against them."[8] Meanwhile he faced them all, and demanded:

"What do you think about the Christ? Whose son is he?"

"David's," they answered without hesitation.

"How is it then that David in the Spirit calls him Lord, saying, 'The Lord said to my Lord, "Sit you at my right hand, until I put your enemies under my feet"' If David, therefore, calls him Lord, in what way is he his son?"

The obvious reply was that David had prophesied the incarnation of God in one of his descendants, who stood before them in this last decisive moment, pleading for their faith. But Annas and his sons hardened their hearts and made their everlasting choice. "And no one was able to answer him a word, nor did anyone dare from that day to question him further."[9]

It was only then, after they had had their last chance and had spurned his love deliberately and forever, that Peter saw the Christ tower above them, and seem to become that judge of the living and the dead that he had proclaimed himself, as he took the verbal offensive against them, and put them all to rout in one of the most terrible scenes in human history. An impotent pallor must have spread over the cadaverous face of Annas and the smug fat one of Caiaphas, as they heard themselves described and castigated, before the very mob they misled and exploited, as no ruling class had ever been or would be.

"The scribes and the pharisees sit in Moses' seat," he said first to the crowd and to his disciples. "Do and observe, therefore, all that they tell you; but do not imitate their actions, for they preach and do not practise. And they tie up heavy and insupportable burdens and lay them on men's shoulders, but they will not put forth a finger of theirs to remove them. And they do all their actions that they may be seen of men; for they widen their phylacteries and enlarge their fringes, and love the places of honour at banquets and the first seats in the synagogues, and to be saluted in the marketplaces, and to be addressed by men as 'Rabbi!' Do not, however, be called 'Rabbi,' for one is your teacher, and you are all brothers. And call no one your father upon earth, for one is your father, he who is in heaven. And do not be called masters, for one is your master, the Christ. But the greatest among you shall be your servant. And whoever exalts himself shall be humbled, and

[8] Luke 20:17-19
[9] Matt 22:46

whoever humbles himself shall be exalted."[10]

Now he had come to the awful and searing climax of his last public utterance. It was a dreadful experience for those who had heard the eight beatitudes three years before to see him turn now toward his frightened but defiant enemies, and hurl upon their heads, like a God dispensing judgment, the thunder of eight deliberate curses:

"Woe to you, scribes and pharisees – hypocrites! because you shut the Kingdom of heaven in men's faces; for you neither enter yourselves, nor allow those that are going in to enter.

Woe to you, scribes and pharisees – hypocrites! for you devour the property of widows under the pretext of making long prayers; for which you shall receive the greater sentence.

Woe to you, scribes and pharisees – hypocrites! for you traverse sea and land to make one convert; and when you succeed, you make him twice as much a son of Gehenna as yourselves!

Woe to you, blind guides! who say, 'If anyone swears by the temple, it is nothing; but if one swears by the gold of the temple, one is bound. Blind fools that you are! Which is greater – the gold, or the temple which has sanctified the gold? ... You blind ones!...

Woe to you, scribes and pharisees – hypocrites! for you pay tithes of mint, anise, and cummin, and have neglected the weightier matters of the Law – justice, mercy, and faith. These latter you ought to have observed, while not neglecting the former. You blind guides, who strain out the gnat and gulp down the camel!

Woe to you, scribes and pharisees – hypocrites! for you clean the outside of the cup and the plate, while within you are full of extortion and incontinence ...

Woe to you, scribes and pharisees – hypocrites! for you are like whitewashed tombs, which outwardly appear handsome, but within are full of dead men's bones, and of all uncleanness. So you, too, outwardly appear to men to be righteous, but inwardly you are crammed with hypocrisy and iniquity.

Woe to you, scribes and pharisees – hypocrites! for you erect the tombs of the prophets, and decorate the monuments of the saints ... Thus you give evidence against yourselves that you are the sons of those who murdered the prophets! Be it yours, then, to fill up the measure of your fathers! You serpents! You breed of vipers! how are you to escape the damnation of Gehenna?

Behold, I myself, therefore, will send you prophets and sages

---

[10] Matt 23: 1-12

152

and teachers; and some of them you will kill and crucify, and some of them you will flog in your synagogues, and pursue from city to city; that upon you may come all the righteous blood shed upon the earth, from the blood of the just Abel down to the blood of Zachariah, son of Barachiah, whom you murdered between the sanctuary and the altar. Indeed. I tell you, all these crimes shall come upon the present generation."[11]

The majestic voice died away, and in the apocalyptic moment that followed, all the thousands stood as if petrified, motionless and silent, waiting. He had finished. A great weariness seemed to have descended upon him. Then he raised his eyes, and spoke the heart-broken words of farewell:

"Jerusalem, Jerusalem, you who kill the prophets, and stone those who are sent to you! How often would I have gathered your children together, as a hen gathers her chickens under her wings; but you would not! Behold, 'Your house shall be left to you desolate.' For I tell you that from this time you shall not see me until you say, 'Blessed is he who comes in the name of the Lord!'"[12]

The effect that this utterance has today on those who know the sequel seems to have been wholly lost upon Peter and his fellow apostles. They may have been drowsy as they leaned against the wall, listening, they may have felt relieved that it was over. Perhaps they had heard some of it so often that they took it for granted. But the lack of understanding they were capable of displaying on such occasions never seemed more obtuse than in the gospel account of what they did as they followed the Lord across one of the temple courts, away from the still hushed and frightened multitude. They were more like a party of sight-seeing tourists than the followers of one who had made his last appeal in vain to those for whom he was about to die. They began to inspect the architecture with appreciative eyes, and to remark upon some of its excellences.

They were especially interested in the size of the marble blocks with which Herod had rebuilt the shrine of Solomon. Some of these were nineteen feet long and half as high. There was one on a corner that must have been seven and a half feet square. Here again we have proof of the fidelity with which these scenes were reported; only life itself could be so crass and unexpected. For one of the twelve (and in Mark's gospel he sounds rather like Peter) actually remarked, after craning his neck as he trooped along beside

[11] Matt 23:13-36
[12] Matt 23:37-39

the Messiah:

"Look, Master, what stones, and what buildings!"

"Do you see all these great buildings?" replied Jesus, sadly. "There shall not be left here one stone upon another that shall not be thrown down!"[13]

Peter found this depressing. The destruction of the temple seemed to him entirely inconsistent with the glorious events of the last three days. It was also connected, in Jewish minds, with the end of the world. He discussed these objections with his brother Andrew and the sons of Zebedee, as they crossed the Kedron valley to the Mount of Olives, and they all agreed to ask the Lord, as soon as they found him alone, to explain his pessimistic remark.

Their opportunity came that evening when they discovered him sitting on the hillside, resting in the gathering dusk, and sorrowfully watching the ancient city array herself in lights, one after another, like a wanton woman putting on jewels for her revels in the very house of doom.

"Tell us, when shall this be?" they asked. "And what shall be the sign when all this is on the eve of accomplishment?"

At great length, the tired God-Man told his simple friends what he had not seen fit to explain to the bureaucrats and emotional mobs in the temple. Jerusalem would be utterly destroyed amid scenes of tribulation unmatched before or after, her people slain or led away captive into all countries; and this in their very lifetime.[14]

The prophets had written of it. Daniel, for instance: "And after sixty-two weeks Christ shall be slain; and the people that shall deny him shall not be his. And a people with their leaders shall come and shall destroy the city and the sanctuary; and the end thereof shall be waste, and after the end of the war the appointed desolation![15] And Moses: "The Lord shall scatter you among all people from the farthest points of the earth to the ends thereof ... Neither shall you be quiet, even in those nations, nor shall there be any rest for the sole of your foot. For the Lord will give you a fearful heart, and languishing eyes, and a soul consumed with pensiveness; and your life shall be as it were hanging before you."[16] And Zachariah: "I will make Jerusalem a burdensome stone to an peoples. All that shall lift it up shall be rent and torn, and all the kingdoms of the

[13] Mark 13:1-3; Luke 21:5-7; Matt 24:1, 2
[14] It happened in 70 A.D.
[15] Daniel 9:26
[16] Deut 28:64-66.

154

earth shall be gathered together against her."

Jesus added that "Jerusalem shall be trodden down by the nations until the times of the nations are completed."[17]

This is arresting enough today as we see the Jews begin to resettle Palestine, and the nations preparing to rend one another over the spoil of the Holy City. But it was an appalling vision of their own future and of that of the world that he unfolded before the four fishermen at his feet. For he well understood that they associated the fall of Jerusalem with the end of time, and his reply covered both events. His apostles must carry his teachings to every part of the earth. Their reward in this life would be to be hated and persecuted by all nations for his sake; even relatives and friends would betray his followers, and they would be hunted down and killed. Yet not a hair of their heads would perish, and in their patience they would possess their souls.[18]

The end of the world would not occur until the gospel had been preached to every nation. One sign of the approaching catastrophe would be the appearance of impostors pretending to be Christ or to speak for him; these would lead many astray, but were not to be believed or followed. There would be wars and the rumours of wars, nation rising against nation, and empire against empire; earthquakes, famine, pestilences. "All these, however, are but the beginning of birth-pangs."

A great and general apostasy from the Church would occur toward the end of the world. "And you shall be hated by all nations for my name's sake," he repeated, as if speaking to the Christians of the last days. "And then many shall fall away; and they will betray one another, and hate one another. And many false prophets will arise and mislead many. And on account of the increasing law-lessness, the love of the majority will be chilled. But he who per-severes to the end, he it is who will be saved."[19]

The next part of the discourse seems to refer both to the coming destruction of Jerusalem and to some frightful event toward the end of time, when men would see "the abomination of desola-tion, spoken of by the Prophet Daniel, standing in the holy place."[20] False Christs and false prophets would next appear, showing great

[17] Luke 21:24
[18] Luke 21:18, 19
[19] Matt. 24:9-14. Pope Leo XIII believed that he saw signs of the great turning away from truth in his encyclical *Divinum Illud,* 4 May 1897. All the Popes since have made similar observations.
[20] Dan 9:27

signs and portents, "so as to mislead, if possible, even the elect." But the faithful were not to follow them. "For as the lightning comes out from the east and shines even to the west, so, too, shall the coming of the Son of Man be."

His coming, however, would follow great affliction, unparalleled in all history. "Unless the Lord had shortened those days, no flesh would be saved: but for the sake of the elect whom he chose, he has shortened the days."[21] After that "the sun shall be darkened, and the moon shall not give her light, and the stars shall fall from the sky, and the powers of the firmament shall be shaken. And then shall appear the sign of the Son of Man in heaven. And then shall all the races of the earth mourn, and they shall witness the Son of Man coming in the clouds of heaven with great power and majesty. And he will send out his angels with a loud-sounding trumpet, and they shall gather his elect from the four winds, from one end of the heavens to the other... ?[22]

"And as were the days of Noah, so shall be the coming of the Son of Man. For as in the days before the deluge they were eating and drinking, marrying and giving in marriage, until the day on which Noah entered the ark, and knew not until the deluge came and swept them all away, so shall be the coming of the Son of Man. Then two men shall be in the field – one is taken and one left. Two women shall be grinding at the handmill – one is taken and one is left. Watch, therefore, for you know not on what day your Lord is coming ... At an unexpected moment the Son of Man will come..."[23]

"But when the Son of Man comes in his glory, and all the angels with him, then he will sit upon the throne of his glory; and before him shall be gathered all nations; and he will separate them one from another as the shepherd separates the sheep from the goats, and he will place the sheep on his right hand, and the goats on his left ... And these shall go away into everlasting punishment; but the righteous into life eternal."[24]

It was dark now, and the magic of night had drawn the irregular lines and disparities of the city into a harmony, glowing with soft lights and humming faintly with music and innumerable voices. Peter was probably growing sleepy as the moon, almost full, began to peep over the shoulder of the hill behind them. The last

---

[21] Mark 13:20

[22] Matt 24:15-31

[23] ibid 24:37-44

[24] ibid, 25:31-33, 46

words of Jesus were ringing in his ears:

"Watch, therefore – for you know not when the master of the house will come, whether in the evening, or at midnight, or at cock-crow, or in the morning – lest coming suddenly he find you sleeping. But what I say to you I may say to all – watch!"[25]

It might have been terrifying and confusing if Peter had allowed his mind to dwell upon it. But it was like him to fix his attention upon the glorious return of the Lord to judge the world and to forget the rest. It was enough for him that he had been promised a place on one of the twelve seats of the mighty.

The Lord's voice was speaking again:

"You know that after two days comes the Passover: and the Son of Man shall be delivered up to be crucified."

Characteristically they ignored the reference to the crucifixion, nor did Jesus stress it further; and when they asked him where they should eat the Passover feast he gave some rather unusual instructions to Peter and John:

"Go into the city, where a man carrying a jar of water will meet you; follow him, and wherever he shall enter, say to the master of the house, the master says, "Where is my guest-room, where I may eat the Passover with my disciples?"' And he himself will show you a large room ready furnished; and there make ready for us."[26]

With these words murmuring in his brain, Peter fell asleep.

[25] Mark 13:35-37
[26] ibid, 24:12-16. John gives the same details.

19

Peter and John went to the city on Wednesday morning, "and found it to be as he had told them."[1] Almost at once they encountered a man, probably a servant, with an earthen water jar on his shoulder. They followed him through the mazes of traffic, up some of the crooked streets, then to the western hill, until they saw him turn into a little court, and enter a certain home. On knocking there and telling their errand, they were admitted. Possibly it was the residence of Nicodemus, or of some relative or disciple of the Lord. Most likely it belonged to the mother of his young friend John Mark.[2]

Following the master of the house up the outdoor stairway, the two fishermen were ushered into a large room in which they saw a table quite sufficient for their purpose, with tapestried couches extending on three sides of it. There were some rich bronze lamps, severely moulded with no images and little ornament; good rugs from the East; and on one wall two swords, memorials perhaps of the part this family had played in the Maccabean War. These last especially, we may be sure, commanded the attention of Simon Peter. Nothing would have suited his frame of mind better than to grasp one of them in his brawny fist, to thrust the Romans out of Jerusalem forever, and to seat his master on the throne of David. Meanwhile their host was giving instructions to his servants to have dinner prepared for thirteen persons, and he assured his visitors that everything would be ready when they and their master arrived.

Peter and John were not the only apostles in the city that day. Even as they left the house on the hill, and made their way back to the business district, they may almost have brushed against one of their brethren who was on his way to the palace of the high priest, hardly a stone's throw distant from where they had been. For Judas Iscariot, after four days of brooding on his humiliation at the dinner in Bethany, had finally resolved the conflict in his soul by a terrible decision.

For a whole year now he had been fighting a losing battle to retain his natural love and loyalty for Jesus without the aid of the supernatural faith he had rejected in the synagogue at Capharnaum. Thus he was at the mercy of an unseen enemy with more than

---

[1] Mark 14:16
[2] cf Acts 12:12

natural resources, and that enemy had beaten him from one temptation to another until he floundered in a confusion to which almost any resolute act seemed preferable. The sermon on the mount had meant as little to him as to many professing Christians of our day. The death of John the Baptizer, the Lord's refusal to be crowned king, his mystifying reply to the demand for a sign, and finally his encouragement of the extravagance of that silly woman at Bethany might have been forgotten if only he had taken advantage of the opportunity that had been foisted upon him on Palm Sunday. On that day and the two following, Judas had hung upon his every word and act. He had not been taken in by what appeared to be his victories. Magnificent though they were, they were verbal and unsubstantial. Moreover, the last pleading and tearful words after the titanic diatribe of Tuesday afternoon were those of a heart-broken and defeated man, not of the regal messiah Judas had been expecting.

What then, of all the miracles? We shall never get to the bottom of the mystery of iniquity that the character of Judas presents. Yet it is plain from the words of Christ both to him and to the temple rulers that faith in him was a secret gift from the Father to the sincere and loving heart; without it a man could see even the raising of Lazarus, and still withhold the assent of his will. "If they will not listen to Moses and the prophets, neither would they believe were one to rise from the dead!" To penetrate this secret further would be to tear the veil from hell and the devil, and once more to pluck from the tree of good and evil knowledge the forbidden fruit which brought death to the world.

Judas could no longer believe in Jesus, but he could believe in the high priests, for they were children of the city of man like himself, and he understood them. These rich, powerful, politically minded prelates would act as soon as it was safe to do so. They would bring about Jesus' destruction, and he would not lift a finger. On the contrary He had unmistakably prophesied his death. And this at least, on probable and rational grounds, Judas could accept.

He may not have desired it consciously. Bad as he was (to give the devil his due), he would probably not have sought it himself until he had been convinced that it was inevitable. That being so, he might as well profit by it. But how? Even the high priests would not dare touch the Lord while admiring crowds surrounded him. Still, if they could arrest him in some quiet, out-of-the-way spot, with no publicity, they would doubtless be willing to reward the man who would put him in their hands. And millionaires with so much at stake could afford to pay generously. Judas could already see himself going away with a fat bag of golden shekels that might enable him to start life again in Rome or Alexandria, where he could forget the reproach in the eyes of Jesus, and all that impractical but haunting talk about another world, and living like birds of the air. He was certainly not disposed to be a fool like Thomas the Twin, and say "Let us die with him!" Lost causes are no part of a businessman's philosophy.

Let us suppose, then, that Judas barely escaped meeting Peter and John as he shrank against the buildings on his way to the palace; and that on inquiring for Annas or Caiaphas he was directed to the temple, where the holy pair were attending another emergency meeting of the sanhedrin. The synoptic gospels indicate, without giving particulars, that he sought them of his own accord and found them: that is all. Likely enough they would be keeping in close touch those days with the leading members of the council. A quorum consisted of only 23 of the 70, and could condemn a man to death by a majority of two. This right, under Roman rule, was only theoretical. In practice, no formal execution could be carried out without the approval and cooperation of Pilate. A stoning by the mob, under the Old Law, might be managed. But in this instance the populace could not be depended upon, and the experiment might be dangerous. It would be better to let Pilate handle the business.

Annas got on very well, behind the scenes, with that indolent politician, and had probably bribed him more than once. Thus he had him in his power, and could make trouble for him with Tiberius if he found it convenient. The only real difficulty was how to get the Nazarene into his hands without public commotion. He and his apostles lodged now at one place, now another. And one of them, his cousin James the Less, was said to look very much like him. It is hardly likely that the experienced old Nasi or prince told all this to the councillors as they sat facing him in a semicircle in the Hall of Hewn Stones; but after their departure, perhaps, he was discussing it with his son-in-law, the high priest, when he heard that one of the friends of Jesus wanted to speak with him.

He had never expected such good fortune as this. Doubtless he made a quick appraisal of Judas, and flattered and reassured him until he had him on record before witnesses as being willing to betray his master. Up to that moment he would have been willing to

160

offer him almost any reasonable bribe, even in gold, and it was
obvious that the fellow expected something of the sort. But Annas
had not become a millionaire by unprofitable acts of generosity.
And at once it flashed upon his mind of subtle cunning that there
was no need for more than a token payment, since Judas had placed
himself completely in their power. If he tried to withdraw now, they
could denounce him to his own associates and leave him exposed
and friendless. This probably explains why they gave him only
thirty silver shekels, the equivalent of about as many dollars in our
money – the standard indemnity, under the Mosaic Law, for a slave
gored by an ox.[3] Once more, too, Caiaphas was unconsciously
fulfilling a prophecy: "And they weighed for my wages thirty
pieces of silver."[4] Perhaps he also meant to insult Jesus by offering
so niggardly a price for him. But Judas had to accept whatever they
gave him. And when the high priest contemptuously dealt out the
coins – one of them conceivably the widow's mite that the Lord had
commended only the day before – it was a broken betrayer that took
them mechanically and stumbled out into the mocking spring
sunshine. Satan had sifted this once able and promising apostle, and
little remained but the chaff of a numb despair when he finally
rejoined his brethren in the garden of Gethsemane.

Nothing is said in the gospels as to how the Lord and the other
apostles spent that fateful Wednesday: possibly as a day of rest,
prayer, and preparation, possibly with their friends in Bethany. But
on the next day, Thursday, they undoubtedly proceeded to the city
to eat the Passover supper in the house where Peter and John had
arranged for it. The sun was already sinking behind the western hill.
The first lights were beginning to twinkle dimly here and there. The
savoury smell of roasting lamb or goat permeated every street.
From open windows and gardens came the murmur of happy
voices, the strumming of lutes and harps. It was a warming thought
that more than a million, perhaps two million Jews were gathered
within those holy walls that evening, ready to offer the Passover
sacrifice to the God of Abraham, and to thank him again for their
deliverance from the Egyptians and from all their enemies.

Arriving at the house on the hill, they were shown to the large
upper room, and Peter, in the best of moods, saw that everything
had been arranged as the host had promised. The good red wine had
been poured from leather bags into brown crockery flagons, and

[3] Exod 21:32
[4] Zach 11:11

stood invitingly on the table. As the distinguished guest and his friends reclined on the couches extending on three sides, the servants brought the meat, the bread, the bitter herbs and condiments. Later they would retire, and leave them to their enjoyment.

Ordinarily the procedure would have been this: the father or whoever presided would send around a cup of wine, saying, "Blessed be you, our Lord God, king of the world, who have created the fruit of the vine." All would then wash their hands according to the pharisaic traditions. A salad of bitter herbs, dipped in vinegar or salt water to commemorate the sufferings of the Hebrews in Egypt, was passed around the table. The ritual dishes were now brought in one after another, while the father explained the significance of each: a broth called the charoseth; a sweet reddish sauce made of nuts, figs, and fruits, to remind them all of the bricks their ancestors had made for Pharaoh; loaves of unleavened bread; the festal offerings, to be dipped in the charoseth and eaten with the bread; and finally, the Passover lamb or goat.

The family now drank a second cup of wine, and sang part of the joyful sequence of psalms known as the Hallel. Then they reclined again about three sides of the table, each on his left side and elbow. The father blessed half a loaf of bread, wrapped it with bitter herbs, dipped it in the charoseth, tasted it, and passed it around, saying, "This is the bread of affliction, which our fathers ate in Egypt." He then blessed the lamb, and ate of it; the rest followed his example. Now the feast was in full course, all talking and laughing as the third cup, the cup of blessing, passed from hand to hand. With the fourth cup the remaining verses of the Hallel were sung, and the feast came to its solemn but joyful conclusion, sometimes with a fifth cup and the chanting of other psalms.

The gospels make plain how Jesus followed this hallowed routine in outline and in spirit, and how, at the same time, he enlarged it to suit his own purpose. A knowledge of that purpose has led artists and preachers to attribute to the apostles the reverence that is felt at the Consecration of the Mass. But the twelve had no such realization before the event; and it is easy to credit the vision of Thérèse Neumann in which she saw them with no appearance of devotion at all, and apparently with no understanding of what was about to happen.[5] This is clear, in fact, from their behaviour as described in one of the gospels.[6] They completely

[5] Von Lama, *op cit.*, 1, 132
[6] Luke 22:24

missed the point of the Lord's opening remark. As he blessed and passed the cup, he said, "Earnestly have I desired to eat this Passover with you before I suffer; for I tell you that I will eat it no more, until it is fulfilled in the kingdom of God." Seizing upon the last words only, the twelve at once fell to wrangling among themselves as to which would be greatest in that kingdom.

It may be, too, that they contended for the places nearest him at the table. He reminded them once more that the greatest among them would be like him, the servant of all. Abashed and subdued, they then reclined. The Lord was in the middle of the left side. John, perhaps at his request, was at his right. Peter, ashamed of himself, went impulsively, perhaps, to the last position, opposite him, on the other side. Judas brazenly took the post of honour at the Lord's left; so at least the context suggests, and it may be that he and Peter had been the chief contenders for it, for the traitor would naturally try to cover up his sense of perfidy by a show of special devotion.

When they were all stretched out in their places, Jesus gave a pointed illustration of what he had just said about serving. He arose and took off his mantle. Then, girding himself with a towel from the serving table, he poured some water into one of the basins left there for the cleansing of hands, and going to Simon Peter, at the end of the table, knelt before him and prepared to wash his fete.

This was indeed a far cry from the disdainful self-ablutions of the pharisees. Peter was overcome with embarrassment and shame, for only servants performed this menial office.

"Lord, are you going to wash my feet?" And he began to arise.

"What I am doing you know not now, but you shall understand it hereafter. If I do not wash you," he added, regarding him steadily, "you shall have no part with me."

Peter then resumed his place, crying:

"Lord, not only my feet, but also my hands and my head!"

"He who has bathed needs only to wash his feet; then indeed, he is entirely clean. And you are clean," he ended, glancing about the table till his eyes fell on Judas, "but not all."

After he had put on his outer garments and reclined in his place, he repeated this hint twice, until all of them became aware of it. "Indeed, indeed, I say to you," he said more pointedly, "one of you will betray me!"

They began looking at one another and speculating. Peter leaned across the table and said to John, who was leaning back upon the Lord's breast, "Tell us of whom he is speaking?" And John asked in turn, "Lord, who is it?"

"It is that one for whom I shall dip the sop and hand it to him."

He dipped the bread and herbs according to the old ritual, and handed it to Judas at his left. To most of those at the table it would look like the usual procedure.

Peter and John exchanged glances. Perhaps they were not greatly surprised. But they were the only ones who knew. This was the terrible moment when satan, according to John, entered into the traitor and possessed him. Until then, perhaps, he had been wavering. Seeing the face of Jesus again, so loving and so patient, he might well wonder how he could have been false to him; and there was still time to throw himself at his feet, to tell everything, to beg forgiveness. Cowardice, pride, shame – it is futile to speculate what prevented his asking for what he undoubtedly would have received. Again we have a mystery that no one has been able to penetrate in nineteen centuries; we can only take the word of Jesus that he was a "son of perdition," and that it would have been better for him if he had never been born. When one after the other demanded, "Can it be I, Lord?" the traitor found a sinister courage in his heart to say, "Is it I, rabbi?" The salutation itself was significant: he was the only one who could not call him "Lord". Yet even then the all-merciful did not expose or denounce him. He said to him quietly, "You have said it. What you are bent upon, do quickly."

Peter and John saw Judas get up suddenly from the table, and go out into the night.

20

Did the traitor leave before or after the most important part of the supper? The question has been debated for centuries by saints and scholars, and is still undetermined. The third Gospel alone seems to indicate his presence at the institution of the Eucharist. The first suggests, at least, that he left before it; and it must be said that the chronology of Matthew, as an eye-witness, is probably more reliable. Perhaps, too, it is more consistent with the delicate charity with which the Lord treated his betrayer at the feast to suppose that he wished to spare him the additional crime of sacrilege, and that this was the very reason why he hastened his going by quietly calling attention to his treachery. It was only just, moreover, to deny him the explanation of the seemingly wild words in the synagogue at Capharnaum the previous year – words that he had secretly rejected, and the other eleven, led by Peter, had accepted on faith.

"Now, as they were eating, Jesus took bread, and blessed, broke, and gave it to the disciples, and said:

'Receive and eat; this is my body. Do this in remembrance of me.'

And taking the cup, he gave thanks, and gave it to them, saying:

'Drink, all of you, of this: for this is my blood, that of the new covenant, which is poured out for many for the remission of sins..:"[1]

It is doubtful whether the eleven understood the full significance of this at the moment. Nevertheless they must have received certain definite impressions which time would soon clarify. There must have flashed across their minds the memory of the dreadful afternoon in the synagogue by the sea, when they had followed him, knowing who he was, even after he had spoken words which seemed irrational, and which he refused to explain.

"Unless you eat of the flesh of the Son of Man and drink his blood, you have no life in yourselves," he had said. "He who eats my flesh and drinks my blood possesses life everlasting, and I will raise him up on the last day. For my flesh is real food, and my blood is real drink. He who eats my flesh and drinks my blood abides in me and I in him."[2]

---

[1] Matt 26:26-29
[2] John 6:53-57

Now they all heard him say that the bread was his flesh, and the wine his blood. It must be true, since he said it. Some of them had seen him change water into wine at Cana; why then could he not change wine into blood? The word "covenant" itself evoked the association of blood in minds familiar with the Old Testament. They all remembered how Moses, in sealing the Old Covenant between God and his people, had poured part of the sacrificial blood on the altar, and had sprinkled the rest on the spectators. Here before them, under the appearance of wine, was the blood of the New Covenant, though none of them had any conception apparently of the manner in which it was to be shed, to complete the sacrifice. If ever Peter ran his fingers through his bushy hair in that gesture attributed to him, it must have been at this moment, when he partially saw, and then perhaps was more confused than ever. For here again was mystery.

Equally puzzling, in parts, were the magnificent discourse and prayer which followed. Some have thought that Jesus uttered these after they left the supper room;[3] but they seem to belong to the feast itself, and to the place where it occurred. He was now to be glorified, he said – and here Peter must have remembered the Transfiguration – yet he was going away, to a place where they could not follow. Very solemnly he then said:

"I give you a new commandment, that you love one another; that just as I have loved you, you also love one another. By this shall all men know that you are my disciples, if you have love for one another."

It was Peter, clumsy as ever, who interrupted the sublime discourse at this point.

"Lord, where are you going?"

"Where I am going you cannot follow me now, but you shall hereafter."

"Lord, why can I not follow you now? I will lay down my life for you!"

"Will you lay down your life for me?" The tender irony was unmistakable. "Indeed, indeed, I say to you, the cock shall not crow until you have thrice denied me."[4]

Peter looked hurt and bewildered. What could he say? The Lord took some of the sting out of the remark by adding, with grave affection, "Simon, Simon, behold, satan begged to have you all that he

[3] John 13:36-38
[4] John 13:36-38

might sift you as wheat. But I prayed for you" – here the Greek text changes to the singular, referring to Peter alone – "that your faith may not fail; and do you, once you have turned, confirm your brethren."

"Lord, with you I am ready to go both to prison and to death!" said Peter.

"I tell you, Peter," the sad voice reiterated, "that the cock shall not crow today, until you have thrice denied that you know me."[5]

All of them were disturbed and mystified.

"Lord, we know not where you are going," objected Thomas. "And how can we know the way?"

"I am the Way, the Truth, and the Life; no one comes to the Father but by me. If you had known me you would have known my Father also; and from now you do know him, and have seen him."

Philip brightened up at this, and said:

"Lord, show us the Father, and it will be enough for us!"

"Have I been so long a time with you," replied Jesus, "and you do not know me? Philip, he who has seen me has seen the Father; how can you say 'Show us the Father?' Do you not believe that I am in the Father, and the Father is in me? ... He who believes in me shall do the works that I do – and greater than these shall he do – because I am going to the Father; and whatever you ask in my name, that I will do ... If you love me, observe my commandments; and I will ask the Father and he will give you another comforter to remain with you forever – the spirit of Truth, whom the world is incapable of receiving, because it neither sees him nor knows him. You know him, because he abides with you and shall be in you ... ."

They were still frankly puzzled, and Jude Thaddeus asked, "Lord, what has happened that you will manifest yourself to us and not to the world?"

Nothing bewildered them more than his insistence on their separation from the world – that fundamental principle that would make impossible any real unity of the human race except on the eternal rock of his teachings and His Church.

"If anyone loves me, he will keep my word," he repeated with emphasis as he developed this idea, "and my Father will love him, and we will love him and make our abode with him ... The Comforter, the Holy Spirit, whom the Father will send in my name, he will teach you all things, and will remind you of all that I have told you. Peace I leave with you, my peace I give you; not as the world gives do I give to you. Let not your heart be troubled, nor let

---

[5] Luke 22:31-34

it be afraid ... The prince of this world is coming, and he has no part in me ..." The Lord compared himself to a vine; they were the branches; to grow they must be pruned; if fruitless, cut off.

"This is my commandment, that you love one another as I have loved you. Greater love has no one than this, that one should lay down one's life for one's friends. You did not choose me, but I chose you ... If the world hates you, know that it has hated me before it hated you. If you were of the world, the world would love its own; but because you are not of the world, but I chose you out of the world, therefore the world hates you. Remember what I said to you before, 'A slave is not greater than his master! If they persecuted me, they will persecute you as well ... If I had not come and spoken to them, they would not have been guilty of sin; but now they have no excuse for their sin ....'"

There could be no true religion without the worship of Christ, with all that it implied of unity and charity. For "he who hates me hates my Father also ... . I have told you these things in order that you may not be scandalized. They will expel you from the synagogues; indeed, the time is coming when whoever murders you will think he is rendering service to God ... I have still many things to say to you, but you can not bear them now. But when he, the spirit of truth, comes, he shall guide you into all truth ... A little while and you behold me no longer, and again a little while and you shall see me."

This was very far from the thoughts of glory that kept recurring to Peter whenever he glanced at the two swords on the wall. It was so far over their heads, in fact, that they began to nudge one another and to ask what he was talking about. He finally told them again that he was going to leave the world, and go to the Father.

"Ah!" they said. "Now you are speaking plainly, and using no figures of speech. Now we know that you know all things, and need none to question you. By this we believe that you did come forth from God."

"Are you now believing?" he retorted ironically. "Why, the hour is coming – yes, it has come – when you shall be scattered each to his own place, and shall leave me alone ..."

This left them no more enlightened than before. But now he was lifting his eyes, and speaking the heavenly prayer that ended the discourse. He was asking especially that they be one with him and with one another – they and all who should believe in him through their word – as he and the Father were one. He prayed not for the world that would hate both them and him, but for them and their unity of thought, love, and action. And with that he broke off suddenly, and asked:

"When I sent you out without purse, wallet, and sandals, were you in need of anything?"

Peter remembered his mission journey.

"Nothing," he said. "Nothing," they all said.

"But now, whoever has a purse, let him take it, and a wallet as well; and whoever has no sword, let him sell his cloak and buy one. For I tell you that this which is written must be fulfilled in me; 'He was even ranked among outlaws: ...'"

The word 'sword' fell pleasantly on the ears of Peter, "Lord, look! here are two swords!"

"That will do," he said.

The fisherman tied one of the blades to his girdle. He had certainly not understood much that had been said, but he thought he understood the meaning of this cold steel of Damascus, this ruler of mobs, this maker of kings, that fell so pleasantly against his stout leg. He was beginning to feel that after all something might have been accomplished that evening. He had been rather drowsy, perhaps, after supper, but he became wide awake and alert now as they all arose to take their departure, and followed the Lord down the outer stairway to the street.

As they strode along under the garden wall of the High Priest Caiaphas, they all sang the latter part of the great Hallel, with its significant reference to "the stone rejected by the builders" only to become "the head of the corner," and no doubt the voice of Jesus was audible above the others. Jerusalem was like an elaborate instrument made up of manly voices chanting the deepest and most moving songs of Israel. A full moon had risen in the east, shining in their faces as they went down the hill. The silver radiance had transmuted the sprawling city of stone and dirt into something magical, ethereal, unearthly, evanescent. There was a trace in the air of that mysterious sadness, that hint of death wedded to youth, of corruption lying in wait for beauty, that often comes with moonlight in early spring.

Singing, the twelve men swung along the main street, thence over the Tyropean Valley to the southeast gate below the temple, and then across the Kedron opposite the tombs of the prophets. They had finished the Hallel now, and were walking in silence along the brook, which probably was beginning to dry up with the advance of the season. About twenty minutes after they had left the supper room, they arrived at the little farm called Gethsemane, on the western slope of the Mount of Olives.

As they paused there, it became evident, in the brilliant light of the moon, that the sadness they had remarked in the Lord all evening had deepened into a profound sorrow. He looked "dismayed and heavy-hearted." The eleven, too, could not help feeling suddenly depressed and uneasy. Jesus left eight of them at the garden gate, and signifying that Peter and the two sons of Zebedee were to follow him, he entered, and went heavily up the hillside some two or three hundred yards, before he stopped.

"My soul is very sorrowful, even unto death," he said. "Stay here and watch."

They saw him go farther up the hillside, a dark and towering figure against the steely grey of the sky, until he had reached the top, perhaps a stone's throw away. There he flung himself on his face, praying. After a little while they distinctly heard him say, with no ordinary intensity of sorrow:

"Abba, all things are possible to you! Remove this cup from me! Nevertheless, not what I will, but what you will!"

This saddened them inexpressibly, but there was nothing they could do about it. So Peter seated himself on the grass and leaned against one of the boulders strewn among the silvery olive trees, while the others followed his example. They were tired, dejected, and surfeited, and the crisp air was growing quite cool. Presently all three were asleep.

Peter never knew how long a time elapsed before he was wakened by the voice of Jesus, saying, "Simon, are you sleeping? Could you not watch one hour? Watch and pray that you may not enter into temptation. The spirit, indeed, is willing, but the flesh is weak."

They all stirred, and tried to arouse themselves. And as Jesus returned to the brow of the hill, they could hear him praying as before: "Father, if it be possible..." When this happened a third time, they remembered nothing more. It was only from young John Mark, who had followed them from the supper room and had been eavesdropping in the garden, that Peter finally learned what had occurred.[6] Upon that prostrate solitary form the hosts of hell were heaping the weight of all human sins and ingratitude until the end

---

[6] This has been inferred, at least, from Luke 22:51-52

of time. Out of the future came the shadows of those for whom his sacrifice would be in vain, to mock and to taunt him. As time shrank away from the infinity of his pain, he seemed to be racked upon a cross that filled the empty sky from pole to pit, and would blacken it till the day of doom. Perhaps he would have died if the Angel of the Agony had not come to comfort him.

Peter knew nothing of this. His great chest heaving, the sword gleaming darkly beside him in the malignant half-light, he slept soundly.

21

He awoke with a start. There was someone standing over him, looking down at him, and as he became wider awake he saw that it was the Lord. But something had happened to him. It was not only that he seemed to sag with infinite weariness and sorrow. His face, too, was different. There was a peculiar dark glitter on it in the refracted moonlight.

Peter sat up, rubbed his eyes, and looked again. He could see plainly now. The brow of Jesus was beaded with drops of blood. It was running down his beard, and dripping upon the ground.[1]

"Sleep on now, and take your rest!" he said. "It is enough; the hour's come. See, the Son of Man is betrayed into the hands of sinners! Arise, let us be going. Behold, my betrayer is at hand."[2]

As Peter stumbled to his feet, he heard farther down the hill the murmur of voices and the tramp of heavy feet on rocks. He could see the flicker of lanterns, the flaring of torches, the glint of moonlight on steel casques, swords, and shields. A detachment of Roman soldiers was coming up the hill with the superintendents of the temple and the palace guard of the high priest, attended by a motley mob from the streets, hastily armed with staves and clubs. As they drew nearer, Peter saw Judas at the head of the column.

They had expected, perhaps, to find the Lord asleep or at prayer. The sight of his tragic figure advancing to meet them in the bright radiance frightened them, armed though they were, and they stopped suddenly.

"Whom are you seeking?" he demanded.

"Jesus the Nazarene!" said some of the palace guard and the mob in Aramaic. "We want Jesus of Nazareth."

"I am he," he answered. And they all reeled backward, and fell to the ground.

Again he asked, "Whom are you seeking?"

"Jesus the Nazarene," they repeated as they scrambled to their feet.

"I told you that I am he. If therefore you seek me, let these go away."[3]

Peter was not at all inclined to escape. The rest of the apostles by this time had come up from below, and were looking on in

---

[1] Luke 22:44
[2] Mark 14:41-42
[3] John 18:4-9

horrified suspense as they strove to understand the scene. They saw their brother Judas advance to where Jesus waited, and heard him say:

"Well, Rabbi!"

"Friend, why are you here?" asked Jesus calmly.[4]

"Hail, Rabbi!" and Judas gave him the kiss agreed upon.

"Judas, do you betray the Son of Man with a kiss?"[5]

The apostles now fully realized what had occurred. Their first impulse was a natural one of bitter anger against the traitor. Nothing is more mistaken than the popular belief that these men took to their heels at once like cowards. On the contrary, they were ready to defend their master against great odds if he give the word. "Lord, shall we strike with the sword?" cried one.[6] Shouts and imprecations in Aramaic clashed in the night air, something like, "Thief! Traitor! The sword! The sword! Down with Judas! Down with the son of the Devil! Thief! Thief!"

This was the very moment, in fact, that Simon Peter had been waiting for. He drew the sword from his thigh, lifted it flashing high above his head, and brought it down with a mighty swish on the enemy nearest to him, who happened to be one Malchus, a servant of the high priest Caiaphas.

Either the fellow moved just in time and almost enough, or Peter, none too experienced a swordsman, missed his aim, for the blow intended to cleave the skull merely clipped the right ear. The burly fisherman was ready to try again, when the Lord's voice fell decisively upon him through all the commotion:

"Put back your sword into its place; for all who take the sword shall perish by the sword. Do you imagine that I cannot call upon my Father, and he will at once place at my disposal more than twelve legions of angels? But how in that case should the Scripture be fulfilled which says that this must be?"[7] Turning to the soldiers and the guard, he said, probably in Greek:

"Bear with them thus far[8] ... Have you come out as though against a robber, with swords and clubs? While I was with you day after day in the temple, you did not raise your hand against me. But this is your hour, and the power of darkness."[9] Meanwhile he healed

---

[4] Mark 26:50

[5] Luke 22:48

[6] *ibid*, 50

[7] Matt 26:51-54

[8] Luke 22:51

[9] *ibid*, 52-53

the ear of Malchus merely by touching it.

A sickening sense of failure and disillusionment now fell upon Peter and the Boanerges. "This is your hour." The Lord did not intend to resist his enemies in any way. "Put up the sword." He was going to let them do what they wished with him. As anger yielded to this realization, the apostles knew they were fighting a lost battle; and panic suddenly seized them. Right and left they bolted among the trees, leaving the master alone with his enemies. Nor did he resist as they seized him roughly, bound his hands with ropes, and dragged him toward the city, by the very route, probably, over which he had come from the supper room. Two marks, still pointed out on a stone of the Kedron bridge, are said to have been made by his knees when his captors knocked him down. It may be that they lugged him through the brook until his tunic was soaked through. There is no doubt that they took him first to be questioned by the real ruler of Jerusalem, gloating Annas, and only afterward to the high priest Caiaphas.

Peter meanwhile had not run very far. All had gone black about him when he was deprived of the use of his sword. The next he knew he was reeling down the hillside, still clutching, perhaps, the bloody weapon. As he stopped for breath, he saw another man who had got there before him, being slimmer and younger; and by good fortune it was his best friend, John. The two conferred hastily. They then followed the mob, the guards, and their captive over the Kedron Valley into the city, and up the western height toward the palace of the high priest.

This must have required no small courage under the circumstances. For on that night the temple rulers would be sure to have every strategic point well guarded, and may also have asked for extra details of the Roman garrison to make sure of controlling any demonstration, if the people should learn what was going on. Through all these hostile forces Peter and John pressed boldly on until they arrived before the house of Caiaphas. Possibly they clung to the hope that the Lord was biding his time, and would still permit them to strike the blow that would set him free. Peter was still thumbing the old sword under his tunic, perhaps, as he strode along in the bright moonlight.

He had to wait outside the palace, for no one was admitted that night unless he was identified by the porter. John, however, being "known to the high priest,"[10] possibly through family connections,

---

[10] John 18:15

went inside to reconnoitre. A few minutes later he came back and told the woman to admit his friend. The remark she made as he started to brush past her suggests that she was aware of John's connection with the Lord, and suspected Peter's.

"Are you also one of this man's disciples?"

"I am not," said Peter.

His lie may have had more craft than cowardice in it. A man does not enter a house full of his enemies because he is afraid. The choleric apostle more likely had some idea of being able to help his lord escape when he pushed his way into a courtyard of perhaps ten by twenty-five paces, and found it packed with palace guards, temple officers, and pensionaries of the sons of Annas. Several of them had gathered in the centre about a brazier full of burning charcoal, for it was nearly midnight, and was growing cold. "And Peter also was standing with them and warming himself." Presently he found a vacant place on a bench. Fantastic shadows, some from the brazier below, some from the moonlight above, were intermingling on the high walls and grotesquely clutching at him as he sat among his master's enemies, holding his hands to the blaze.

Peter would not have been allowed inside the house, he had to be content with hearing; but it was more than enough. John meanwhile had probably been admitted to the large room where Annas and Caiaphas had assembled as many members of the sanhedrin as they could find, probably a quorum at least of venal men who had their instructions, and were prepared in advance to return a verdict of guilty at a signal from their president where he sat beside the high priest. It was Caiaphas, however, who conducted the interrogation, in all the purple and gold splendour of his office. As the wicks of the oil lamps flickered in the night wind, the light flashed from the horn on his brow and the aphod on his breast to the still bloody and glistening face of the prisoner, who stood before him in a plain dark robe, humble, shackled, and silent.

In his eagerness to destroy this man, Caiaphas had paid no attention to the laws forbidding such trials by night, or outside the temple precincts. He had even gone so far as to bring in some paid liars who were willing to testify that "we ourselves heard him say, 'I will demolish this temple that is made with hands and in the course of three days will erect another made without hands'"; but the discrepancies in their evidence were so obvious that no one believed them. Jesus said nothing. "Have you no reply to make?" cried the high priest in exasperation. "What about the evidence these men bring against you?" The godlike silence of the prisoner was more impressive than any denial. It was evident that thus far Caiaphas had failed.

He now decided to use the old device of the dilemma, which the pharisees had so often employed and Jesus had so skilfully parried. With crafty insolence he stepped forward to present a question like a two-edged sword. If Jesus answered "Yes," he could be accused as a blasphemer; if "No," as an impostor.

"Are you the Christ, the Son of the Blessed One?"

"If I were to tell you so, you would not believe me; and if I were to ask you, you would not answer me."

The calm majesty of this seemed to give the speaker an advantage. His accuser was in bad faith, and should have known the answer. Jesus had not condescended to give it. But Caiaphas knew that there was another way to put the question so that he would not refuse to answer. And seizing upon this last weapon, he hurled it with vindictive power, shouting:

"I put you upon your oath by the Living God to tell us whether you are the Christ, the Son of God."[11]

"I AM," said Jesus. "And I tell you more: hereafter you shall see the Son of Man seated at the right hand of power, and coming in the clouds of heaven!"[12]

The irony of this reversal was breathtaking. In answering the question Jesus had become the judge, pronouncing sentence on Caiaphas; and he presented to him, in turn, a dreadful dilemma. The high priest must either worship him as the Son of God, or demand his death for blasphemy under the law of Moses.[13] The silence was suffocating. It was shattered by the scream of ripping cloth as the high priest tore his outer and inner garments irreparably, as the law provided, and cried, in malignant tones that shuddered through the lower court into the street:

"What further need have we of witnesses? You have heard the blasphemy." And turning toward the elders of the council, he demanded:

"What is your opinion?"

"Death! Let him die the death!" The chorus was unanimous.[14]

Peter sat stupefied as some of the mob around him began push-

[11] Matt 26:63
[12] Mark 14:62, Matt 26:64
[13] Deut 17:2-7
[14] Mark 14:64

ing their way inside to join the servants and guards who had already begun to insult and beat the condemned. They cuffed him; one smote him across the mouth; others slapped him with open palms, crying, "Prophesy to us, O Christ! Who is the one that struck you?" Hell itself seemed to rise in mockery about the bedraggled and shackled figure of the Son of Man. The enlarged shadows flung on the walls by the waning moonlight, the flickering torches and the darker glow of the charcoal were like devils clutching at the stars he had made. Distorted faces of his creatures leered and cursed at the saviour of the world. Foul mouths spat in the face of the Son of God.

This was the background against which Peter made his second and third denials. Until that moment he had always managed to expect some figurative explanation of the Lord's prediction that he would be mocked and condemned. Now the realization of its literal truth descended upon him with cataclysmic effect, and with it the sickening certainty that he was going to die, for otherwise he would never have submitted to such indignities. It was all plain now. And the fear of death, which had made Peter grow faint on the sea of Galilee, returned to envelop him physically and morally, until he felt cold to the marrow of his bones, to the depth of his soul. Crouching in his seat, he tried to get nearer the fire. He saw close by the servant Malchus, whose ear he had struck in the Garden, and wished he could crawl into some hole in the earth and hide. He was so preoccupied with his own misery that he probably did not notice the commotion within, as the guards began to lead their captive toward the court and thence to the filthy hole in the cellar where he would be cast to spend the rest of the night. Peter may have begun to chatter nervously to those about him, as men sometimes do under the influence of fear, and thus to draw attention to himself and to his Galilean brogue.

"And the maid saw him, and began to tell the bystanders, 'This is one of them.' But he again denied it. And after a little while again the bystanders said to Peter, 'You certainly are one of them, for you are a Galilean.' But he began to utter imprecations and to swear an oath, 'I do not know this man you are speaking about!' And immediately for the second time, the cock crew."[15]

"Then the Lord turned and looked at Peter; and Peter remembered the Lord's word, how he had said to him, 'Before the cock crows today you will thrice deny me.' And going out, he wept bitterly."[16]

---

[15] Mark 14:69-72
[16] Luke 22:61-62

Years later, when men saw deep furrows on his cheeks, they said they had been worn by the tears he had never ceased to shed for that moment. Those tears themselves were evidence that he had not lost the faith which Jesus himself had promised at the supper to pray for. When divine grace had been withdrawn to let him be humbled for his rash presumption and to teach him many lessons for the future, he had yielded, under a sudden and irresistible temptation, to a fear that he might have to share the suffering accepted by his Lord. Cowardice made him lie and curse. And with those falsehoods and imprecations already smothered by sobs of remorse, he stumbled out of the court into the street and was swallowed up by the vast obscurity of that hellish night.

Where he went or what he did no one has ever known. For some forty-eight hours or more he disappears from the history of the Passion. It is futile to speculate, as some have done, whether he walked through the countryside like a maniac for countless hours, or threw himself face down in some dark room in a sort of coma of despair. It was not like Peter to behave thus. It is at least a tenable hypothesis that as soon as he recovered from his panic, he continued to follow his Lord from a distance, even to the last. The hints in the New Testament are few and slight, but worth considering. Peter himself wrote years later that he was "a witness of the sufferings of Christ,"[17] and Luke tells us that "*all* his acquaintances" saw the last torments and death of Jesus "at a distance."[18] It stands to reason that when Peter was so easily found by Mary Magdalen two days later, he could not have been very far from the other apostles in the interim, or out of their ken. He did not go to the Mount of Golgotha with John, because he was ashamed to face the beautiful and silken innocence of the Blessed Mother whose son he had denied. But he loved Jesus, now in his remorse more than ever; and it is inconceivable that he could have torn himself away from the knowledge of what was happening to him. The chances are that when the cold wind failed, and a brazen dawn brought back the parched breath of the Dead Sea and the desert to Jerusalem, Peter was somewhere in the edge of the crowd that saw the trial before Pilate in front of the Citadel Antonia, between the reluctant sunrise and a sickly full moon that hung now in the west, like the unburied corpse of an unspeakable night.

The account which Mark must have got from Peter's lips

---

[17] 1 Pet 5:1
[18] Luke 23:49, my italics

sounds like that of an eye-witness, but one with only a general view of the scene; while John's contains many circumstantial details. Peter heard less of that dramatic conversation, but he noticed what went on in the multitude. He saw that it was the chief priests and their agents who "instigated the crowd to demand that he should rather grant them the discharge of Barabbas:" He saw his Master crowned with thorns, smudged with filth and His own blood, mockingly clothed in purple like a fool, struck and spat upon and reverenced in jest as King of the Jews. If he did not hear the "*Abba schabek lahon*" – "Father, forgive them, for they know not what they do!" – as John did, he would never forget those other Aramaic words, howling words of hate and ridicule, that came down to him on the hot motionless air: "Hail, King of the Jews! Hail, Messiah! Tell us who struck you? Hail, Majesty!" He saw Annas and Caiaphas, like over-dressed devils in priestly robes, fanning the fury they had kindled in the mob, blowing it into the face of their victim and of the politician whose dastardly judgment they were resolved to dictate.

"Crucify him! Crucify him! His blood be upon us and on our children!" All morning the hellish cries resounded between the citadel and the temple. The blows of the scourging, the weak and bloody body of the Christ bending to take up the weight of the cross, the slow painful procession through the narrow stifling streets, the three crosses on the hill – surely Peter himself could not have escaped from all that; surely he felt in his own miserable soul the bite of the nails, the breath of scorn and ingratitude, the thirst, the choking, the loneliness of the utterly forsaken, the god-forsaken. Surely he heard that last cry that came shivering down from Calvary against the doomed city, as the unnatural dusk blackened into premature night, and death possessed the world. When lightning clove the murky sky, and the earth trembled under foot, while scribes and pharisees fled for cover and the dead arose to gibber in the empty streets, then and then only did Peter fly headlong from what he had seen, from what he had done, from his own guilty self, thinking that everything was about to pass away in a chaos of flame. He may have felt a despairing sort of relief in the thought, as he ran, that at any moment the mountains would crash down on him and bury him in the eternal obloquy he deserved. Base, worthless Simon Peter! Vile, rash, presuming boastful fool! Nothingness distilled from stinking pride! Thus with every drop of blood that seeped from the lifeless body on the cross, the soul of Simon Peter was purged of the deadly poison of self-love.

22

When Peter found his way at last, late Friday evening perhaps, to the house on the hill where they had eaten the passover supper, he probably found most of his brethren there, for the sabbath had already begun, and this was to be their headquarters, as the *Acts* make plain, for some time to come. Stumbling in, pale and wild-eyed, he would naturally expect to be scorned for the triple cowardice that had been the fruit of his boasting. "Spit on me, brothers!" he might well say. "I denied the Lord, just as he said!" And it is possible that instead of contempt he encountered consolation and sympathy, which might be even harder to bear. None of them had reason to be proud of themselves. "Forget it, Simon!" Thomas or Matthew might say. "We all ran away. We were all cowards – all but John."

If John was the only one who had some reason to taunt him, he would also be the last to do so. It was he, most likely, who brought his friend back to something like a normal state of mind. He probably took him away from the cenacle to some other house where they could talk quietly. This is suggested by the fact that the two were together early Sunday morning, and not with the other apostles, when Mary Magdalen went to look for them.[1] Where were they, then? The inference seems plain. The dying Christ had committed his mother to the care of his beloved disciple, since she had no other children, and John had taken her to the house of one of his relatives, where she would be safe from all annoyance. It seems reasonable to suppose, therefore, that when she learned that Peter also had arrived here, a broken and disconsolate man who would never forgive himself, she sent for him, and gave him, out of the constancy of her own sorrowful heart, new hope and courage.

Yes, the Lord was dead; there was no doubt about it. Toward sundown the Roman legionaries had gone to break the legs of the three crucified men. This was not as barbarous as it seemed, rather it was an act of mercy, a *coup de grâce* to shorten the long torment of a death that otherwise might take twenty to thirty hours. Thus they dealt with the two thieves. But when they came to the one in the middle, the one called the king of the Jews, they saw that he had already expired. One of them, to make doubly sure, drove a lance into his body from the right side to the heart, for with the blood that

---

[1] Luke 24:10-12; John 20:1-2

gushed forth came water from the pericardium. John himself had seen this, and had since thought of the old prophecies: "They shall look on him whom they pierced,"[2] and "Not a bone shall be broken."[3]

The high priests, moreover, in their anxiety to make sure of the death of their victim, had helped to establish the fact. At sundown the two had gone to the Roman procurator to ask that the bodies be removed lest the sabbath be broken. They assured him that all were dead. Pilate doubted this, and sent for the centurion in charge of the executions. When he learned that the three were dead beyond any possible doubt, he gave permission for the removal of the bodies.

Hearing of this, one of the secret disciples, the rich merchant, Joseph of Arimathea, a member of the sanhedrin, had gone boldly to Pilate at sundown to demand the body and to offer to bury it in a tomb of his own in the hillside nearby. This he had done with the help of Nicodemus, who, having found his courage at last, had brought a hundred pounds of myrrh and aloes to anoint the sacred corpse for burial according to Jewish custom. John himself and the Blessed Mother had assisted at the sad rites, and the men had then rolled a huge stone against the door of the tomb to protect its contents from desecration or from the jackals and hyenas that could be heard howling in the hills at the rising of the moon.

It was John also, very likely, who told Peter some of the other consequences of the tragedy for which they were all grieving. The fate of Judas was what might have been expected, yet it was no less shocking to think about. On realizing what he had done, he had taken the thirty silver shekels back to Annas and Caiaphas. Hypocrites that they were, they had contemptuously refused to accept the price of blood. Judas had dashed the coins on the stone floor, and going to a high ledge overhanging the Kedron Brook, had hanged himself to a tree. There his body had swung in the fierce wind, far over the hissing waters in the gorge, until, the rope breaking, it had plunged like satan falling from heaven, and had burst asunder on the rocks. This and many other strange events were being talked about all over the city. People were in an extraordinary ferment of dejection and fear. What troubled them most was that at the very moment of the Lord's death the heavy woollen veil of the temple sanctuary had been ripped like old parchment, as by a mighty unseen hand, from top to bottom.[4]

---

[2] Zach 12:10

[3] Num 9:12; Exod 12:46

[4] Besides the Gospels, four other sources independently confirm the story of some notable catastrophe in the Temple at this time, foreshadowing its destruction:

Many good Jews were saying that they would all rue that evil day's work. Some perhaps wished they had interfered to stop it; but the priests and pharisees had the advantages of surprise, resolution, and organization; now that Jesus was dead, no one was likely to oppose them.

If such were the feelings of comparative strangers, there were no words to describe the anguish of the apostles, to say nothing of his Blessed Mother. For three years these men had been in the company of the Messiah night and day: they had seen his miracles, hung upon his every word, and fairly lived upon his love as if it had been the air they breathed. Now they faced a dark and uncertain future in which none of them had the slightest expectation of ever seeing him again.[5]

There was a great deal of other news, no doubt. But by this time the harassed mind of Peter had been lulled into a drowsy stupor by the kind voice of his friend John, and he was soon deep in the sleep of exhaustion. It is evident that on the next day, Saturday, he remained indoors, for the gospel notes that all the disciples of Jesus, good Jews as they were, "rested according to the commandment" on that dismal Sabbath.[6]

Not so the high priests and the pharisees. Despite all their lip-service to the commandment on which so many of their complaints against the Lord had been grounded, they were not so squeamish about breaking it when their own desires or interests were involved. Early that Saturday morning they called Pilate from the Praetorium once more, and said:

"Sir, we remember that that impostor said when still alive, 'After three days I shall rise again: Order, therefore, the tomb to be made secure until the third day, lest possibly his disciples should come and steal him away, and tell the people he has risen from the dead; and then this final fraud would be worse than the former."[7]

Was Annas really afraid that the disciples would steal the body of Jesus? In that case would he not have had them arrested and at least threatened if not punished? More likely he felt that without their master these humble fishermen and artisans would be quite harmless. More likely he feared that the power he had discerned in that man might manifest itself in some embarrassing way even after his death. Unbelievers grant to superstition what they withhold

Tacitus, Josephus, the Talmud and the apocryphal Gospel according to the Hebrews. Cf. Edersheim, *op. cit.* II, 610, and his references.
[5] So it appears from John 20:9-10, 13; Luke 24:19-21 etc
[6] Luke 23:56
[7] Matt 27:63-65

182

from faith: like Herod, in the instance noted above; like those
scribes who could attribute the miracles of Jesus to devils, but not
to God; like Pilate, who could believe his wife's dream but not the
living Christ before him. Similarly it was only after Jesus had raised
Lazarus from the dead that Annas had seriously set about planning
to kill him rather than worship him. And now, with Pilate's
contemptuous permission, he went to Golgotha and carefully posted
a watch, either of Roman soldiers or of his own palace guard,[8] with
strict orders not to let any one approach the tomb and its huge
stone. Thus unwittingly he made certain that the evidence for what
was about to happen should be unimpeachable. It is another strange
paradox to think of: the enemies of Jesus fearing, if not believing,
that he might burst from the tomb: his own apostles having no
expectation, apparently, that he would do so.[9]

So passed the long and tearful sabbath. On the following night,
nine of the apostles were asleep in the house, let us suppose, of
John Mark's mother; the women from Galilee were in another
house nearby, and John and Peter were likewise resting in the house
where the Mother of the Lord was lodged. But there was one person
in that home who did not slumber. Mary arose in the middle of the
right to weep, perhaps, and to pray long and fervently in that
sublime forgetfulness of self which had been her habit since early
childhood. Not only had the Almighty sent angels to speak to her,
but he had become incarnate in her and had lain in her arms as a
warm child and as a cold corpse. And being human, with such
familiarity with the divine, she was torn by more than ordinary
sorrow; it was actually as if the sword predicted by Simeon had been
plunged into her heart. While she offered this grief to the Father,
accepting whatever might happen to her now, she became aware, in
the state of contemplation or ecstasy that had come upon her, of a
presence in the room. She saw her son standing before her, the
wounds in his hands and feet, the marks of the thorns on his brow, a
tender and revealing smile on his face. For he had come to take away
her misery, and to explain to her that he had just risen from the grave.
Such is the old Christian tradition, confirmed by a remarkable
revelation by Jesus himself to Saint Teresa of Avila in 1570.[10]

Peter and John knew nothing of this when they were roused
from deep slumber in the early dawn. They were told that Mary

[8] The Greek is "Take a guard:" the Vulgate, "You have guard.
[9] When they first heard of it, they refused to believe it.
[10] Mercedes de Dios, no. 15, in *Las relaciones espirituales*, B.M.C. t. II, 49, 50.

Magdalen and two or three others were waiting outside, and must see them at once. On going out the two apostles found the group of women in an extraordinary state of excitement. And the story they told was startling, to say the least. They had risen before dawn and had gone to the garden of Gethsemane to anoint the Lord's body with some sweet spices they had prepared. On the way it occurred to them to wonder how they would be able to roll away so heavy a stone. When they got there, they saw at once that it had been moved. The sun was just peeping over the crest of Mount Olivet. The guards were nowhere to be seen, but just inside the open door of the sepulchre a young man in white was sitting as if waiting for them. He told them that Jesus had risen as he had promised, and would meet them all in Galilee. This they were to tell Peter especially.

Fearful and joyful at the same time and still only half comprehending, they had hurried back to the city and had gone to the Cenacle to rouse the apostles who had been sleeping there: Thomas and Matthew, the two James, Bartholomew and Philip, Jude, Simon and Andrew. "But these words seemed to their minds an idle tale, and they did not believe them."[11]

Mary Magdalen learned where Peter was and ran to tell him and John. From John's account it does not appear that they grasped the fact of the resurrection any more than their brethren had; they understood her to say that someone had taken away the body. But that was enough.

"Peter, therefore, and the other disciple set out and went to the tomb. Now the two were running together; but the other disciple outran Peter, and arrived first at the tomb, and stooping down saw the linen cloths lying; nevertheless he did not enter. Simon Peter, therefore, came following him and entered the tomb, and viewed the linen cloths that lay there, and the napkin that had been on his head, not lying with the linen cloths, but folded up in a separate place by itself. Then the other disciple accordingly, who had arrived first at the tomb, also entered; and he saw, and believed. For as yet they had not understood the scripture, that he must rise from the dead."[12]

Mary returned to the tomb alone, apparently, and after encountering two angels saw through her tears a man whom she supposed to be a gardener. The immortal scene never loses its freshness and charm:

"Woman, why do you weep? Whom are you seeking?"

[11] Luke 24:11
[12] John 20:3-10

"Sir, if you have removed him, tell me where you have laid him, and I will take him away."

"Mary!" said Jesus.

"Rabboni!"[13]

And he sent her back to the apostles to confirm the news of the resurrection. Apparently, too, he showed himself to Simon Peter: one account in fact makes it appear that his first visit, after the one to his mother, was to the fisherman who was to be the head of his Church.[14] Certainly there must have been no ordinary excitement in Jerusalem that Sunday. Everywhere the disciples of Jesus were saying, "The Lord has risen, and has appeared to Simon!"

There was a most unusual activity, of course, about the temple and the palaces of the high priests. Before the sun was up, their guards had come running from the tomb near Calvary to wake them with an incredible tale. The ground, they insisted, had shaken under them. Then they had seen a man with a face like lightning and raiment white as snow push back the great stone with no effort at all, and sit on it. Terrified, they had fallen on their faces like so many dead men; but as soon as they were able, they had crawled away, and had then rushed breathlessly to tell their employers.

The conduct of Annas seems to confirm the terrible suspicion that forces itself upon us. His satanic heart, in the inscrutable depth of its iniquity, had deliberately rejected Jesus, well knowing who he was. And since he had been expecting something of this sort, he believed the story of the guards. The logical procedure, had he doubted it, would have been to arrest both them and the apostles, and to investigate, with Pilate's help, who had taken the body and where it had been hidden. This would have been easy enough had such a theft occurred. But it is more and more plain, as one weighs the words and acts of this wretched man, why the Christ had spoken with such unwonted severity to him and his chief henchmen.

No recourse was had to Pilate, who had already shown that he suspected the motive of the high priests. Instead, a futile meeting of the leading members of the sanhedrin was called in the first moments of alarm. "And after consultations they gave the soldiers a large sum of money, and said, "Tell people, 'His disciples came during the night and stole him while we were asleep.' And should this come to the governor's ears, we shall clear you before him, and rid you of responsibility." So they took the money and did as they were

---

[13] *ibid,* 11-20

[14] 1 Cor 15:5

directed, and that tale spread among the Jews, and is current until the present day." So wrote Matthew, who, was in Jerusalem at the time. Saint Justin Martyr insisted that the priests and pharisees had sent their emissaries all over the world with this false account of the Resurrection, and that their successors were still doing it in his time.[15] And improbable though it was that a few fishermen would have dared steal the body from under the very noses of armed guards, whether awake or asleep, the story was gradually accepted far and wide among Jews, most of whom were victims of the plutocracy that controlled, with its wealth and authority, the chief sources of public information.

Peter and his fellow apostles, on the other hand, became more and more convinced that their master had truly died and had truly risen. In fact they were so sure of it that they spent the rest of their lives going about the world teaching it as the chief and fundamental reason why men should accept him as the Christ. To men of their sort with almost no resources this meant a perpetual and staggering record of self-sacrifice, with constant hardship, suffering, persecution, and nothing to look forward to at the end but a bloody death like his. Such men do not ordinarily get themselves crucified or beheaded for an illusion, much less for a lie.

The resurrection itself, furthermore, was not their only basis for belief in it. Jesus appeared not only to his mother and to Peter, but to Cleophas and another disciple on the road to Emmaus. He appeared to all the apostles except Thomas, and then to all together; and the incredulity of the Twin has given us, providentially, the only convincing and conclusive evidence to refute those later dissenters who claimed that only a ghost had been seen, and not the risen body of the Saviour. They had all seen him come through the walls, like a spirit, when the doors were bolted. Yet doubting Thomas felt the nail-holes in the flesh of his hands, and the wound in his warm side before he fell on his knees and cried, "My Lord and my God!" And all of them could feel his breath when he said, "Receive the Holy Spirit; whose sins you forgive, they are forgiven them; and whose sins you retain. they are retained."[16] Finally, He was seen by at least five hundred persons,[17] including many disciples and others, at the Mount of Beatitude in Galilee, where the Eleven went in obedience to the command they received from him through Mary Magdalen.

---

[15] *Dialogue with Trypho*
[16] John 20:19-23
[17] 1 Cor 15:6 Saint Paul appeals to many of them as witnesses, still living.

23

It was a long time since Peter had been in his native Galilee; and something in the spring air, in the blue sky, and in the deep clear water called to his blood, and invited him to find rest from the conflict of the past year, in the childhood peace that lingers where it has been known. Everything seemed the same: the hundreds of boats careening on the lake, the murmur by day and the ring of lamps by night in the cities that girdled its shores; such simple joys as the sound of bell over the water, or that of a shofar horn on the roof of the synagogue at Capharnaum. Evidently Peter returned to his own house there, perhaps to be welcomed by the good old mother-in-law and a faithful servant. With him were Thomas the Twin, Bartholomew of Cana, the two sons of Zebedee, and two unnamed disciples.[1]

Late one afternoon they were sitting on the hillside, not far from the wharves, talking. They had a great deal to recall. Perhaps they were discussing the apparitions of the Lord, particularly the most recent one of which there were so many Galilean witnesses, and wondering how soon he would be coming in the glory he had so often mentioned, to restore the kingdom of Israel; for this, in their minds, was still the issue and the end. There were many other things to be explained, too. But they knew that he had risen from the dead, and that sooner or later they would see him again.

Peter lazily scrutinized the sea and the sky. He stretched his long arms and yawned.

"I am going fishing," he said.[2]

"We'll go with you," said the others. And strolling down to the shore, they found a boat, perhaps one of his own, keeled over just where he and Andrew had left it. Someone, either a hired man or old Zebedee himself, must have calked and painted it, and barqued the net, for everything was in readiness, and they had only to shove off as the gorgeous dusk began to paint lavishly, both overhead and beneath, with bold strokes of purple and gold, crimson and amethyst.

It was a warm evening, without much wind. Simon Peter cast off his clothes, and stood naked at the tiller. It was good to feel the coolness of the breeze in his face, the sting of the spray on his body.

---

[1] John 21:2, 3
[2] *ibid*

Perhaps a vague impression came over him, as he responded to those boyhood stimuli, that he had been living through some fantastic and elaborate dream that seemed to have gone on for three years. It was precious, painful, delightful, terrible, cataclysmic, celestial, but it was past. Here on the quiet sea of Galilee there was no conflict except with the elements; no greed, no cruelty, no treachery, no disillusionment. What if after all he settled down again now to be a fisherman? There could be worse lives. He guided the barque into deep water, and as the sunset faded into night, they shot their net.

It is John the son of Zebedee who tells the rest of this inimitable story.

"And during that night they caught nothing.

When, however, day was now breaking, Jesus stood on the shore; nevertheless the disciples did not know it was Jesus. Jesus, therefore called to them:

'Young men, have you anything to eat?'

'No,' they answered him.

'Cast the net on the right side of the boat,' he told them, 'and you shall find something!'

They accordingly cast it, and they had not strength enough to haul it in, owing to the multitude of fishes. That disciple therefore whom Jesus loved said to Peter:

'It is the Lord!'

When Simon Peter therefore heard that it was the Lord, he tied his tunic about him for he was stripped – and threw himself into the sea. The other disciples, however, came in the boat, for they were not far from the land – say about a hundred yards distant – towing the net full of fishes. So when they had got out upon the land, they saw a charcoal fire set, with fish laid upon it and some bread.

"Jesus said to them, 'Bring some of the fish you have just caught.

Simon Peter accordingly went up and hauled the net upon the land full of large fishes, one hundred and fifty-three; and although there were so many, the net was not broken.

'Come, break your fast,' said Jesus to them. And none of the disciples ventured to ask him, 'Who are you?' knowing that it was the Lord. And Jesus went and took the bread and gave it to them, and the fish likewise ...

So when they had broken their fast, Jesus said to Simon Peter:

'Simon, son of John, do you love me more than these do?'

'Yes, Lord,' said he; 'You know that I love you.'

He said to him, 'Feed my lambs.'

He said to him a second time, 'Simon, son of John, do you love me?

'Yes, Lord,' he answered him; 'You know that I love you.'

He said to him, 'Be shepherd over my sheep.'

For the third time he said to him, 'Simon, son of John, do you love me?'

Peter was grieved because he asked him the third time, 'Do you love me?' and he said to him, 'Lord, you know all things: You know that I love you!'

He said to him, 'Feed my sheep.'

'Indeed, indeed, I say to you, when you were young, you dressed yourself and went wherever you had a wish; but when you grow old, you shall stretch out your hands and another shall bind you and carry you where you have no desire to go.' Now he said this to intimate by what death he should glorify God. And having said this he added, 'Follow me.'"

Here apparently, Jesus arose and walked away a little distance, and Peter followed. Presently he saw that John, too, was walking after them, and he said:

"Lord, and what about this man?"

"If it be my will that he remain until I come, what is it to you? You follow me."

Afterwards they all discussed this remarkable incident many times, and they came to the conclusion, which was fairly obvious, that the Lord had given Peter an opportunity to atone by a triple affirmation of love for his triple denial. Nor did they fail to notice the change that his answers had revealed in Peter. There was no longer any of that rash and self-confident truculence in him. Instead of boasting that he loved the Lord more than his brethren did, he appealed to the Lord's own knowledge of his heart and of all things. For Peter's fall had taught him what it was meant to teach: profound humility, without which there could be no true affection. And so none of the others begrudged him the leadership that was now so plainly confirmed upon him.

The words of Jesus had indicated that he was to preside not only over the Church in general, but over its leaders: he was to feed the sheep as well as the lambs. But if any were still inclined to resent his primacy, they must have been glad enough to leave it to him when they considered what he would have to pay for it in the end. They had seen Jesus dragged through Jerusalem and hanging bloodily between heaven and earth, and they knew from his words that Peter would be similarly bound, and would stretch out his hands upon a felon's cross as he breathed out his soul. Some of them said that Jesus had promised John, on the other hand, the gift of immortality. The son of Zebedee took pains to deny this. "Jesus did not, however, tell him that he should not die, but 'If it be my will that he remain until I come, what is that to you?'"[3]

Peter and his guests went back to Jerusalem and rejoined their fellow apostles. And one evening, about six weeks after the Resurrection, they were startled and delighted again by the appearance of Jesus in their midst as they were about to eat supper in the house on the hill. Thérèse Neumann "saw" this event in one of the most detailed of her visions, on 28 May 1927, and left an account which, whatever the final explanation of it may be, certainly helps one to visualize the scene. Philip was serving. He placed a large and a small fish on a brown platter, and divided them, holding each one by the head, with "a broad knife-like bone somewhat curved at the farther end." Having passed out the portions, he then took one for himself and reclined.

Suddenly Jesus appeared in the centre of the room, back of Peter and John. He spoke a few words of greeting, and they answered as they arose to make a place for him at the table. Philip gave him bread on a platter, and placed a piece of the fish on the bread. Jesus arose, blessed the food, then reclined and ate. Philip then gave the brown crock – wide in the middle, narrow at top and bottom – to the Lord, who drank of it and passed it to Peter. Each drank but once, and in a half-reclining position. Jesus then spoke to them briefly but earnestly.

Philip now left the room and returned with some honey in the comb on two platters, one of which he offered first to the Lord. It was passed around, and all ate, breaking off pieces of the comb and wiping their hands on cloths which they wore. Jesus had a white garment now instead of his usual brown one, but no cloth; he used the one that John held out to him.

Jesus spoke again. Then there was a general discussion in which Peter, as usual, had the most to say. A curious detail is that the Lord stood when he spoke, while the others, in so doing, remained seated. Finally he addressed them more solemnly and at length. They all arose and went out, Peter going first, followed by

---

[3] John 21:1-23

190

the Lord and John. It was about four o'clock in the morning as they filed through the sleeping city over the familiar route across the Kedron Valley, toward Bethany.

It was morning, but rather cloudy, when they all assembled on the central height of the Mount of Olives, Jesus standing on a stone, his mother nearby, and about ten other women, including Mary Magdalen and Veronica, before him. There were probably a hundred men there: the apostles and many disciples, including Lazarus and a Roman centurion on horseback, besides other legionaries.

These visions in no way conflict with the less detailed accounts by Mark and Luke. Thérèse did not understand the Aramaic words she heard; but the Evangelists tell us what the Lord's final instructions were. They make it plain that even then the eleven had not wholly divested themselves of their concept of a nationalistic Jewish messiah. They thought that Jesus had taken them to that high place to proclaim himself king of the Jews of the world. For some of them said, earnestly:

"Lord, will you at this time restore the kingdom of Israel?" "It is not for you," he replied, "to know the times or periods which the Father has fixed by his own authority. But you shall receive power when the Holy Spirit descends upon you; and you shall be my witnesses both in Jerusalem and in all Judea and Samaria, and to the remotest part of the earth."[4]

"All authority is given to me in heaven and on earth. Go, therefore, and make disciples of all the nations, baptizing them in the name of the Father and of the Son and of the Holy Spirit..."[5]

"Go out into the world, and proclaim the gospel to all creation. He who believes and is baptized shall be saved, but he who believes not shall be condemned. And these signs shall accompany those who believe: In my name they shall cast out demons; they shall speak in new tongues; they shall handle serpents; and if they drink any deadly thing, it shall in no way hurt them; they shall lay hands upon the sick, and they shall recover." [6]

"These are my words which I spoke to you while I was still with you: 'All that is written about me in the law of Moses, in the prophets and in the psalms must be fulfilled ... Thus it is written that the Christ should suffer, and rise again from the dead on the

[4] Acts 6:1-8
[5] Matt 28:18
[6] Mark 16:15-18

third day; and that repentance and remission of sins should be proclaimed in his name to all the nations, beginning from Jerusalem. And you are witnesses to these things. And I will send upon you the promise of my Father. But you are to stay in the city until you are invested with power from on high?[7] ... And lo, I am with you throughout all time, even until the consummation of the world."[8]

After this, if we may believe Thérèse Neumann, he spoke a few words to his mother. Spreading out his pierced hands, he looked to heaven, and then began slowly to rise from the ground. Once more his eyes affectionately sought those of Mary, and rested a moment on the eleven, before they were turned upward again. The wounds on his hands and feet glistened above and below the marks of the nails. They could be seen glowing for a long time as he ascended somewhat obliquely toward the east, growing smaller and smaller until at last a little cloud covered him and he disappeared.[9]

Many of those who watched began to weep – Lazarus most of all, according to the visionary, and Peter and the centurion least. While they stared at the empty sky, the red brim of the sun appeared on the eastern hill-top. Two angels, like radiant youths with long hair, stood before them, speaking in unison. This accords with Luke's account, which represents them as saying:

"Men of Galilee, why do you stand gazing up into heaven? This Jesus who has been taken away from you into heaven, will so come in the way that you have seen him go into heaven."[10]

Both vanished. The friends of Jesus and his Blessed Mother returned very joyfully to Jerusalem, and went to the temple to pray, and then to the Upper Room.

Peter had his answer now. He knew at last what it would mean to be a fisher of men.

[7] Luke 29:44-53
[8] Matt 28:20
[9] Von Lama, *op. cit. Further Chronicles of Thérèse Neumann*, pp. 185-194.
[10] Acts 1:11

24

"Now the day of Pentecost having arrived, they were all together in one place, when suddenly a sound came from heaven like the rush of a mighty wind; and it filled the whole house where they were sitting. And there appeared to them tongues as of fire, which parted and settled upon each of them. And they were all filled with the Holy Spirit, and began to speak in foreign tongues, according as the Spirit gave them utterance."[1]

Peter felt an irresistible impulse to tell everybody in the world the truth that had suddenly become clear and complete to him; and rushing out of the supper room like a man beside himself with joy, he presently realized that he was on a street, with the other ten not far away, and a large crowd surging around them. For the roaring sound had been audible throughout Jerusalem, and people had come running from all sides, expecting signs of an earthquake or some other public calamity. It was a most cosmopolitan crowd, including not only Jerusalemites but Jews from all parts of the world who had come for the Passover – "Parthians and Medes and Elamites, and inhabitants of Mesopotamia, of Judea and Cappadocia, of Pontus and Asia, of Phrygia and Pamphylia, of Egypt and the country of Libya about Cyrene, and visitors from Rome, both Jews and proselytes, Cretans and Arabians." These pilgrims were especially astonished when they heard eleven rather ordinary looking men addressing them in their own tongues.

"Drunk!" said some of the sophisticates of the town. "They are filled up with new wine."

This gave Peter the opportunity for his maiden speech. He had made no preparation for it, yet here he was addressing a huge audience with terse power and perfect self-possession. Passages from the scriptures that he had studied in boyhood seemed to come tumbling out of his well-stored mind without effort, and to arrange themselves harmoniously in his argument. And if he retained a trace of his native clumsiness, it only heightened the effect of utter sincerity:

"Men of Judea, and all you residents of Jerusalem!" he cried. "Let this be known to you, and pay attention to my words! For these men are not drunk, as you imagine, since it is but nine o'clock in the morning. On the contrary, this is the manifestation which was

---

[1] Acts 2:1-4

predicted by the prophet Joel:

"'And it shall be in the latter days – God says – that I will pour out a portion of my Spirit upon all flesh; and your sons and daughters shall prophesy and your young men shall see visions, and your old men shall dream dreams. Yes, and upon my servants and my hand-maids in those days will I pour out a portion of my spirit, and they shall prophesy. And I will display portents in the heaven above, and signs on the earth beneath, blood and fire and a cloud of smoke. The sun shall be transformed to darkness, and the moon to blood, before the day of the Lord comes, that great and luminous day. And it shall be that whoever calls on the name of the Lord shall be saved.'[2]

Men of Israel, listen to these words! Jesus of Nazareth – a Man made known to you by God by means of miracles and wonders and signs which God worked by him in your midst, as you yourselves know – this man, delivered up by the settled design and fore-knowledge of God, you murdered, crucifying him by the hands of lawless men. But God raised him up, having destroyed the pangs of death, because it was impossible that he should be held fast by it. For David says concerning him: 'I beheld the Lord always before my face; for he is on my right hand that I may not be disturbed. My heart therefore was glad, and my tongue exulted; moreover my flesh too shall rest in hope: because you will not leave my soul to the abode of the dead, nor will you suffer your holy One to see corruption. You have made known to me the paths of life; you will make me full of joy with your countenance.'

Brethren, I may say to you with assurance regarding the patri-arch David that he died and was buried, and his tomb is with us up to the present day. Since, then, he was a prophet, and knew that God had sworn to him with an oath that 'of the fruit of his loins One should sit upon his throne,' he spoke with foresight concerning the resurrection of the Christ, that neither was he left to the abode of the dead,' nor did his flesh see corruption. This Jesus God raised up, of which we all are witnesses. Being exalted therefore by the right hand of God, and having received from the Father the promised Holy Spirit, he has poured forth this which you see and hear. For David did not ascend into the heavens; but he himself says: 'The Lord said to my Lord: Sit at my right hand, until I make your enemies a stool for your feet.'

Let the whole house of Israel therefore know most certainly that

---

[2] Joel 2:28; 3:1-5

God has made him – this Jesus whom you crucified – both Lord and Christ."

Peter stopped for breath. Indeed, he had said all that he had to say, and with such complete success that "they were pierced to the heart." Jewish voices all over the square cried out to him and to the other ten, "What are we to do, brethren?"

Peter answered promptly and with authority. "Repent, and be baptized every one of you in the name of Jesus Christ for the remission of your sins; and you shall receive the gift of the Holy Spirit. For the promise is to you and to your children, and to all who are far away, whomever the Lord our God shall call to him." He said many other things, repeating again and again, "Save yourselves from this perverse generation!" By nightfall he had received three thousand of these Jews, both local and foreign, into the Church.[3]

What had happened to Peter to give him this new power over himself and others? Obviously, what occurs more secretly and perhaps less lavishly to all Christians when they receive the sacrament of Confirmation. The Holy Spirit promised by the Lord had come to dwell with him in a special manner. His own words indicate that the idea of that indwelling, whose consummation had just brought him to spiritual maturity, had not been wholly foreign to him since childhood. There were many adumbrations of the doctrine of the Holy Trinity in the Old Testament. Before Christ revealed it, however, it would have been difficult for most Jews to understand it, particularly when they were engaged in defending the truth of God's unity against an idolatrous world – though he himself implied that a master in Israel, like Nicodemus, should have understood the Scriptures better.

Peter had been aware for some time, in a rather confused way, that the writings of the prophets were jewelled with broad hints that God the Father, in whom power excels, would send God the Son, the Messiah in whom truth excels, to sweep away all misunderstandings and to reconcile man to himself. Now he saw clearly that this had happened; and that the Father and Son, moreover, had sent the Holy Spirit, in whom love excels, to create a perfect understanding, and to remain forever with the Church, protecting it from error and disunion. Not that he had failed to manifest himself under the Old Law: it was now plain that he had dwelt by grace in the souls of the prophets, and had overshadowed the incomparable woman who was to be mother of the incarnate Son. Yet he would

---

[3] Acts 2:5-41

communicate himself much more profusely, as Peter pointed out in his initial sermon, in the messianic age: he would pour his gifts first on the house of Israel, and then on all flesh.

Peter saw more deeply now into the mystery of Christ, the consummation and fulfilment of the mystery of Israel, which it included. The faith of the chosen people was not invented by men or devils, as the pagan cults were, but had been handed down by the Creator, the one true God – their God – through Abraham, Isaac, Jacob, Moses, and all the prophets. It was like a living and growing tree which would flower, as the prophets consistently taught, in the Incarnation of the Son of God who would also be a son of David. The ceremonial precepts were meant to remind the Hebrews that he was coming; hence they would end when he came. But he would not come to destroy the essentials of the law or to establish a new religion. On the contrary, he would insist, and he did insist, on every last jot and tittle of the revealed truth; and far from destroying or displacing the house of Israel, he had now completed it, as a cornerstone completes a building. The Church then, was and is the perfected Israel.

In these first days, too, it was thoroughly Jewish in membership. Its worshippers in no way looked upon themselves as innovators. As cells in the mystical body of Christ they were Jews more than ever before, fulfilling the best hopes and traditions of their fathers. It is significant that John described the followers of Annas and Caiaphas in the great repudiation of Him as "those who call themselves Jews, and are not, but lie."[4] The converts of the apostles continued to worship in the temple and the synagogues, and to observe the Mosaic Law as best they could, with no thought, apparently, of ever doing otherwise.

It was the mystery of Christ, too, fulfilling the mystery of Israel, that drew these devout Jews together on the first day of the week after their visits to the temple. But they met for something more than the commemoration of the resurrection. They met to witness and to take part in the ultimate and perfect sacrifice of which the oblations in the temple, solemn though they were, had long been but prefigurings and preparations.

Indeed, all cults, from the beginning of the world until now (except pure Buddhism, Mohammedanism, and Protestantism) have recognized in sacrifice the highest form of prayer, commanded by God himself in the morning of the world. Pagan rites, however debased, were reminiscences of this primitive universal religion.

---

[4] Rev 3:9

The Jews alone for centuries had kept it clean and holy by the safeguards of the Mosaic Law. The time had come for the redemption of Israel, and through Israel of all mankind, by the supreme and perfect sacrifice of history. It was one which demanded no ordinary victim. The revolt of man, as an offence against infinite majesty, required an expiation of infinite worth. But the God of Abraham had not forgotten his promises. Remembering that Abraham had not spared his only son, through love of him, he did not spare his only Son in his love for Abraham's children. So Jesus gave his blood on the Cross for Israel and for all mankind.

Such a Victim ought to be offered by no common priest. When Caiaphas and his followers made void the ancient high priesthood of Israel by crying "We have no king but Caesar!" the king of the Jews took on himself the office that had been Aaron's. And it was plain now to Peter that he was also the promised high priest according to the order of Melchisedech, who had blessed Abraham, and on whose sacrifice the sun would never set. Jesus had indicated in veiled fashion in the synagogue at Capharnaum that he would perpetuate his sacrifice by giving his flesh to eat and his blood to drink – and this, he insisted, literally. At the Last Supper he had revealed the meaning of the promise, and had kept it, by establishing the eucharistic sacrifice. The flesh and blood would be under the appearances of bread and wine, but would truly be there. With each sacrifice the incarnation and crucifixion would be re-enacted and perpetuated until the end of time, when the house of Israel (the completed Church, the Mystical Body of Christ) would be drawn up into the new Jerusalem of eternal felicity.

A sacrifice so sublime that human minds could comprehend it only as mystery had need of ritualistic preparation. And it was natural that these Jews who followed Peter into the primitive Church should find it in the traditions of their own people. They prepared for it, in fact, with a typical synagogue service, in which the holy Hebrew books were read, the Hebrew psalms were sung, and the apostles, like the elders in the synagogue, gave homilies and explanations. The people answered "Amen" in Hebrew after each prayer, just as their fathers had done. These Jewish elements, leading up to the re-enactment of the sacrifice of the Last Supper (which is also the repeated sacrifice of the Cross) still constitute the liturgical framework of the Mass. The words of Isaiah, "Holy, Holy, Holy, Lord God of Hosts," chanted by Jewish Christians twenty-five years after the death of Peter, still preface the most

198

solemn part of it.[5] After the consecration of the bread and wine, the priest still asks the Father "to look with favour on these offerings and accept them as once you accepted the gifts of your servant Abel, the sacrifice of Abraham, our father in faith, and the bread and wine offered by your priest Melchisedech."

One early innovation was the Agape or Love-Feast, followed by prophesying, speaking in various tongues, or healing the sick; but these non-essentials were dropped when increasing numbers led to various abuses. No change was ever tolerated, however, in the important parts of the ceremony. For these Jewish Christians accepted the words of Jesus, "This is my Body ... This is my Blood" not in any figurative or symbolic sense, but in all the literalness on which he had insisted. This is evident from the words of one of Peter's chief collaborators:

"For I received from the Lord what I delivered also to you, that the Lord Jesus, the night he was betrayed, took bread, and having given thanks, broke it, and said, 'This is my Body which is for you; do this in memory of me.' In like manner also the cup, at the end of supper, saying, "This cup is the new covenant in my Blood; do this as often as you drink it, in memory of me: For as often as you eat this bread and drink the cup, you proclaim the death of the Lord until he comes. So that whoever eats the bread or drinks the cup of the Lord unworthily shall be guilty of the Body and Blood of the Lord. But let a man examine himself, and so let him eat of the bread and drink of the cup; for he who eats and drinks, eats and drinks judgment to himself, if he does not discern the body."[6]

There is no essential difference between this early literal interpretation of the Mass and the one that Saint Justin the Martyr was to write, less than a century after Peter's death, for the Emperor Antoninus:

"When the president has given thanks and all the people have answered, those whom we call deacons give the bread and wine and water for which the thanksgiving has been made to be tasted by those who are present, and they carry them to those who are absent. This food is called by us the Eucharist.[7]... No one is allowed to partake of it but him who believes our doctrines to be true, and who has been

<hr/>
[5] The "*Sanctus, Sanctus, Sanctus*": Is 6: 3. The three "Holys" are believed to refer to the three divine Persons in the Trinity.
[6] 1 Cor 11:23-29
[7] The first known to use this word (ευχαριστία) was Saint Ignatius of Antioch, in his letter to the Smyrnians, about 107 A.D.: "The Eucharist is the flesh of Our Saviour Jesus Christ" etc.

baptized in the laver of regeneration for remission of sins, and lives up to what Christ has taught. For we take these not as common bread and common drink, but just as Jesus Christ our Saviour, being incarnate by the word of God, had both flesh and blood for our salvation, so we are taught that this food, by which our flesh and blood are nourished, over which thanks have been given by the prayers in his own words, is the flesh and blood of the incarnate Jesus."[8]

It is interesting to notice how this crowning expression of the mystery of Christ, fulfilling his promise at Capharnaum – "My flesh is real food, and my blood is real drink" – began to transform his sincere followers, under the guidance of the Holy Spirit, both individually and collectively. They became conspicuous for their charity to all men, and particularly to one another. They, lived up to his teachings so faithfully that they were exceedingly popular among their fellow citizens, "possessing favour with all the people."[9] They were worshipping in the temple on Saturdays and "breaking bread" at home or in the house on the hill on Sundays. In other matters, too, they were living to an astonishing degree on the supernatural plane that had seemed so difficult to Peter when he had first heard of it in the Sermon on the Mount.

They now interpreted this according to the counsel Jesus had given the rich young man to "sell whatever you have, and give to the poor, and you shall possess treasure in heaven: and come, follow Me!"[10] As the author of the *Acts* recorded it, "all the believers were together and had everything in common; and selling their possessions and belongings they distributed the proceeds to all, according to the needs of each one."[11] This statement, in fact, he took pains to repeat, as if to forestall any misunderstanding: "Now the multitude of the believers were of one heart and soul; and not one claimed any of his property as his own, but everything was common to them ... And great grace rested on them all."[12]

These first Christians could be called communists in all truth if the word had not been appropriated by those who were to make a cruel travesty and caricature of it, giving it a connotation as far from the primitive reality as hell is from heaven. They probably would have been greatly astonished to hear themselves described, in this matter also, as "revolutionaries." For Jews had always been cons-

---

[8] *Apol* I, ch 65 and ch 66.
[9] Acts 2:47
[10] Mark 10:21
[11] Acts 2:44
[12] *ibid*, 4:32-34

picuous for mutual generosity, as compared to pagans. They had shared the necessities of life with one another in the wilderness, where "he who gathered much had nothing over, and he who gathered little had no lack";[13] while hoarders found that their manna, over and above an omer, had putrefied overnight. From the most ancient times the poor had been encouraged to gather the grain left in the corners of fields, and to follow the harvesters, like Ruth, as gleaners. Price-fixing in Peter's time was the accepted expedient to prevent inflation, with all its cruel consequences to the poor. And whatever may be said of the rapacity of the sons of Annas, there were other rich persons in Israel who were not only liberal but lavish in what they set aside for the misfortunate, for education, for the national cause and for religion. They supported poor students in the academies of Jerusalem, and that meant most of them. Some Jews, unlike the hypocrites denounced by our Lord for having trumpets sounded before them when they gave alms, were capable of a rare delicacy in their benefactions. They secretly enabled well-to-do persons who had misfortunes, to live on the same scale as before. The great Hillel, who supported himself and his family on a pittance, is said to have hired a horse and even an outrider for a certain decayed rich man.[14]

If there is eastern exaggeration in some of these anecdotes, at least they illustrate how lofty was the Jewish ideal which the first Christians of Jerusalem had inherited. It is ridiculous to compare their performance with any species of marxism or socialism, which begins by spurning their premise, the love of God, and ends by reducing the poor to worse slavery under a more concentrated plutocracy, by fraud or violence very different in spirit from the voluntary sharing of Peter and his converts. That spirit will not be found in any socialistic regime, but it will be seen flourishing in convents and monasteries. The Church still commends this mode of life to all who are capable of living it, as Christ commended it to the rich young man who went away sorrowful. She urges the wealthy to divide their surplus with the poor, as he did; and while she also insists on the right of private ownership (as he did), she consistently denies that the owner may use his property to the detriment of others or of the community as a whole. Peter made it clear, furthermore, that the sharing of goods was not compulsory.

Thus far everything had gone better than he might have expected. Converts were coming in daily. All the people were im-

---

[13] 2 Cor 8:15 the reference is to Exod 16:18
[14] Edersheim, *op. cit.* I, 118, 130

pressed by the beautiful lives of his flock. And the men who were most to blame for the Lord's death, and most resolved not to benefit by it, had done nothing to interfere. Perhaps Annas felt that there was no reason to fear a few Galileans who had given no evidence of possessing such powers as that man had unquestionably had. But when Peter performed his first miracle, all was changed.

"Peter and John were once going up to the Temple at the ninth hour of prayer. Now a certain man, lame from his birth, used to be carried and laid daily at the entrance to the temple known as the Beautiful Gate, to beg alms of those going into the temple. He, seeing Peter and John about to go into the temple, asked to receive alms. But Peter, with John, fixing his gaze upon him, said, 'Look at us.' He accordingly gave attention to them, expecting to receive something from them.

But Peter said, 'Silver and gold I do not possess, but what I have, that I will give you. In the name of Jesus Christ of Nazareth, walk!' And seizing him by his right hand he lifted him up. And at once his feet and ankles were strengthened; and leaping up he stood and walked, and entered the temple with them – walking and leaping and praising God.

Now all the people saw him walking and praising God; and they recognized him to be the same who customarily sat begging at the Beautiful Gate of the temple. And they were filled with astonishment and ecstasy over what had befallen him. Now while he held fast to Peter and John, all the people, lost in wonder, ran crowding toward them in the portico known as Solomon's."

Standing in the very place where he had so often heard the Lord's voice reverberating from column to column, Peter found himself face to face with thousands of people. Yet he was not a bit frightened or embarrassed as he proceeded, in his heavy Galilean brogue, to deliver his second sermon:

"Men of Israel! why do you wonder at this man or why do you stare at us, as though by our own power or piety we had enabled him to walk? The God of Abraham and of Isaac and of Jacob, the God of our fathers has glorified his servant Jesus, whom you delivered up and denied in the presence of Pilate when he was determined to release him. But as for you, you denied the holy and just one, and demanded a murderer to be granted to you, while you murdered the author of life; but God raised him from the dead, of which we ourselves are witnesses. And his name, through faith in his name, has given vigour to this man, whom you see and know;

yes, the faith which is through him has given him this perfect soundness in the presence of you all.

And now, brethren, I know that you as well as your rulers did it through ignorance. But God thus accomplished what he foretold through the mouths of all the prophets – that his Christ should suffer. Repent, therefore, and be converted, that your sins be blotted out; so that seasons of refreshment may come from the presence of the Lord, and that he may send the Christ who has been appointed for you – Jesus whom the heavens must receive until the era of the restoration of all things, which God has spoken of through the mouth of his holy prophets who have been from of old.

Moses, for instance, said, 'The Lord your God will raise up for you from among your brethren a prophet like me; listen to him in all that he may say to you. And it shall be that every soul that will not listen to that prophet shall be exterminated from among the people.' And all the prophets, from Samuel and those who came after, as many indeed, as have spoken, they, too, have announced these days. It is you who are the sons of the prophets, and of the covenant which God ratified with our forefathers, saying to Abraham: 'And in my seed shall all the races of the earth be blessed: God, having raised up his servant, has sent him first to you to bless you, when one and all you turn away from your iniquities.'"

Questions probably were asked, and Peter was still explaining and exhorting when the reflected sunlight faded from the marble magnificence of Solomon's Court. Suddenly there was a ripple in the crowd, and a little phalanx distinguished by brighter colours forced its way through to where the two apostles stood with the ragged beggar. It was the prefect of the temple, with some priests and some fellow-sadducees of Annas, all "deeply annoyed." Before anyone could protest, they laid violent hands upon the three and dragged them away to a cell, probably under the treasury, where they locked them up for the night.

"But many of those who had heard the discourse believed; and the number of the men reached about five thousand."[15]

---

[15] Acts 4:4

25

It was a dramatic encounter that followed next morning in the hall of hewn stone. Peter's miracle and second sermon had created a situation which reminded the priests and pharisees only too vividly of the last Passover week. If his conversions continued at this rate, all Jerusalem would soon be following him. Annas was so alarmed that he summoned a hasty meeting of the sanhedrin; and feeling the need that day of all the resources he could find in the city of man, he surrounded himself with an imposing array of "princes, ancients, and scribes," including his sons John and Alexander and his son-in-law Caiaphas.[1] He himself, again in the robes of the high priest, for he had resumed his old office, was an impressive figure as he stood waiting to interrogate and judge the recreants who had been summoned before him. On the surface it might seem as if Moses and Aaron, King David and the Maccabees stood almost visibly beside this impersonation of the Jewish theocracy, holding up his hands and threatening his adversaries with extinction.

Yet the two somewhat unkempt and unwashed Galilean fishermen, set before him with a mangy beggar who no longer limped, knew what most of the spectators of that scene were unaware of. Here was the Vicar of Christ face to face at last with his archenemy and chief murderer. Here was the head of the city of God on earth confronting a potentate of the city of man, which was the city of satan. And he was a different Peter, this crop-haired sturdy man with the sparse red beard, from the inept and awkward apostle whom Annas had seen at the heels of that Man in the temple during the recent Passover, if indeed he had done him the honour to notice him. Peter had received, in distinguished measure, the seven gifts of the Holy Spirit, one of which is fortitude. There was something indefinably impressive in his sturdy silence, even under his dusty tunic, and Annas probably found it disquieting and hard to lay hold of as he peered down at him with pretended disdain and real curiosity. His opening question was singularly lame and cautious. It was obvious that, knowing the answer as he did, he was only playing for time.

"By what power or in what name have you done this?" he demanded.

---

[1] Acts 4:5

Peter, "filled with the Holy Spirit," answered without hesitation:

"Princes of the people and ancients, if we are under examination today regarding a benefit to an infirm man – by what means he has been cured – let it be known to you all and to all the people of Israel, that by the name of Jesus Christ the Nazarene, whom you crucified, whom God raised from the dead, by him this man stands in your presence, well. He is the stone rejected by the builders which has become the cornerstone. And there is salvation in no other, for there is not another name under heaven given among men by which we must be saved."[2]

Annas had expected nothing as forthright and fearless. It evoked disagreeable memories of an earthquake, a temple veil torn, an empty tomb, above all, perhaps, something strangely invulnerable about that Man when he was looking down from the cross at those who were mocking him, Annas among them. There was a bit of the same sort of fearlessness in this fisherman. And beside him was the beggar, a man in his forties, whom they had seen for years sitting in his rags by the Beautiful Gate – there he was, fully cured. The adroit old high priest could think of nothing to say. To gain time he had the accused and the mendicant removed from the council chamber, while the sanhedrin went into executive session.

Annas came to the point at once. He took no pains to hide from his fellow-criminals the appalling depth of his hypocrisy. Just as he had decided on the death of Jesus after the raising of Lazarus, so now he resolved to silence the apostles, not because they had been shown to be impostors, but because they had presented unanswerable proof to the contrary.

"What shall we do with these men?" he or one of his spokesmen asked. "For that a notable miracle has been done through them is manifest to all the inhabitants of Jerusalem, and we cannot deny it. But that it may spread no farther among the people, let us warn them with threats to speak no more to any man in this name."

A great deal more may have been said. But Annas had already impressed upon most of the elders the fear of losing their own power and wealth if the teachings of Jesus were given a fair hearing before the Jewish people. Having made themselves his accomplices in the crime of Passover week, they could hardly withdraw from this vicarious re-enactment of it. They readily assented, and the three culprits were brought back to the council room. The high priest then "forbade them to speak or teach at all in the name of Jesus."

---

[2] Acts 4:8-9

"Judge whether it is right in God's sight to listen to you rather than to God!" replied Peter and John. "For we cannot do otherwise than tell what we have seen and heard."

It was difficult to answer this. Annas seems to have done no more than to repeat his previous command, reinforced by a rather vague threat. Then he discharged the two, "finding no way to bring them to punishment, on account of the people, because all were glorifying God for what had occurred."

Peter and John, heedless of the angry looks that followed them, hastened from the chamber and the temple to the other side of the city to report to their friends. They were received with un-restrained rejoicing. All of them together – the apostles, the holy women from Galilee, the Mother of the Lord – gave fervent thanks to God for their delivery, while one of them, who sounds rather like Peter himself, offered a prayer suggested by some scriptural quotations that came to his mind:

"Lord, you are he who made heaven and earth and the sea and all that are in them;[3] who by the Holy Spirit, by the mouth of our father David your servant, did say: 'Why did the heathen rage, and the people devise what is vain? The kings of the earth stood ready and the princes were gathered in one against the Lord and against his Christ.'[4] For in truth in this very city both Herod and Pontius Pilate, with the gentiles and the people of Israel, were combined against your holy servant Jesus, whom you have anointed, in order to affect whatever your hand in your purpose predetermined should be done. And now, Lord, behold their threats and grant to your servants to speak your word with all boldness, while you extend your hand to heal: and that signs and wonders may be performed through the name of your holy servant Jesus."[5]

The first result of his arrest was to make Peter bolder than ever in preaching the gospel in the temple and wherever else he could find an audience. Another was to enhance his authority among the brethren. Not that this had ever been questioned. Not even the shameful aberration of the triple denial had destroyed their respect for his fundamentally honest and loyal character, and especially for the divine commission he had received. In the *Acts* it was always he who took the initiative. Even before Pentecost he had announced to the others the suicide of Judas, and had proposed the lottery which

---

[3] Acts 4:13-31, referring to Exod 20:2

[4] Ps 2:1:2

[5] Acts 4:13, 31

resulted in the choice of Matthias. He was the logical spokesman for all after the descent of the Holy Spirit. It did not require the sensational success of his first two sermons to make his brethren see in him the Vicar of Christ.

The cure of the lame beggar, and his cool defiance of Annas and the pharisees, brought him a prestige that extended far beyond the ranks of his own followers. He was the most popular man in Jerusalem, probably the most sought-after Jew in the world. It was almost like those first days in Capharnaum, when the Lord had performed so many miracles in his house. Wherever he went, he was surrounded by the sick, the lame, the deaf, the blind, the possessed, people bearing stricken children in their arms, crowds eager to see him and to hear him speak. "They even carried the sick out into the streets in order that as Peter came by, his shadow at least might alight on some one of them."[6] Not only Peter but all his brethren performed wonders when they met to pray and preach in Solomon's Portico. The converts now were numbered by "multitudes," according to the *Acts*: and "crowds also flocked together from the towns about Jerusalem, bringing sick persons and those troubled with foul spirits, all of whom were cured."

The climax of these golden days of Peter's early apostolate, and the high-water mark of his prestige and authority, was the curious incident of Ananias and his wife Sapphira. Like all the other converts, these prosperous new members of the mystical Body of Christ accepted the principle of the sharing of worldly goods. They were under no obligation to sell all or even a part of their real estate; though to be sure there must have been some pressure of public opinion toward this end, since, as the *Acts* say, "no one claimed any of his property as his own" and "none among them was in need, for all who were owners of lands or houses sold them, and bringing the proceeds of the sale laid them at the apostles' feet." One of those who did so was a tall, distinguished, heavily bearded youth, a Levite named Joseph, son of a well-to-do Jew of Cyprus, who sold some land he had in Jerusalem and handed the proceeds to Peter, taking, with his baptism, the name of Barnabas, or Son of Consolation. He then lived on whatever the apostles saw fit to hand back to him for his daily maintenance; and this was the spirit of the whole Church. Ananias and his wife, however, were the sort of Christians who like to eat their cake and have it too: who desire the glory without the cross, the reputation for sanctity without self-

---

[6] *ibid*, 5:15

sacrifice. They even went so far as to sell some of their property. But since "we live in a practical world," since "one must be realistic," and so on, they concealed a good part of the proceeds, and the husband piously laid at Peter's feet only enough to gain, as he supposed, an honourable standing in the zealous and venerated community.

How the keeper of the Keys knew of the deception is not stated. There is no mistaking, however, the tone of majestic assurance that had come to him with the gifts of Pentecost:

"Ananias, why has satan tempted your heart to lie to the Holy Spirit, and to deduct some of the proceeds of the land? While it remained unsold, did it not remain your own? and even when sold, was it not under your own control? Why have you conceived this transaction in your heart? You have not lied to men, but to God."

On hearing these words Ananias dropped dead. "And the young men, rising, wrapped him up, and carried him out and buried him."

Sapphira had been shopping, perhaps, in the meantime, and did not know what had happened to her husband. When she called on Peter, three hours later, he said:

"Tell me, did you sell the land for so much?"

"Yes, for so much."

"How is it," said Peter, "that you have conspired together to tempt the Spirit of the Lord? Behold, the feet of those who have been burying your husband are at the door, and they shall carry you out."

She fell at his feet without a word. "And the young men on entering found her dead, and they took her out and buried her by her husband. And great fear came upon the whole Church, and upon all who heard these facts."[7] Many must have recalled the sternness with which Jesus had warned them against offending the Holy Spirit. There was a great deal in this primitive Jewish Christian Church of that holy austerity which had sometimes made Moses so terrible to the enemies of the Most High.

There is no evidence that all this power and popularity turned the head of Simon Peter. If ever he was tempted to go back to his old careless boasting and brash self-confidence, surely there would rise before him the reproachful eyes of the Christ, the bloody scourge, the black cross, and himself reeling from the palace of Caiaphas with the brackish taste of a lie in his mouth. But it is

---

[7] Acts 4:32- Acts 5:11

doubtful whether his days of prosperity lasted long enough to expose him seriously to such a temptation of the flesh. Annas and his sons, despite appearances, were not yet defeated. They kept well informed and on the alert, for it was plain that if things went on in this way much longer, all their power would be at an end. So at least they feared; and one day they decided to take the initiative even at the risk of popular displeasure. They had the twelve apostles arrested in Solomon's Portico, and clapped into a dungeon under the treasury. The next morning, having summoned a meeting of the sanhedrin, they sent some of the temple guards to fetch them, and place them on trial.

A little while later the officers returned, looking abashed and confused, without any prisoners.

"We found the prison closed and perfectly secure," they said, "and the keepers stationed at the doors; but on opening it we found no one within!"

Annas and the temple prefect were angry and incredulous, but the fact was so, and while they were still seeking an explanation for it, one of their agents came in and said:

"Why, the men whom you put in prison are in the Temple, standing and teaching the people!"

This they found to be true. An angel had set the twelve free in the last hours of the night, and had told them to return to the temple and preach; and they had been doing this since daybreak.[8]

The temple prefect and his officers again apprehended Peter and his companions in the Portico of Solomon and led them to the hall of hewn stone. But they were careful to do this as courteously as possible, without violence, for they were afraid of being stoned to death by the crowd, which was huge and hostile. Thus it came about that Peter stood face to face a second time with the cold, ruthless, implacable enemy of his master.

"We gave you strict orders," said Annas, "not to teach in his name. Yet here you have filled Jerusalem with your doctrine, and intend to bring this man's blood upon us!"

To this striking remark the apostle replied with a dogged repetition of what he had said before:

"We must obey God rather than men. The God of our fathers raised up Jesus whom you murdered by hanging upon a tree. Him has God exalted with his own right hand to be Prince and Saviour, to give repentance to Israel and forgiveness of sins. And we are

[8] Acts 5:19

witnesses of these facts; and so is the Holy Spirit whom God has given to those who obey him."

Annas was furious. He felt now that he must rid himself of this man even at the risk of offending the Jews. Once he was out of the way, they would forget him. He faced the sanhedrin, as Caiaphas had on a previous occasion, and demanded the death of all twelve.

It happened that on that day there was a man in the council who could still call his soul his own. He was a pharisee and doctor of the Law, and one of the few who still commanded universal respect: Gamaliel, nephew to the great Hillel, and head of a famous school in Jerusalem. He suggested clearing the chamber, so that they might debate the proposition laid before them by the high priest. As soon as they were in executive session he addressed them at some length, recalling, like the scholar and statesman he was, several notable historical examples of pseudo-messianic movements that had come to nothing.

"If this design or movement be from men," he argued, "it will be wrecked. But if it be from God, you will not be able to put them down; and perhaps you may even find yourselves in conflict with God!"

Gamaliel was so generally esteemed, and his plea so evidently in the best tradition of Israel, that Annas, supple old politician that he was, deemed it wise to withdraw his demand for the time being. He recalled the twelve, forbade them once more to speak in the name of Jesus, and then told the temple guards to give them all a good flogging and let them go.

A scourging in those days was no trifling penalty. From Roman hands it usually meant fifty lashes with leather thongs tipped with knuckle bones which sometimes left the flesh in bloody strips and gashes; this was what our Lord endured under Pilate's orders. Jewish law was more merciful, but not sentimentally so. Moses had decreed that the number of blows should not exceed forty, "lest your brother depart shamefully torn before your eyes."[9] The prisoner, stripped to the waist, commonly received thirty-nine stripes, which one of the judges carefully counted: thirteen on the breast and as many on each shoulder. The whip was made of two leather straps, one of calf skin divided in four, the other of ass's skin, in two thongs. Such was the punishment now inflicted upon Peter and his eleven companions, one after another.

Strange to say, he began to feel, under the burning pain and

---

[9] Deut 25:3

humiliation, a glow of joy, and so did they all. Remembering the words of Jesus, "The servant is not greater than his master," and the terrible sound of the blows that had fallen on his silent form, they rejoiced at the thought that at last they were being allowed to share a little in his sufferings. This brought them a courage so invincible that when they were finally thrust forth from the treasury dungeons, the spectators noticed, with astonishment, that they were laughing and joking together, and they staggered into the street, "rejoicing that they were considered worthy to be treated with indignity for that name. And every day in the temple and at home they never ceased teaching and proclaiming Jesus as the Christ."

Peter had good reason to feel elated. He had had evidence that the gates of hell should not prevail against the Church he had been chosen to lead. Annas had desired to kill him, and had not dared to do so. More than ever he and his companions "continued to speak the Word of God with boldness," and they saw the numbers of the faithful increase every day.

Such rapid expansion, to be sure, presented a few perplexing problems. Some of the Grecian Jews, for instance, were complaining that the widows among them did not receive the same relief as those of Judea. The difficulty was easily solved, however, by the appointment of seven assistants or deacons, to whom the Holy Spirit was imparted by the laying on of hands. This left the apostles free to devote all their time, as before, to prayer and to preaching, and with such success that even rabbis and priests began coming into the Church in large numbers.[10]

---

[10] Acts 6:7

26

The most promising of the new deacons was young Stephen. Nothing is known of his previous life except that he was chosen for his faith, wisdom, and "attested character." From his mastery of Greek it has been assumed that he was a Hellenistic Jew, born in Greece of Hebrew parents, but this is not certain. Nor is there any proof that he obtained his uncommon eloquence and knowledge of the scriptures at the school of Gamaliel. There were other wise and good men in Jerusalem from whom he might have received, as he did, the best of what the pharisees had to offer: an extensive knowledge of the law, an intense zeal for it, and a determination never to compromise with what appeared to be error.

How he freed himself from their misconceptions and exaggerations we do not know. Perhaps as a young student he heard the last discourse of Jesus in the temple, saw him dragged through the streets, stood at the foot of the cross, watched him die – and then understood, better than his teachers had, all that he had read of the sufferings of the messiah. At all events, his conversion made him into a purposeful, dynamic Christian who saw that nothing was so important as to carry out his commands for the perfection of Israel. He began to express his views in the synagogues, and naturally, having a good knowledge of Greek, found his way especially to the assemblies of the Hellenistic Jews, who, having returned from the diaspora, preferred, like those of other places, to worship by themselves. There were some 480 of these alien synagogues in Jerusalem. Stephen went most frequently to those of the Jews from Alexandria, Cyrene, Asia Minor, and Cilicia. Wherever he had an opportunity, he arose and told the congregations in burning words what he knew about the Christ who had come and had been put to death. And among these pilgrim Jews, who had always been more amenable to the messianic teachings than their brethren of the Holy City, he was making many converts.

There were times, however, when the zeal of the young preacher must have given a little uneasiness to the leading apostles. Sometimes there were riots and fist-fights in the synagogues after he had spoken. This would hardly seem necessary to older men who had been making distinct progress by more peaceful means. James the Less, cousin of the Lord, was a conservative of the conservatives, noted among them all for the perfection with which he continued to observe the Mosaic precepts, while following, just as scrupulously, the teachings and practices of Christ. James the Elder and his brother John were no less loyal to the Law. Peter, with all his rashness of temperament, had always been cautious and traditional in his thinking, sometimes too much so; and no doubt at fifty he felt the sobering effect of authority and responsibility. He had had the last word in giving Stephen permission to preach. It was his duty to see that the youth did not interrupt, by excessive or misguided zeal, the work that had been going on so well. It goes almost without saying that he resolved to keep an eye on him. He and John may even have gone to hear him in one foreign synagogue or another.

Stephen had a particular gift for enraging the pharisees. Perhaps it was because, having been trained by them, he knew all their arguments, their strength and their weakness; and with his conversion the Holy Spirit had given him the grace to expose their misunderstanding of Moses, sometimes sincere, sometimes hypocritical, with logic that they could not refute. He gave particular offence to a young pharisee from Tarsus in Cilicia, who was known as Saul among the Jews, for he belonged to the tribe of Benjamin, and as Paul among the Gentiles, since his father was a Roman citizen, probably of Galilean origin. Though his family were well-to-do, he had been taught a useful trade, like every good Jew, and if necessary could earn his living making tents, or weaving the mohair of which they were constructed. His interests were intellectual, however, and he had studied, doubtless with brilliant success, at the school of Gamaliel. It is likely that he had returned to Cilicia before the Crucifixion, and was now back in Jerusalem, perhaps for further studies, for the first time since that event – let us say a year or two later. Naturally he accepted from his fellow pharisees the version they had been giving of the Nazarene and his followers; and for both he had conceived so passionate a hatred that he would not listen to a word in their favour. If Stephen had been his friend and fellow student, it is still easier to understand how bitterly he would resent his conversion, looking upon him, as other pharisees did, as a renegade and a traitor. But no such supposition is necessary to explain his hatred. He detested all Nazarenes, and Stephen was one of the most militant. They were two of a kind, these young Israelites: hard-thinking, fearless, utterly sincere. When they took opposite sides on the most vital question in the world, there was bound to be an explosion.

There is no evidence that either Saul or Peter was present on the fateful day when Stephen spoke in the synagogue known as that of the Freedmen, which had been established by the liberated descendants of the Jewish captives of war whom Pompey had taken to Rome. Some of the pharisees challenged him, and he replied so vigorously that "they were not able to withstand the wisdom and the Spirit with which he spoke."[1] From the context it seems probable that he quoted some of the words of Christ predicting the destruction of the temple of Jerusalem, and asserting that the pharisees had been false to the teachings of Moses and the other prophets. As usual, many of the congregation were convinced, and signified their intention to be baptized.

This provoked a reaction very similar to the one elicited by the same statements when they had been flung at the Sons of Annas. No doubt there were faithful puppets of the high priests on hand to arrange the affair, and to report everything to headquarters. They paid some professional liars to go about the city saying, "We have heard him utter blasphemous statements against Moses and against God," and to make the same accusations to Annas and leading members of the council. When all was in readiness, they hired a mob to waylay the young deacon and apparently to treat him roughly before dragging him to the temple. A meeting of the sanhedrin was hastily convoked. Stephen was placed on trial for blasphemy, the worst crime of which a man could be accused. There were not lacking witnesses who declared, "This man never ceases uttering speeches against the Holy Place and the Law; for we have heard him say that this Jesus the Nazarene will destroy this place, and change the customs which Moses transmitted to us."[2]

It would be strange indeed if Peter and John, on hearing of all this, did not hasten to the hall of hewn stone in the Temple to defend their young deacon, or at least to follow the proceedings. They may have stood almost next to Saul of Tarsus, watching Annas conduct the investigation and direct the verdict. It can hardly have escaped their notice that history was repeating itself with a strangely symbolic fidelity. The false witnesses were saying exactly what had been said against the Lord. Stephen was being tried under the very same law of Moses that had been invoked, though not directly enforced, against Him:

"When there shall be found among you within any of your

[1] Acts 6:10
[2] Acts 6:11-14

gates ... man or woman that do evil in the sight of the Lord your God, and transgress his covenant, so as to go and serve strange gods, and adore them ... and this is told to you, and hearing it you have inquired diligently, and found it to be true, and that the abomination is committed in Israel, you shall bring forth the man or the woman to the gates of your city, and they shall be stoned. By the mouth of two or three witnesses shall he die that is to be slain. Let no man be put to death, when only one bears witness against him. The hands of the witnesses shall be first upon him to kill him, and afterwards the hands of the rest of the people, that you may take away the evil out of the midst of you."[3]

This was the law that Annas got Pilate to enforce, fearing that he himself would be the target for the stones of the mob. He had no reason for such a precaution in the present instance. Hence, after the indictment had been read and the witnesses heard, he advanced with brisk confidence to where the young deacon stood, and demanded almost triumphantly:

"Are these things so?"

It was in answer to this question that Stephen, his face glowing like that of an angel so that all in the room remarked on it, made his immortal speech. The first part of it was so lucid an exposition of traditional Jewish history that all the assembled councillors, scribes, and pharisees, however indignant, felt obliged to listen in silence. It was all so correct and so orthodox that they had no excuse to interrupt it. The holy names of Abraham, of Isaac, of Jacob, and of Joseph fell from his lips like a familiar music, and Moses lived and prophesied again in his eloquent cadences. It was only toward the end that their faces whitened with anger as they began to see that he was reminding them of the lapses in faith for which their fathers had been justly punished from time to time: the worship of the golden calf, the sacrifice of their own children to Moloch. It was too late now to stop him. They listened even when on reaching the climax of his speech he cried in a voice that rang through the stately chamber:

"You stiff-necked race, uncircumcised in heart and ears! You are always resisting the Holy Spirit! As your forefathers did, so do you! Which of the prophets did not your fathers persecute? and they murdered those who foretold the coming of the just One, of whom you have now yourselves become betrayers and murderers – you who received the Law as it was ordained by angels, and did not observe it."

---

[3] Deut 17:2-7

This was substantially what the just One himself had said within those very walls. The result was very similar. "They were cut to the heart, and ground their teeth at him." Stephen seemed no longer to see them. His face was radiant again, his eyes turned toward heaven. Rapt in an ecstasy, he was allowed to see a vision of Jesus, approving and encouraging him; and "being full of the Holy Spirit," he cried joyfully, "Behold, I see the heavens opened, and the Son of Man standing at the right hand of God!"

His enemies seized upon this as an admission of his guilt under the Law, for he was proclaiming that Jesus was God. A bedlam-like scene followed. The councillors and chief pharisees stopped their ears and drowned the echoes of the youthful voice with screams of horror and rage. Garments were torn and flung into the air. Clenched fists were raised. Then they "rushed upon him with one accord," and pushed him from the chamber.

Outside strong temple guards seized and bound him. The false witnesses laid their hands on his head, and as many others as could reach him did likewise. They dragged him through the courts and down through the city among the bazaars and hucksters, the caravans of camels and asses, the throngs of citizens and pilgrims, toward the Damascus Gate at the north.

Peter and John, in the likely event of being helpless witnesses to this scene, must have followed the screaming mob with a strange awareness of living over, with the fidelity of a dream, a portion of the ineradicable past. For now they were following the very route over which Jesus had carried his cross. They went over the stones on which his blood had fallen, through the identical gate, and along the same road toward Calvary. Just before they reached the mount, the mob left the highway and swarmed across a barren field to a skull-like rock, bleak and forbidding, near the grotto of Jeremiah. At one side of it, like the gaping jaw, was a pit surrounded by piles of stones. This was the Beth ha Segilah, the ancient place of stoning. Here the woman taken in adultery would have died like many others. Here Jesus himself might have perished if Annas had not feared the mob and if the Father had not chosen rather to let him be enthroned in death against the blackening sky.

If Peter followed thus far, he must have seen that the execution was in charge of a stern young man who now took his stand with folded arms on a pile of rocks, while the leading witnesses and others removed their outer garments – mantles, tunics, phylacteries – and laid them at his feet. This was the young pharisee from

Tarsus in Cilicia. It may be, then, that Peter now had his first glimpse of the man he was to know as Paul. He was about thirty, pale, short, sickly-looking, prematurely bald, his broad shoulders suggesting great endurance and strength, his dark intelligent eyes glowing with anger. "So Saul was consenting to his murder" by guarding the garments; and as he gave the word, they cast Stephen into the pit, and began picking up stones. If Saul had glanced up the hill, he would have seen the place where the three crosses had stood not many months before. But he saw only Stephen, and Stephen saw nothing but the glorious Christ in the blue heaven. The stones were hurled. They thudded against the young body, the head, the face, till the victim swayed and grew faint. "Lord Jesus, receive my spirit!" they heard him say. Then, falling on his knees, he cried in a loud voice, "Lord, lay not this sin to their charge!" And with that he died.[4] The rocks still crashed upon the quivering corpse.

Stephen's death was the signal for the first general persecution of the infant Church. It began that very day; and those who had been called angels for their brotherly love now heard themselves denounced as apostates, idolaters, and blasphemers. They were threatened, scorned, beaten, cast out of employment, hounded from their homes. Many fled to Lydda and Joppa, to Samaria, even as far as Antioch, Damascus, Phoenicia, and Cyprus.

No one waited on the pavement now for Peter's shadow to restore him to health. Yet the head of the Church proved himself, under this first severe test, to be a good shepherd and not a hireling. He may have had to discontinue preaching in the temple, or even worshipping there. The twelve may have continued their prayers and the breaking of bread in secret with the mother of the Lord and a few faithful disciples. Nothing is said as to this; all that is clear is that they stayed at their posts and faced the popular indignation that the pharisees had managed to fan against them.

From the brethren in exile Peter received disturbing accounts indicating that the persecution had not been confined to Jerusalem by any means. Saul of Tarsus had taken advantage of the notoriety he had gained on the occasion of Stephen's death to place himself at the head of the movement, and had become the agent and chief inquisitor for the high priests and the sanhedrin. Like a lion that has tasted blood, he went raging through the city from house to house, inquiring for Christians and dragging them off to dungeons, where he tried to force them to apostatize and in some instances had them

---

[4] Acts 7:60

put to death.[5] After that he scoured the small towns of Judea with an army of spies and temple guards at his command. Anonymous denunciations, secret hearings, midnight raids, threats, floggings – woe to the poor Christian who found himself in the path of this fanatical zealot of the Law! Finally, to the relief of all the faithful in the holy city, he took himself off to Damascus, still "breathing threats and murder," and fully resolved to bring back the refugees there for trial in Jerusalem.

If all this was a perpetual sorrow and worry to Peter, there was a brighter aspect which soon caught his attention. Persecution was making the Church grow faster than ever. Philip the Deacon, for example, was preaching with notable success in Samaria, where he had gone to minister to the fugitives from Jerusalem. "And the people gave unanimous heed to Philip's utterances, when they heard him and saw the miracles he performed. For from many of those possessed the foul spirits came out, shrieking with a loud voice; and many who were paralyzed and lame were cured. So there was great rejoicing in that town."[6]

Among those he baptized was a curious character known as Simon Magus, who, in addition to several unusually clever sleight-of-hand performances, seems to have organized something like a small religious sect, whose members attributed more than human powers to him. Nor did Simon object when people of high and low degree began saying, "This man is that power of God which is called great." In the deacon from Jerusalem, however, he soon recognized a superior, and professing to believe all that he said, he became not only a convert but "a close attendant" upon him. He was particularly interested in any miracles or cures that Philip performed, and watched him intently to discover how each trick was done. The less his curiosity was satisfied, the more his fervour increased.

When Peter and John heard of the success of Philip, they decided to visit the converts in Samaria and to administer the sacrament of Confirmation to them. Accordingly they took the old familiar route along the main Roman highway between the mountains, and after two or three days walked down the lordly avenue between two rows of columns into the city they had often seen from a distance perched on its eminence, but had never before visited. Probably they found lodgings with some of the refugees from

---

[5] So he stated later to King Agrippa: Acts 26:10
[6] Acts 8:4-8

Jerusalem, and after breaking bread with them, went from house to house, examining the converts, and imparting the Holy Spirit to them by the laying on of hands. Sometimes this evoked the phenomena that often followed the reception of the Sacrament: prophecies, speaking in unknown tongues, the healing of maladies.

Simon Magus was usually on hand, and was deeply impressed. It is not clear whether or not he was confirmed. But he had higher aspirations. He wanted to be able to do what Peter did, as a professional accomplishment of evident commercial value. One day he laid a handful or bag of silver coins before him, and said:

"Give this power to me also, so that upon whomever I may lay my hands, he may receive the Holy Spirit."

Peter's answer, though verbal, might be called the first known decree against simony:

"To perdition with you and your silver, because you have thought to obtain the gift of God with money! You have no part nor lot in this matter, for your heart is not right before God. Repent therefore of this your wickedness, and pray the Lord that if it may be, this purpose of your heart may be forgiven you. For I see that you are in the gall of bitterness and in the bondage of iniquity!"

Simon's reply was too meek and prompt to be wholly convincing.

"Pray yourselves to the Lord for me," he said unctuously, "that nothing of what you have said may come upon me." The sequel suggests that he may have been less afraid of the Lord than of what the apostle might be able to do with those mysterious powers of his.

Peter and John had now completed their mission, however, and were anxious to return to Jerusalem, to see whether any further misfortunes had fallen upon the Church there. To their great relief they found conditions notably improved. With the departure of Saul for Syria, the persecution had lost much of its virulence. It had also been bruited about that the new Emperor Tiberius was inclined to look with some favour on the followers of Jesus Christ. Having heard from Pilate, perhaps, of the miracles he had wrought even in death, the imperial syncretist proposed to enrol him among the Roman gods, and it may be that this broad-minded gesture had some restraining influence upon the Sons of Annas, who in worldly affairs at least managed to know which way the wind was blowing. Finally, there was the news from their fellow apostle Philip (not the deacon), who, on the way from Jerusalem to Gaza, had converted and baptized a highly important eunuch[7] of Hebrew faith, the treasurer to Candace, Queen of Ethiopia, thus planting and watering the tree of faith that was to flourish for centuries in North Africa, until the frost of compromise should kill it. Philip meanwhile made many other conversions as he went on his victorious way, preaching in various towns all the way to Caesarea.

The most sensational development, of course, was the conversion of Saul. In fact the news was so unexpected that Peter and his fellow apostles were inclined to doubt it. This was the attitude, naturally, of most of the brethren at Jerusalem. "They were all afraid of him, not believing him to be a disciple."[8] There was always the possibility that Annas or the pharisees might be setting a new trap for them.

The story grew more astonishing as further details began to arrive. The persecutor had been struck blind as he approached Damascus, and claimed to have heard the Lord himself speak to him. A Christian named Ananias had baptized him, having been told in a vision to do so, and Saul's sight had been restored. Almost at once, then, to the amazement of both Jews and Christians, he had begun to preach Christ in the synagogues. This was almost too much. And now he was said to be on his way to Jerusalem.

The only one who believed at once in the conversion of Saul was the tall Levite from Cyprus, Joseph, who was now called Barnabas. Perhaps he too had been a student at the school of Gamaliel, and had known Paul personally. He could vouch for one thing, then: the man's utter sincerity. He had persecuted the Church because he had believed it to be evil. If its true character were revealed to him, he would undoubtedly defend it to the death. Perhaps Barnabas, too, had seen the death of Stephen, and had noticed that when he said, "Lord, lay not this sin to their charge," he had looked at Saul, as if he had been praying especially for him.

Peter said nothing. He remembered how the Lord's eyes had met his that night. He would wait and see.

---

[7] He was not necessary a physical eunuch. Eunuchs had been employed so much in royal positions of trust that the term had come to mean nothing more than one who held such a place.

[8] Acts 9:26

27

Peter left Jerusalem, it seems, before Saul arrived. He had decided upon another episcopal visitation, this time to the exiles near the Mediterranean coast, especially in Lydda and Joppa. It took them three or four days to cover the intervening fifty miles, following the western road from Jerusalem, now through rocky gorges, now along the edges of cliffs three-thousand feet above the sea. On either side were bleak, bare, and sun-parched mountains. But after he had passed Emmaus, he began to see occasional olive groves on the high rocky terraces, and sloping pastures on which sheep and goats nibbled the meagre grass. Finally descending to the coastal plain, he passed through the teeming market town of Ramleh (Arimathea) and arrived, perhaps at the end of the third day, at Lydda.

In this large town, the spoil of so many wars, he had no difficulty in finding a lodging and a hearty welcome with some of the fugitives from Jerusalem. There was great joy among them when he laid his hands on one Aeneas, who had been bed-ridden with paralysis for eight years, and instantly restored him to health. The news spread to Sharon and other nearby towns, and finally as far as Joppa. Everyone wanted to see and hear him. He never refused an appeal if he could help it. There were not enough hours in the day for his work, but his rugged frame seemed inexhaustible.

One day he received a visit from some of the faithful at Joppa, who begged him for the love of God to go with them at once, and to lay his hands on one of their neighbours named Tabitha, or Dorcas, who had died. She was indispensable to the community, having spent all her time in prayer and works of benevolence. They had heard of Peter's healing powers, and had no doubt they would be adequate in this instance.

Here was faith with a vengeance. Peter must have found it rather frightening. Yet it was not any power of his, but that of the Lord that effected cures. Hence, after fervently consulting him in prayer he agreed to make the attempt, and set forth with the men from Joppa. It was hardly more than half a day's walk to that sea-port over the main Roman highway where chariots rumbled inces-santly at urgent speed, and caravans of camels and asses carried fruit and grain from the south to be loaded on ships. As the travellers approached the Mediterranean, the air grew cool and fresh, its salt tang mingling with the fragrance from groves of almonds, oranges, figs, and olives on both sides of the road. Thus the Vicar of Christ came to the town that is now the Arab enclave of Jaffa, surrounded by the Jewish state centred in Tel Aviv.

His guides took him at once to the house of Dorcas in one of the suburbs, on a little street lined with olive and mulberry trees. He entered, and going upstairs, saw the woman's body where it had been washed and laid out by the disciples. "And all the widows stood round him weeping, and showing the gowns and cloaks which Dorcas had made while she was with them.

"But Peter, having put them all out, knelt down and prayed. Then, turning to the body, he said, 'Tabitha, rise!' And she opened her eyes, and seeing Peter, sat up; and he gave her his hand and raised her up, and calling the holy ones and the widows presented her alive. And it became known all through Joppa, and many believed in the Lord."[1]

It goes almost without saying that this miracle gave Peter even more celebrity, if possible, than the cure of the lame man had in Jerusalem. But he had learned his lesson too well to take to himself any praise that belonged to the One in whose name he had worked. There was a great deal to do also, in Joppa. Peter remained some time there, preaching, directing, baptizing, confirming, visiting and healing the sick. He lived in the older and more crowded part of the city near the waterfront, in a small, one-story house belonging to one Simon the Tanner. Pilgrims still notice the well and the stone basin of his trade nearby, and the outer stairway leading to a roof and a diminutive lighthouse.

Peter spent many quiet hours on that small eminence. It commanded a good view both of the city and of the harbour, both of which were rather unusual. Joppa was a typical eastern seaport in one way, noisy and picturesque, filthy and beautiful by turns. Built on a high rock jutting into the water, it rose above the nearby bazaars, with their odours of camels, asses, and goats, and their hubbub of merchants, beggars, travellers and shoppers, into a crest of gardens and orchards, brilliant and aromatic against the blue Mediterranean sky. It is safe to imagine, however, that the eyes of the tired apostle more often sought the void of the Great Sea. It was to this harbour that the cedars of Lebanon had been towed on their way to the Temple at Jerusalem. It was to one of those rocks rising from the perilous reefs yonder that Andromeda was said to have

---

[1] Acts 9:2-42

been chained. It was from these wharves that the prophet Jonah had set out for Tharsis in Spain. Old and well-seasoned, even in Peter's time, the place had a charm and a mystery all of its own; yet nothing so wonderful as the power that resided in the rather tired and silent old man who sat in the sun on the roof.

It was not for sight-seeing or recreation, however, that he climbed the rickety stairs every three hours or so. He had seen enough of this world, and since Pentecost had known how to value it. He had always been a man of prayer. Now he had probably reached an advanced state of asceticism and contemplation. An early tradition says that he ate barely enough of the cheapest and coarsest food – a handful or two of dried peas or beans – to keep body and soul together. When he was not actively accomplishing the duties of his office, he was conversing with God either in vocal prayer or in that higher form without words which sometimes leads mystics to visions and ecstasies foreshadowing the delights of his presence in heaven. Peter was too reticent and too humble to leave any record of the spiritual desolations and consolations that must have been his portion. But it is evident from the *Acts* that he had attained a high degree of sanctity, and that on that modest roof he probably enjoyed experiences which, if he had taken the trouble to record them, would have had an important place in the history of mystical theology.

One of them, however, did find a chronicler. On a certain day about noon he went to the housetop to pray. He was probably lost in contemplation for a long time, for he became hungry, and asked those downstairs for some food. While they were preparing it, "he fell into an ecstasy; and he beheld heaven opened, and a kind of vessel descending, as it were, a great sheet let down by the four corners to the earth, in which were all kinds of quadrupeds and reptiles of the land, and birds of the sky. And a voice came to him, 'Rise, Peter, kill and eat.' But Peter said, 'By no means, Lord; for I have never eaten anything profane or unclean: Then a voice came to him again a second time, 'What God has made clean, do not you treat as profane.' This occurred three times, and immediately the vessel was taken up into heaven."[2]

He was still wondering what all this could mean when he heard a knocking downstairs, and the sound of voices. Someone was asking if Simon, surnamed Peter, lodged there. And within himself the voice of the Holy Spirit was saying:

---

[2] Acts 10:9-16.

"Behold three men are inquiring for you. Now, then, rise and go down, and accompany them without hesitation; for I have sent them."

Peter obeyed, and was considerably surprised to find a Roman soldier in uniform, with two other men who looked like servants.

"Here I am," he said, "the one you are looking for; what is the reason of your coming?"

The legionary replied:

"The Centurion Cornelius, a just and God-fearing man, whose character is well attested by the whole Jewish nation, has received a declaration by a holy angel that he should send for you to come to his house, and listen to instructions from you."

Peter invited them in, gave them some refreshment, and asked for further particulars. Cornelius was a centurion in the Italian Cohort probably the *Cohors II Italica civium Romanorum* – which had been stationed in Syria and was now part of the imperial garrison at Caesarea Maritima, the official residence of Pilate, some thirty miles north of Joppa. He was noted for his piety, his charity to the poor, and his kindness to the Jews in general. In fact he went so far, evidently, as to observe part at least of the Mosaic Law, though he does not seem to have been a circumcised proselyte. While keeping the ninth hour of prayer on the previous afternoon (at three o'clock), he had seen a man in shining robes who, suddenly appearing from nowhere, had said:

"Cornelius, your prayers and your alms have ascended as a memorial in the sight of God. So now send men to Joppa to fetch Simon who is surnamed Peter. He is lodging with one Simon, a tanner, whose house is by the seaside."

Peter was astonished, but his own vision had left him no choice; and early next morning he set out for the north with the three messengers and six of the brethren from Joppa. They reached Caesarea on the following day – not the Caesarea Philippi near which he had made his confession of faith, but Caesarea Maritima, one of the most radiant pagan cities, rising in a shimmer of white marble from the shore of the Great Sea as one more evidence of Herod's passion for building and his flattery of Augustus. Proceeding at once to the house of the centurion, they found him waiting with many relations and friends whom he had invited for the occasion.

Cornelius came out to meet his guest, and fell on his knees before him with profound veneration. Peter raised him up, saying bluntly:

"Stand up. I myself also am a man."

This was a bit embarrassing, but it was nothing to what he felt when he went inside with his host and found himself surrounded by gentiles, most of them probably Italians. Never in his life had he had anything to do with such people. But with the voice of the Holy Spirit still ringing in his ears, he said:

"You yourselves know how contrary it is to established custom for a man that is a Jew to associate with or visit a foreigner; but God has shown me that I should call no man profane or unclean. Therefore, I have come without hesitation on being sent for. May I ask, then, for what reason you have sent for me?"

Cornelius explained, adding, "So at once I sent for you, and you have been very kind in coming. Now therefore we are all here in the presence of God to listen to all that has been commanded you by the Lord."

Peter set forth, in a few rugged words whose full importance he could hardly have been fully aware of, the catholicity of the Church and the equality of all races within her fold.

"Truly I perceive," he said, "that God is no respecter of persons; on the contrary, in every nation whoever fears him and acts uprightly is acceptable to him. He sent the Word to the sons of Israel, proclaiming good tidings of peace through Jesus Christ, who is Lord of all.

You yourselves know the account which was published throughout all Judea – beginning from Galilee after the baptism which John preached – about Jesus of Nazareth; how God anointed him with the Holy Spirit and with power; how he went about doing good and curing all who were tyrannized over by the devil, for God was with him. And we ourselves are witnesses of all he did in the country of the Jews and in Jerusalem. But they put him to death by hanging him on a tree. Then God raised up the third day, and granted him to become visible, not indeed to all the people, but to witnesses pre-ordained by God, that is, to ourselves who ate and drank with him after he had risen from the dead.

"And he commanded us to proclaim to the people, and to give our testimony, that he is the one whom God has constituted judge of the living and the dead. All the prophets bear witness to him, that everyone who believes in him shall receive forgiveness of sins through his name."

The Holy Spirit, meanwhile, in his desire for souls, did not wait for him to finish, much less to baptize any of those in the room, but poured himself out in all his charismatic generosity, until the six Jewish Christians who had come from Joppa were amazed to hear the Gentiles "speaking in strange tongues and magnifying God".

Peter was delighted. "Can anyone refuse water," he cried, "that these should not be baptized who have received the Holy Spirit as well as ourselves?" He administered the sacrament without further delay. For several days thereafter he remained at the house of Cornelius, teaching and perhaps confirming gentile converts. For the first time in his life he ate non-kosher food, and thought nothing of it.

The news of this got to Jerusalem before he did, and caused no small scandal. When he finally arrived (how or when we are not told) he was criticized to his face by angry brethren, faithful circumcised Christians, one of whom probably was James the Less.

"You have visited uncircumcised men and eaten with them."[3]

That was all they said. The bald statement of fact suggested the enormity of the offence. The Church was still so Jewish in membership and in consciousness that the mere accusation of such a thing stirred it to the depths of indignation. Yet the moral authority of Peter, as Vicar of Christ, was sufficient to sweep aside their protest with a few frank words, and with it the whole dead weight of pharisaic tradition. He told them exactly what had happened at Joppa and Caesarea, and they listened. "If then," he concluded, "God granted the same gift to them as to ourselves when we believed in the Lord Jesus Christ, who was I that I should be able to hinder God?"

There was no answer to this, and they all agreed that he had done well. Not only that, but they glorified the Lord, saying, "Then God has also bestowed on the Gentiles life-giving repentance!" A stupendous, unprecedented thing had happened in Israel.

It must have been about this time that Peter finally met Paul of Tarsus, who had just arrived in Jerusalem after a long retreat in Arabia. Unfortunately for our historical curiosity, the evangelists, absorbed in more important considerations, left not a word about the first conversation between these two great Jews. On the surface, at least, they seemed as different as oil and water. The only description of Paul comes from his own fluent pen. He wrote of his "mean presence," his feeble bodily appearance, his contemptible diction, his suffering from "a thorn in the flesh, a messenger of satan to beat me,"[4] which may have been a chronic malaria, or some other

[3] Acts 11:3
[4] 2 Cor *passim*

disease. Yet tireless energies and boundless endurance smouldered in his warped and stunted body, and in his dark intense eyes burned the flame that had given such sublime vigour and beauty to the scriptures of Israel, and almost superhuman courage and wisdom to the prophets. He had also something of the self-assurance and poise of one born rich (even though his father may have disinherited him after his conversion), and he was proud not only of his race, but of his Roman citizenship.

Towering above this sturdy gnome of a man stood Peter, as rugged and ungainly as one of his native Galilean hills. He had the deliberate and casual ease of men who work out-of-doors. There was always something of the sea and the sun and the west wind about him, something, too, of the hidden storms that lay waiting to fall on the smiling waters of Galilee. It is conceivable that his first impression of the man before him was one of aversion, which Paul reciprocated. The physically powerful instinctively patronize the physically contemptible, all the more so if they feel in them some intellectual or other superiority. Peter's slower and less instructed mind was bound to be confused and irritated by Paul's rapid and nervous speech, by his habit of stuttering, by his rhetorical abstractions, and most of all, perhaps, by a habit he had acquired from the pharisees of multiplying enumerations and fine distinctions. It was not always easy to understand what he was trying to say. Furthermore, Peter had been warned not to trust him too far. Likely enough he let his guest do most of the talking.

Paul probably told him the details of his conversion, and what followed. His first impulse, after regaining his sight and being baptized, had been to preach in the synagogues of Damascus. But such a sudden change was bound to be misunderstood, for the Jewish Christians could not believe in his sincerity, and the followers of Annas regarded him as a turncoat; some of them, indeed, swore to expunge him from the face of the earth. It was to escape from them and to think out his own thoughts that he had gone to Arabia. There he had lived for three years on the edge of the desert, supporting himself by his trade, re-reading the holy scriptures in the light of his new experience, praying, and fasting.

As Peter listened, he began to like his visitor better. There was something spontaneous and honest about his manner and his speech. And rhetorical ornaments and subtle dialectic by no means destroyed the truth of what he had to say. The kernel of his thought was the same as Peter's, in fact: Christ first, last, and always: Christ yesterday, today, and tomorrow: Christ as the crown, seal, fulfilment, and interpreter of all the prophets; life with Christ and in Christ, here and forever. If he was pretending, he was doing it with consummate skill.

Paul must have said a great deal also about the universality of the Church. He was convinced that the Jewish nationalism of the pharisees, with all their insistence upon minute ceremonial observances, should be discarded, so that all mankind, Gentiles, women, slaves, everybody, could be drawn into the Mystical Body of Christ and saved. A few weeks ago Peter might have been scandalized by such talk. If he had heard it before his journey to Joppa, he would have been sure that Paul was a wolf in sheep's clothing. Now, in the light of his own experience and revelation, it became the very thing that convinced him of the man's sincerity. Thus on the rock of Christ and in the light the Holy Spirit had imparted to both of them, two men so different in origin, temperament, and training became fast friends. They spent two full weeks together, during which no doubt Peter laid his hands on Paul, conveying to him the powers of an apostle and a bishop.

Once his doubts were removed, the Keeper of the Keys was willing enough to talk in his turn; and we know how voluble he could be when it suited him. He was ready now to answer the thousand questions that sprang from the keen mind of the little man who seemed to have an insatiable hunger for knowledge. Day after day as the two sat on the roof after prayer looking over the housetops of Jerusalem, he told all that he remembered of Jesus, his life, his death, his teachings. And likely enough he took his visitor to see all the principal scenes of that story.

"Here is where he stood when he scourged the money-changers ... This is where he called them hypocrites ... This is where he saved the life of the sinful woman ... Here he sat at supper, and I was here, and John was there ... This is where I slept, and he was just above there, praying ... . That is the high priest's palace; that lower court is where I denied him, and then I heard the cock crow and saw him looking at me ... Here is the place they crucified him ... I was down there in the crowd ... This is the spot where he arose from the ground, and went up that way until we could see him no more." Imagination and common sense both suggest some such conversations during those fifteen days. It was probably Peter, too, who gave Paul many details concerning the Eucharist in addition to what he had already learned from revelation[5] and Peter who introduced him to the mother of the Lord, of whom his disciple Luke was to be the chronicler.

The other apostles were not so sure about the sincerity of the convert. Things had been going very well lately. The persecution had died down, the ranks were growing, the future looked promising again. And now this newcomer, of whom they knew so little, was going about the synagogues lashing out at the pharisees and scribes with a violence that painfully recalled the brief and splendid adventure of Stephen. James the Less felt that Paul was saying things that had better be left unsaid, or expressed more tactfully. Even Peter became uneasy, despite the liking he had taken for the man, and may have joined the sons of Zebedee in asking him to be a little more moderate. They were experienced in this work, and he was not. They may even have suggested that he leave Jerusalem for a while to those who had already laid the foundations there.

The inference from one of Paul's later statements[6] is that he refused to take this advice. Instead, he went to the temple, and complained to the Lord until he fell into an ecstasy. Then he heard him say:

"Make haste and get quickly out of Jerusalem, because they will not accept your evidence concerning me."

"Lord," he replied, "they themselves know that I used to imprison and flog in every synagogue those who believed in you; and that when the blood of your martyr Stephen was shed, I myself was standing by and approving, and keeping the garments of his murderers."

"Go!" said the voice: "for I will send you far away to the Gentiles."[7]

So Paul left the city, and went back to Tarsus. If Peter had any regrets, he left no record of them. Most of the disciples, except Barnabas, felt relieved.

---

[5] Paul tells of his visit to Peter in Gal 1:18
[6] Acts 22:17-21
[7] ibid

28

Peter was disturbed over the news from Antioch. The Church there had been founded by some Jews of Cyprus and Cyrene who had fled from Jerusalem after the death of Stephen, and had been prospering wonderfully. There had been glowing reports of conversions, cures, and miracles. Lately, however, these harmonies had been interspersed with too many discords. The issue was the one that Peter himself had raised by baptizing Cornelius. With such an example before them, the zealous refugees at Antioch had accepted not only fellow Jews but many Greeks, thus establishing the first community of believers that could be called "Gentile," and the first in history, by the way, to apply to itself the word "Christian."

So far so good. But the problem at Antioch was far more complicated than the one at Caesarea. The Gentiles saw no reason why they should be circumcised as well as baptized, or subjected to the burden of the countless minor precepts of the Mosaic tradition. Some of the Jewish believers agreed with them, others violently disagreed; and the conservatives became known as "Judaizers." Besides these two groups there were the unbelieving Jews of the synagogue, who welcomed the opportunity to widen the breach in the Christian ranks. Certain pharisees were said to have gone so far as to pretend conversion, that they might pursue this object from the inside. Disputes were frequent and bitter, and it was high time for someone in authority to intervene.

Peter accordingly sent Barnabas to Antioch as an apostolic delegate. He was just the man for the task. As a native of Cyprus he would have an initial advantage in a community so largely recruited from that place; furthermore, he was gentle and conciliatory, and there was something about his tall majestic presence and luxuriant black beard that commanded respect everywhere – in fact, on one occasion the pagans at Lystra tried to worship him, mistaking him for Zeus, and Paul for Hermes.[1]

The reports he sent back from Antioch seemed to justify the confidence of Peter, James the Elder, and John. He had composed differences and was increasing the number of the faithful, both Jewish and Gentile. One week there was a small commotion when Agabus, a visitor from Jerusalem with a gift of prophecy, was

---

[1] Acts 14:12

prompted to announce at the Agape before the breaking of the bread that there would soon be a severe famine throughout the world. Despite this dismal note the Syrian community continued to flourish.

Peter's attention must have been distracted from the situation at Antioch, not long after this, to a more troublesome one in Jerusalem, one that threatened him personally in no gentle way. For a new persecution had begun there in the year 44 A.D. under the direct instigation of King Herod Antipas, with some cooperation, no doubt, from the chief priests and pharisees. The old rake, who had murdered John the Baptizer and had cast a purple cloak on the Redeemer in mockery, had lately made an ostentatious show of practising the religion of the Prophets. Every day he was seen offering a sacrifice in the temple. And presently he began to manifest indignation against the Nazarenes who, according to the sons of Annas, were enemies of God and of Moses. It may be that he found it useful to blame them for the famine that scourged Palestine and all the world, exactly as Agabus had foretold, in 44 A.D. Whatever the details, he certainly decided to make no ordinary gesture of friendship to the rulers of the Temple and the synagogues of unbelief. He had James the Elder seized and beheaded.

"Then, as he saw that this pleased the Jews, he proceeded to seize Peter also. It was the days of unleavened bread. And having arrested him he put him in prison, committing him to the custody of four detachments of four soldiers each, intending after the Passover to bring him out to the people. So Peter was confined in the prison; but prayer was made fervently by the church to God in his behalf.

"When Herod, however, was about to produce him, Peter was that very night sleeping bound with two chains between two soldiers, and sentinels before the door were guarding the prison, when behold, an angel of the Lord stood by him, and light illuminated the cell; and striking Peter on the side he roused him, saying, 'Rise up quickly,' whereupon his chains fell from his hands. "The angel then said to him, 'Gird yourself and fasten on your sandals;' and he did so. Then he said to him, 'Throw your cloak around yourself, and follow me.'

He accordingly went out following him; yet he failed to realize that what was done by the angel was actual, but supposed that he was seeing a vision. Passing then the first and second guards, they came to the iron gate leading into the city, which opened to them of its own accord; and they went out and passed on through one street, when all at once the angel departed from him. Then Peter coming to himself said:

'Now I know of a certainty that the Lord has sent his angel, and delivered me from the hand of Herod, and from all the expectation of the Jewish people.'

Then on reflection he went to the house of Mary the mother of John surnamed Mark, where many were assembled and praying. And when he knocked at the door of the gateway, a little girl named Rhoda came to answer; and recognizing Peter's voice she was so delighted that she did not open the gate, but ran in and told that Peter was standing at the entrance.

'You are out of your mind!' they told her; but she insisted that it was so. Then they said, 'It is his angel.'

But Peter kept on knocking, and when they had opened they saw him and were astonished. But motioning to them with his hand to be silent, he related how the Lord had brought him out of prison; adding, 'Bring this news to James and to the brethren'; and taking his departure he went to another place.[2]

The "other place" to which Peter fled, either through Samaria and Caesarea Philippi, or by the coastal road near Tyre and Sidon, was probably Antioch. There he learned that Herod, after ordering the execution of the sixteen guards, had departed for Caesarea, where, on allowing himself to be venerated as a god by the Tyrians and Sidonians, he presently expired, smitten by an angel of the Lord and eaten by worms.[3] There, too, according to one of the oldest and most persistent traditions, Peter set up his primary episcopal see or chair, whence he ruled the universal Church for a long time; some say three years, some seven. A statement in Paul's letter to the Galatians definitely establishes his presence in the city;[4] and his prolonged stay was asserted by Eusebius, Origen, Saint Gregory the Great, Saint John Chrysostom and many others.

Antioch the Glorious offered no ordinary opportunities to the head of a Church destined to be universal, at a moment when he could no longer remain safely in Jerusalem, and was not yet ready to go to Rome. Queen of the East, City of the Moon, it was the third largest of the Empire, most pleasantly and advantageously situated on the south bank of the broad Orontes below the foothills of the Amanus, about thirty miles from the port of Seleucis and the Great

[2] Acts 12:1-17
[3] Acts 18-23
[4] Gal 2:11

Sea. To a stranger entering it for the first time from such a tortuous and haphazard metropolis as Jerusalem, it must have seemed marvellously arranged, for it was laid out like a modern city in rectangles based on four broad avenues running east and west. The most southerly was the magnificent Corso, a boulevard between massive colonnades with separate lanes for heavy commercial traffic and the chariots or fashionable coaches of the rich, and covered porticoes on either side for pedestrians. Peter could hardly believe his eyes when he strolled along in the evening and saw it illuminated with oil lamps from end to end. The gorgeous buildings, too, were something to remember: palaces, theatres, temples, baths, aqueducts; and the various gardens jewelled with fountains, cascades, and rare statuary were unrivalled even in Rome and Alexandria.

Thoughtful Peter soon savoured something more important behind these dazzling appearances. He saw that there were three distinct worlds in this fabulously rich and cynical community, and that its half million inhabitants were divided by invisible walls as high as heaven and as deep as hell.

The pagans were well-fed, witty, and light-hearted; they cared for nothing but money, horse-racing, gladiatorial games, and sensual indulgences which were euphemistically named for that Grove of Daphne in the southwest suburb, that concealed so much depravity.

Side by side with these sybarites lived a community of Jews so large that only Jerusalem and Alexandria could boast of numerical superiority. They shared in the prosperity of their neighbours, but cleaving to their own faith and customs, and worshipped in a magnificent synagogue adorned with the trophies that Antiochus Epiphanes had stolen from the temple at Jerusalem.

It was to this busy and cultured Jewish community that the Cypriot Jews from Jerusalem had gone after the martyrdom of Stephen, first worshipping in the gorgeous synagogue and breaking bread at home, and later, as dissension grew, establishing their own houses of prayer. Most of them lived in a rather modest quarter called Epiphania which has completely vanished, though an ancient tradition places it on or near Singon Street close to the Pantheon. It was somewhere in that neighbourhood, probably, that Peter found a simple lodging with the one or two brethren who doubtless had accompanied him from Jerusalem. There he quietly completed the organization of the Antiochan Church, exchanged a few priceless letters, now lost, with his fellow apostles in the holy city, poured oil on the spiritual waters troubled by the dispute between the Gentile Christians and the Judaizers, and set up the universal see to which the brethren scattered far and wide constantly appealed.

The most urgent of his tasks probably seemed the arbitration of the dangerous dispute that had divided the flock into two zealous and often acrimonious factions. He was doing his best, but he was not succeeding very well, for he was too much of a Jew, despite his brief triumph with Cornelius, to feel at home with any but his own people; there was little in him of Paul's facile ability to be "all things to all men." Possibly it was this very thought that reminded him of the earnest little tentmaker from whom he had parted, with mixed sentiments, at Jerusalem. He remembered that Paul was conscious of having a special mission to the Gentiles, even as Peter himself had to his fellow Hebrews. It is very likely, therefore, that he decided to summon him to Antioch and try what his eloquence could do among the less amenable of the Greek and Syrian Christians. It is plain from the *Acts*,[5] at any rate, that about this time Barnabas left Antioch to hunt for Paul in Tarsus. Who would be likely to send him on this mission but Peter himself?

Barnabas found Paul at his old home in Cilicia and brought him back to Antioch. Soon afterwards the two left for Jerusalem, again probably under Peter's direction, to help relieve the sufferers from the famine, which was especially severe there. A few weeks later they returned to Antioch, bringing with them young John Mark, who was a cousin to Barnabas and apparently was full of enthusiasm for Paul's missionary ideas.

It is at least a tenable hypothesis that the famous and often exaggerated quarrel to which the Apostle of the Gentiles alludes in his letter to the Galatians occurred at this time. Many modern Catholic as well as Protestant writers place it later, after the Council of Jerusalem; but Saint Augustine's contrary opinion still has its probability, both psychologically and historically. Peter, on first going to Syria, had associated freely with the Gentile Christians. He had prayed with them, talked with them, and even shared un-koshered food with them. This gave acute offence to some of the more rigorous Jewish Christians. Peter was unable to placate these Judaizers as he had the brethren at Jerusalem after the baptism of Cornelius. They had been fortified by the arguments of certain astute pharisees and by the example of James the Less, now bishop

---

[5] Acts 11:23, 25

234

of Jerusalem, whom they regarded as their leader. Peter had placed himself officially on record against their position. Yet in a moment of weakness he deferred to them, to maintain harmony, and stopped eating with the Gentiles. Perhaps he went away on a missionary journey and forgot all about the incident.

Not so Paul. He was highly indignant when he returned from Jerusalem and heard of this. Years later, in defending his apostolate against the Judaizers, he recalled the circumstances to his disciples in Galatia:

"But when Kephas came to Antioch I withstood him to the face, because he was self-condemned. For before the arrival of some of James's people he used to eat with the Gentiles; but when they came he drew away and separated himself, fearing those of the circumcision. And the rest of the Jews fell in with his pretence, so that even Barnabas was carried away into their dissimulation.

And when I saw that their conduct was not straightforward according to the truth of the Gospel, I said to Kephas before them all:

'If you, who are a Jew, live like a Gentile and not like a Jew, how is it that you compel the Gentiles to live like Jews?'"[6]

Paul saw clearly and felt intensely, and doubtless justified himself to Peter in language fully as incisive as that of his letters. Man is not justified by the works of the Law, but by the faith of Jesus Christ.[7] ... By means of the Law I died to the Law, that I might live to God ... I do not set aside the grace of God: for if justification comes through the Law, then Christ died to no purpose!"[8] The promise of God was given to Abraham and to his descendant, Christ, not to his descendants, the Jews. The Law of Moses was given them 430 years later, and was meant to last only until Christ came.[9] In the Church of Christ there could be "neither Jew nor Greek, neither slave nor freeman, nor male and female."[10] Again, he demanded, "Is God the God of Jews only? Is he not also the God of Gentiles? Yes, of Gentiles as well, as indeed it is one God who justifies the circumcised by faith, and the uncircumcised through the same faith. Do we then nullify the Law through the faith? By no means! On the contrary, we corroborate the Law." [11]

---

[6] Gal 2:11-15
[7] ibid, 3:16
[8] ibid, 2:19-21
[9] Gal:3:16, 17, 24
[10] ibid, 3:28
[11] Rom 3:29-31

Peter knew that Paul was right, and admitted it humbly, though perhaps a little gruffly. He knew from divine revelation that his personal conduct had been inconsistent with the principles he had laid down for the guidance of the Church in Jerusalem. He had yielded either to a mistaken charity or to the old timidity which was the reverse side of his temperamental rashness.

Paul, too, was very human. Long after his curtain lecture to Peter and even after the Council of Jerusalem we find him circumcising young Timothy, to avoid offending the Judaizers,[12] and shaving his own head under the Nazarite vow to make an impression on them in the temple.[13] But Peter was learning, as Paul, too, would learn, not to expect from others more perfection than he discovered in himself. He would never perhaps feel quite at ease with this man. Years later he referred to the letters in which "our dear brother Paul" had spoken "according to the wisdom granted him," adding that "in them are some things difficult to understand, which the ignorant and unsettled distort, as they do other scriptures also, to their own ruin."[14] Yet if 'love covers a multitude of sins', as Peter reminds us in another epistle,[15] it is certainly potent with the mere eccentricities and divergences of temperament; and this is the last we hear of any discord between two great and holy men.

It was doubtless with Peter's blessing that Paul departed from Antioch soon after to undertake his first missionary journey, accompanied by Barnabas and Mark. Both of them parted from him later, finding his pace and methods too extreme. Mark returned to Jerusalem, and later attached himself to Peter, who called him "my son Mark." Nothing could stop Paul, however, once he had begun a task. He vanished for many months into the pagan wilds where the voice of Christ had sent his restless person on the quest for souls.

How long the head of the Church remained in Antioch after their departure it is futile to inquire. The only definite and undisputed historical fact about him, from then on, was his presence in Jerusalem five or six years later. But powerful traditions and logical inferences suggest that in the interim, using Antioch as his base, he made one or more missionary journeys of his own. His first encyclical letter, addressed to "the sojourners of the Dispersion," that is to say Jewish Christians in Pontus, Galatia, Bithynia, Cappadocia, and Asia Minor,

---

[12] Acts 16:3
[13] *ibid*, 20-26
[14] 2 Pet 3:15-16
[15] 1 Pet 4:9

is regarded as evidence that he himself had gone to those places and had converted many of the lost sheep of Israel, perhaps after Paul had turned indignantly from them to the Asiatic Gentiles.

If Peter had had Paul's exuberant gift of self-expression, it might appear that his life was just as dramatic and colourful, if not more so. Instead of keeping his trials and sufferings to himself, he might have told us how he also laboured for the faith "in afflictions, in necessities, in difficulties, in blows, in prisons, in riots, in labours, in vigils, in fasting, in chastity, in knowledge, in long suffering.[16] He might have given ample confirmation to Paul's observation that "I think God has caused us apostles to seem lowest of all, as though doomed to death; for we are made a spectacle to the world, both to angels and to men. We are fools for Christ's sake, while you are wise in Christ; we are feeble, while you are strong; you are in honour, while we are in contempt. Up to this present hour we suffer both hunger and thirst, and are ill-clad, and beaten, and are homeless wanderers; and we work hard, labouring with our own hands. Being reviled we bless; under persecution we endure; in face of slander, we entreat. We have become like the refuse of the world, the off-scouring of all, even until now."[17]

Peter also, perhaps, could say, "I am in labours more abundantly, in prisons more frequently, in floggings beyond measure, often in the midst of death! From Jews five times I received forty lashes less one. Thrice I was beaten with rods; once I was stoned; thrice I was shipwrecked; a night and a day I have passed on the sea; in frequent journeys, in dangers from rivers, in dangers from robbers, in dangers from my own nation, in dangers from Gentiles, in dangers in town, in dangers in the desert, in dangers at sea, in dangers among false brethren; in labour and hardship, in wakefulness often, in hunger and thirst, in frequent fasting, in cold and nakedness. Besides these external things, there is my daily anxiety – the care of all the churches ... The God and Father of the Lord Jesus, who is blessed forevermore, knows that I do not lie!"[18]

After all his unrecorded adventures Peter finally arrived, as many traditions and converging pieces of evidence establish, in Rome.[19] It is not so easy to conjecture how he got there. He may

---

[16] 2 Cor 6:4-6 1

[17] 1 Cor 4:9-13

[18] 2 Cor 11:23-3

[19] Protestant as well as Catholic scholarship now accepts this. See for example the strong assertion of Dr. F. H. Chase, Anglican bishop of Ely, in Pope, *Aids to the*

237

have gone to Pontus to preach to the Jews who had refused to hear Paul. He may then have proceeded to Ephesus on the great Roman road that ran straight from the East to that city of Diana; and there he may have taken a ship to Greece, traversing the isthmus on foot, and then crossing the Adriatic in another vessel. His presence in Corinth was a local tradition of such antiquity that Denis of Corinth wrote of it as of a notorious fact to Pope Soter in 171 A.D.[20] On the other hand he may have sailed straight west through the Mediterranean. If Luke had travelled with him instead of with Paul, we might have had a fascinating account of this momentous voyage.

Assuming that he went the easier way, he might have left sometime between the middle of March and mid-November, on any one of the hundred and twenty ships that put out from Alexandria for the west every year: the best would be one of the imperial corn ships to Puteoli. Accustomed to handling boats, the old fisherman of Galilee would walk about the decks in amazement, taking in every detail. For this was no fishing smack, but a mighty hulk of five-hundred tons or more, two-hundred feet long and fifty in the beam, with a pair of mighty paddles for steering, one on each side of the stern, and on her bow the golden figurehead of some pagan god. It was something to see a sailor going up like a monkey to take his post on the high crow's nest, and to watch the fluttering out of the huge mainsail, made of canvas strips joined by leather, with the foresail and topsail following.

In good weather such a ship would make the voyage in eight or nine days, even with a heavy cargo. One carried a huge Egyptian obelisk and 400,000 bushels of wheat besides her passengers. Another bore as many as 1,200 persons from Alexandria to Rome. This was exceptional. The average was more like the 500 mentioned by Josephus, or the 276 on the memorable voyage of Paul. As long as possible the skipper would hug the shore, guiding her south of Crete, or crossing to Rhodes in Asia Minor, thence due west. Or he would follow the coast of Palestine to Caesarea or Seleucia (the harbour of Antioch) and then, passing north or south of Cyprus, would brave the full power of the Great Sea.

Study of the Bible, London, 1922-1930, IV, 296. "That St. Peter visited Rome," said Dr. George Edmundson in one of the Bampton Lectures in 1913, "is admitted by everyone who studies the evidence in a fair and reasonable spirit." The evidence is overwhelming, despite some forced conjectures, in Barnes, *Christianity at Rome in the Apostolic Age* (London, 1938), *St. Peter in Rome, etc.,* 1900, etc.; and of course Fouard, *St. Pierre et les premières aunées du Christianisme,* Paris, 1893.
[20] Pope, *op. cit.* IV, 92, and his references.

It could be very rough sailing in foul weather. Luke's account of Paul's journey,[21] culminating in the wreck on the coast of Malta, suggests the risk that Peter assumed when he finally made up his mind to carry the gospel of Christ to the political and military centre of the world. Weeks or months may have elapsed before he finally saw Rhegium rising from the sea. The next day his ship would pass through the Straits of Messina, and on the one following would nose into the Gulf of Puteoli, where the masts were like a forest undulating with wind and water. Around the green shores above the deep blue, like a string of square pearls, he saw marble villas on the lovely estates of Baiae and Misenum. Above them all, in the background, dark, green and silent, arose the vine-clad height of Mount Vesuvius.

---

[21] Acts 27:4-20

29

He was not without company and guidance as he went ashore through all the bedlam of the docks of Puteoli and started on his way north.

Besides the one or two disciples who had accompanied him from Antioch, he had doubtless become acquainted on board with several other Jews, some of whom had been in Rome before and were going there again. They had already told him, no doubt, that it could take six or seven days to walk the 130 miles from Puteoli. With a little party of fellow Hebrews, all bearded and dressed very much like him, he walked along the side of the well-paved road, with vineyards and olive groves on either side, to where it merged, at the end of the day, with the larger one from Brundisium, the Via Appia.

He had heard much of this highway, but he could hardly have imagined, until he went on from Capua next morning, what a cross-section of humanity it presented, and how true it was that all roads led to Rome. Sitting by the roadside to munch his simple dinner, he saw the whole world strutting or whirling past. A sheikh from Persia, a camel driver from Arabia, a snake charmer from India, a Syrian bringing the newest carved idols from Antioch (all the rage in Italy), a Jewish pedler with his well assorted pack, black slaves from Numidia, blond ones from Britannia, some handsome young gladiators under guard on their way to an amphitheatre, a company of Praetorians or a troop of cavalry, a Roman noble reading or dicing in his brilliant coach with its two scarlet-clad outriders, a heavily painted and perfumed matron in a litter carried by six Cappadocians in gaudy livery – this was only part of what came and went there, day after day. It was nothing unusual to see a cortege of imperial chariots, heavily guarded, whirling a sickly and deformed old man to inspect his new harbour at Ostium. If there was a handsome woman with him, doubtless she was his third wife Messalina, a murderess whose adulteries, fabulous in number and bestiality, were known to everyone but Claudius. Perhaps as they vanished in a thunder of wheels and hooves, the lords of the world left a cloud of dust powdering the old man in dark Jewish garb who was on the way to visit their metropolis.

The next day, after passing Formia, and wondering perhaps who was the Cicero said to have been murdered in his villa there, the travellers crossed the Pontine marshes, bide the barge-canal of Augustus, to Forum Appia, where they would probably have to spend the night. But not to sleep. The Romans had no hotels in the modern sense. These "inns" on the Appian Way were nothing but shacks with unfurnished beds crowded together, with filthy wine taverns adjoining; and in the literature of the time the owners appear as thieves, gamblers, and panders, the maids as witches and harlots. What with the mosquitoes from the malarial swamps, the crawling vermin, the croaking frogs, the ribald songs, and guffaws of muleteers, this place was worse than the hovels of Jericho or the caves by the Dead Sea. It was no small relief to leave it behind and to push on to the heights of Velitrae and the Alban Hills.

The following day brought the wayfarers to Aricia and the soil of Latium; the next, to the mournful Campagna and the first glimpse, in the hazy distance, of a sombre mass of brownish and yellowish buildings, relieved by white flashes against the Alban and Sabine Hills. And that was Rome. Christ was coming at last to preach and suffer in the capital of the world, under the guise of a tired man who was doggedly completing his long journey between the urns and epitaphs of noble dead Romans and the graves of his humbler brethren in the Jewish catacombs.

Entering by the Capena Cate, the travellers would soon hear, if it was afternoon, the growling of wild beasts and the roaring of the spectators in the Circus Maximus, and after skirting the east side of the Palatine Hill, would enter the Forum through the Via Sacra.

What were the thoughts of such a man as Peter as he stood looking for the first time at that historic mart and meeting place to which all roads led? I doubt whether he was much impressed by the temples of Vesta and Castor, high above him at the left, or by the temple of Concord directly in front, or the Senate adjoining it, or the Record Office and the temples of Jupiter and Juno beyond. He had seen the matchless pagan shrines and public buildings of Antioch and Caesarea Philippi. "The gods of the heathen are devils," wrote King David, and their works would not stand.

The keen-eyed Vicar of Christ was more interested in the people who came and went by the thousands. Every social class was represented. Money lenders and bankers, hurrying to or from their offices at the north of the Forum, almost stepped upon the loungers who squatted on the lava pavement to play at dice or backgammon, or the urchins matching fingers exactly as they do today. It was not long before one learned that the grave men with purple stripes showing on their tunics beneath their astonishing togas were senators coming from a meeting in the temple of Castor. The stately ladies with similar purple bands on their gowns were senators' wives. Equestrians and men of business were gathering around a pillar to read the latest intelligences from the provinces or the senate in the Daily News, an official bulletin like an abbreviated and carefully censored modern newspaper. Hawkers with ear-splitting voices were inviting the passers-by to see the one-eyed woman from Cappodocia or the two-headed boy from Galatia. Many cults and races, too, were passing, unconsciously, in review before the visitors from Jerusalem. There were priests of Isis from Egypt, fakirs from the banks of the Ganges, blue-eyed merchants from eastern Spain, slaves of diverse colours on whose backs rested the foundations of empery.

To a Jew trained from childhood to see the directing hand of God in everything, there was something more than coincidence in the unification of the known world under the Empire at the very moment when the Messiah was about to offer the sacrifice of himself for all men. The intellectual conquest of Rome by Greek culture had given the apostles an opportunity to address mankind in the language the great Hebrew scholars had used in the Septuagint. The order and peace imposed by the Caesars had made it possible for them to travel on excellent roads from the Ganges to Britain, from Puteoli to the Rhine; and if their disciples did not have the gift of tongues that they had received in the first outpouring of the Holy Spirit, they could speak to men of every, race and nation in a universal idiom. Even with such advantages, however, the task of converting the pagan masses was going to be difficult. The slaves and sybarites that Peter had passed on the Via Appis would be willing to listen and to say, as the Athenians said to Paul, "We will hear you again on this subject." They were inclined to believe, superstitiously, that all religions might have some truth and efficacy. This broadmindedness made it almost a hopeless endeavour to persuade them that there was only one true God, one true religion. Peter was glad that his particular mission was to the Jews, not like Paul's to the Gentiles.

Even more fortunate for him and for the Church than the *Pax Romana* was the universal dispersion of the chosen people. When Christ was born, they were scattered, according to Josephus and Philo, to every inhabited land on earth. Paul would convert many gentiles, but even his first converts had been invariably Jews; and Peter could see the wise intent of God in casting his people far and wide to serve as intermediaries for the communication of his Word to the heathen. The debt that the Church owes to these persecuted exiles can hardly be exaggerated. Their own faith included the premises of Christianity, and as it pointed toward the messiah, they were Christians by anticipation whether they realized it or not. Not only that, but their temperament made them admirable instruments for its diffusion. Intense, intelligent, hard working, they were not, as a rule, softened by indulgence as the pagans were; and they were not afraid of difficulty.

Happily there was a large and growing community of Hebrews in Rome when Peter arrived. It seems to have originated with the captives of war that Pompey took there in 65 B.C. When Christ was born, there were about eight thousand. Within half a century the number had increased to sixty thousand. The more prosperous had become well-to-do merchants, factors, or bankers, and lived in houses scattered throughout the fourteen districts into which Augustus had divided the city; some even had positions in the imperial court. But the vast majority were still poor, hard-working people – hucksters, small traders, poets, actors, labourers – crowded together in the fourteenth district, a low and unhealthy congeries of slums west of the Tiber. It was plain to the Vicar of Christ that this was the place to begin his labours. He would go to the fourteen synagogues of Rome and tell his fellow Jews what he had seen and heard. So he betook himself to the ghetto across the Tiber, according to ancient tradition, and found himself a room there.

It is possible that he lived with or near Aquila and his wife Priscilla, two Jewish tent-makers from Pontus[1] who probably owed their conversion to him. And as the Romans had no conception of the dignity of labour, they were probably reduced, like most other artisans, to finding quarters in one of the massive tenements called *insulae* or "islands," which housed most of the despised lower classes. These were rickety fire-traps four or five stories high, each occupying an entire block between streets so narrow that Juvenal, living among the pigeons' nests near the roof, could almost shake hands with his neighbour across the way. The first floor was often occupied by shops, whose owners added to the confusion of the ill-smelling alleys, scattered with rubbish and garbage, by displaying their wares outside. Occasionally one of the upper stories would be an apartment, like a modern flat; but most of them were divided into single rooms, where the occupants could only sleep and eat,

---

[1] Acts 18:2

with no light but that of wax candles and what seeped in otherwise from the gloomy exteriors. The noise was terrific, especially at night, when wagons, prohibited during the day by an imperial edict, added their rattle to the cacophony of a thousand other nuisances that made sleep so difficult. In the summer the heat was intolerable.

Danger lent spice if not contentment to this life. The Tiber had a way of overflowing after heavy rains, and the *insulae*, being mostly in the lower districts, collapsed with slight provocation over the heads of their occupants. A fire could start from an overturned candle, and quickly consume a whole block, sometimes an entire quarter, like so much paper. With such primitive fire apparatus as pails, siphons and wet blankets the imperial watch were often at a disadvantage. But life was cheap, and nobody seemed to care.

These people, having lost the primitive and universal concept of a creator and a life with rewards and punishments after death, were coming to look upon themselves as animals; but as man can never be a mere beast, they were living on a still lower level in many respects. To be sure, the fantastic banquets with their *vomitoria* were probably more exceptional than they have been made to appear. The average well-to-do family dined moderately and decorously, discussing lines of Ovid or Horace, the latest witticism of Petronius Arbiter, or the newest *sententia* of Seneca, as they sipped their Falernian wine. They had their elaborate baths, their games, their investments. But the old days of Latium were gone.

Two good indices which are really one – the family and the position of woman – augured badly for the future. Although Roman women were still freer than in the pagan East, and a few enjoyed a dignity and respect comparable to that of Jewish matrons, this was changing rapidly with the increase of divorce, adultery, abnormal vice, and the resulting disintegration of family life. The efforts of the Caesars to arrest the falling birth rate by edict were as futile as Canute's command to the North Sea. Among the contributing causes were probably abortion and contraception, which must have been evils of long standing when Saint Augustine denounced them three centuries later.[2] Deformed children were killed or exposed at birth. With the growing contempt for human life and personality, suicide and other forms of "euthanasia" were common. The empire was beginning to die of broadmindedness, as Chesterton said somewhere, before it had reached physical maturity. It had no gasoline or

---

[2] *De Nuptiis.* For a detailed account of Roman life and customs, see Tucker, *Life in the Roman World of Nero and St. Paul,* New York, Macmillan, 1929 reprint.

electricity, but in other respects it was quite "modern."

As for the lower orders with whom Peter presumably was more familiar, the middle class was rapidly crumbling away between the upper and under millstones of concentrated wealth and hopeless cringing poverty. Its ancient industry, patience, broad humour and devotion to the Lares and Penates of the home were yielding to the general corruption, while heavier and heavier taxes forced its members down into the greasy ranks of the proletariat.

The poor, both slaves and freemen, were the children and bondsmen of despair. The former had no rights whatever, and could be killed by their masters with impunity. They did most of the household and farm work, besides assisting in other occupations. Free workmen had to compete with their labour, with disastrous effect on wages. Sated with government corn and animal pleasures, these hopeless wretches of both categories sat herded day after day in the foul theatres or better, if they could, in the Circus Maximus and other stadia (the Colosseum was not yet built) and screamed, "Give him the steel!" when a gladiator was disarmed, or flushed with pleasure to see a slave torn to ribbons by a hungry lion. They had whipped their bored minds and tired nerves to the last of the depravities that began with lechery and ended with a perverted enjoyment of bloodshed for its own sake.

It was no hardship to turn from all this to the Jews, who had kept their own mysterious vigour and integrity to a gratifying degree. The inscriptions in their cemeteries still offer mute testimony that they lived on a far higher plane than their pagan neighbours. Their homes were shrines compared to such dens as Plautus presents, for example, in the *Menaechmi*. Every Saturday they repaired to their synagogues to hear the words that the creator had spoken to Moses and had placed on the tongues of his other prophets, and to lift their hearts to him in prayer. They were probably more devout, man for man, than their brethren in Palestine. The nostalgia of exile sharpens perceptions and deepens old loyalties. The satirists wrote with contempt of most Jews as hawkers, rag-pickers, old clothes dealers, dirty and odorous, with swarms of tattered children. But they paid tribute to their mutual charity and their reverence for marriage.[3]

If Peter had left an account of his visit to one of these synagogues on his first sabbath in Rome, we may be sure it would not differ greatly from the experience of Paul. As a guest he arose

---

[3] e.g. Tacitus, *Hist.* V, S.

at the invitation of the president to comment on the day's reading from the scriptures. He went to the point at once, bluntly and boldly telling the congregation that the Messiah had come, had died, risen, and ascended to heaven; that he had been an eye-witness of his glory and his sufferings, and had come to tell them that they might have eternal life in his Name. Some of them may have heard rumours to the same effect from Jerusalem, but whether incredulous or not, they were fascinated by this opportunity to hear the sensational story at firsthand, and they listened courteously, avidly, until he had finished. They asked questions and he replied. Some went to see him at his lodgings, and several believed him. Tradition has it that he baptized these converts in the Tiber nearby. It was almost as muddy as the lower Jordan, especially after a rain. The essential requirement, however, had been met, and the Christian community of Rome had been born. The believers continued to pray in the synagogue, but they gathered elsewhere for the Agape and the breaking of the Bread. In the course of time they were joined by gentile converts.

In the synagogues were doubtless men of pharisaic traditions who found it difficult to believe that the messiah could be as Peter described him, or that He would curtail the hundreds of ceremonial precepts in any way. At first they were at a loss; but as time went on they received answers from home. They were now in a position to tell the congregation that the most respected men in Judea regarded this stranger as a jail-bird and a disturber of the peace, an enemy of God and Moses, whose purpose obviously was to destroy the Jewish nation. Disputes and demonstrations occurred when he appeared in the synagogues. The Christian Jews and Peter replied. All over the city there were fist fights, riots, clamours and hootings, in which the Christians, being fewer, undoubtedly fared badly.

News of this got to the Capitoline Hill, and action was prompt. If there was anything the Caesars had a right to boast about, it was their service to peace and order. The Jews were respected but not popular in Rome. As an alien race who in the main refused to compromise with syncretism, and clung to their own national cult with a determination that seemed stubborn and bigoted, they were disliked and perhaps a little bit feared. They had been the victims, too, of many cruel slanders, especially from the stentorian mouth of the notorious Jew-baiter Apion, who had come from Alexandria, after similar efforts there, to stir up popular hatred against them. He accused them of ritual murder, cannibalism, and various obscene rites such as worshipping the head of an ass behind locked doors. Fortunately Tiberius had refused to believe these lies, and had discredited Apion by calling him "the tinkling cymbal of the world." Some of the malice remained darkly in circulation, however, waiting for a crisis to bring it to the surface. When the sacred peace was broken, and the offenders were found to be Jews in every instance, Claudius, sometime in 49 A.D., ordered them all banished, according to Suetonius. Dio Cassius says that the order was rescinded. Before this happened, if it did happen, swarms of Jews fled from the city and from Italy, as the *Acts* make plain.

The imperial police made no distinction between Jews who had accepted the revelation of Christ and those who had refused to do so. A Jew was a Jew to them; they were all alike, queer people, foreigners, disturbers. We are to imagine the strange spectacle, then, of the Apostle Peter, his converts Aquila and Priscilla, and other believers hurrying through the Capena Gate with many Hebrew fugitives, whose resentment against them had caused the disaster. Change and travel were nothing new, however, to these people. Their mobility was astonishing. The following year we find Aquila and his wife as far away as Corinth, as hosts to their fellow-tentmaker, the Apostle Paul.

Peter, too, boarded a ship at Ostium or Puteoli, and sailed for the east. It is tradition that includes him among the exiles. But it is historical fact that he reappeared in Jerusalem a few months later, in 49 or 50 A.D.

30

His arrival could not have been timed better. It was plain to all the apostles that the Church must define her position on the question raised by the Judaizers, and as if blown mysteriously together by the breath of the Holy Spirit to carry out his will, they appeared in Jerusalem one after another from missionary fields far and wide. Paul had just come up through Samaria, after his second journey, bringing with him Barnabas and a young gentile convert from Crete named Titus. He had had another dispute with the champions of circumcision at Antioch and, fortified by a revelation and the appeals of his brethren, he was resolved upon a fight to the finish. Now the presence of Peter the Rock made it possible to hold the first formal Council of the Catholic Church.

On the surface the issue seemed to be one of mere formalities. The Judaizers felt that when they had borne the brunt of the conflict, keeping the Mosaic Law as fully as possible in addition to their duties as Christians, it was only fair that the gentiles do likewise. They argued that the Lord had come to fulfil, not destroy the Law, and that he himself had been circumcised. They pointed to James the Less, bishop of Jerusalem, as a brilliant example. He was so devout, so charitable, so reverent in the temple that he was said to be as popular among Jews as among the Christians.

The other faction, of which Paul, with the prestige of his great labours, was becoming the leader, pointed out that the Judaizers themselves were unable to keep the hundreds of ceremonial precepts; that these meant that Christ was coming, and with his coming were fulfilled and abolished. They cited his example regarding sabbath observance and washing before meals. They had another argument, hard to answer, in Peter's vision at Joppa. It was clear that the Lord, having been rejected by a majority of his people, wished to admit the gentiles to his Church; and circumcision, for example, was an unnecessary obstacle.

The real issue went much deeper. It was the fundamental one that Saint Athanasius disclosed beneath the false face of the still more dangerous form of Judaizing known as Arianism. It was the affirmation or denial of the deity of Jesus Christ. If he was truly God, the Church he had founded was the one true world religion, with his authority to teach, define, and interpret. The teachings of Abraham and Moses, who were only men, must be secondary and

248

relative. But if the full Law was indispensable to salvation, as the Judaizers seemed to regard it, the sacrifice of Christ was unnecessary and meaningless. "The blood of bulls and goats was powerless to take away sins."[1] Not so the blood of Christ.

To "trample on the Son of God" and "disregard the blood of the Covenant," cried Paul with passion, was an unpardonable crime. Regardless of what the intentions of the Judaizers were, their teachings pointed toward a repudiation of Christ's authority, implying at least a denial of who he is. Instead of spreading the blessing of Abraham to all nations, the Church would remain a Jewish nationalistic faction within the synagogue. It would wither away and die. In fact there were already secret unbelievers among the Judaizers. Paul complained of pharisees who pretended conversion to bore from within, "brethren surreptitiously introduced, who stole in to spy out our freedom, which we possess in Christ Jesus, in order to reduce us to bondage."[2]

The preliminary discussions were long and bitter. Some of the leading Judaizers tried to shout Paul down, others cried that he should have Timothy and other converts circumcised at once "and enjoin them to observe the Law of Moses!"[3] Paul replied with cutting and glowing logic. It was a satisfaction to remember later that he had yielded to them "not even for an hour."[4] But he took the precaution to go at once to make sure that Peter, James, and John, "the recognized pillars," were on his side. This was the time when they confirmed his special mission to the gentiles and gave him and Barnabas "the right hand of fellowship."[5]

When the Council finally began after an Agape and what we would call a Mass, there was another long debate which the writer of the *Acts* passes over lightly, fearing perhaps to open old wounds. But from Paul's remarks about the pharisees and Judaizers, we may be sure they laid down the claims of the complete Old Law in no timid or uncertain fashion.

Peter then arose and made a short masterly address:

"Brethren, you know that a while ago God made choice among you that through my mouth the gentiles should hear the message of the gospel and believe. And God, who knows the heart, gave evidence in their behalf by granting the Holy Spirit to them, just as

[1] Heb 10:4
[2] Gal 2:4
[3] Acts 15:5
[4] Gal loc. cit.
[5] ibid

he did to us; and he made no distinction between us and them, but purified their hearts by the faith. Now, therefore, why do you call God's act into question by placing a yoke upon the necks of the disciples, which neither our fathers nor we were able to bear? But on the contrary, we believe that we are to be saved through the grace of the Lord Jesus Christ, even as they."

Perhaps the Judaizers had expected Peter to waver as he had at Antioch. But he was speaking officially now as head of the Church, and his presence was so venerable, his authority so unquestioned, his position so clear that they could think of no reply; and "the whole assembly was silent"[6] Barnabas and Paul now told the wonderful story of the Gentiles who had come into the Church during their journey in Asia Minor. James the Less, Bishop of Jerusalem, then arose, the last hope of the party of the circumcision. They did not know that he was in almost perfect agreement with Peter, Paul, and John.

"Brethren, listen to me!" he said. "Simon has related how God first visited the Gentiles, to take from among them a people for his name. And the words of the prophets accord with this; as it is written: 'After this I will return, and rebuild the fallen tent of David, and will rebuild its ruins, and will re-erect it; that the rest of mankind may seek out the Lord, and all the gentiles upon whom my name is called, says the Lord, who makes these things known from of old:

"Therefore my judgment is, not to disquiet those converted to God from among the gentiles, but to write to them to abstain from the defilement of idols, from fornication, from what is strangled, and from blood. For Moses from ancient times has his preachers in every town, being read in the synagogues every Sabbath."[7]

Peter accepted the slight concession, for he was anxious to make it as easy as possible for the Judaizers to remain in the Church, and for Jews to enter. Nothing remained but for the Council to agree unanimously upon its policy. It did so in the following letter:

"The Apostles and Presbyters, Brethren

To the Brethren of the Gentiles living at Antioch, Syria and Cilicia:

Greeting.

As we have heard that some, coming out from among us, to

[6] Acts 15:12
[7] Acts 15:14-21

whom we gave no such instructions, have been disturbing you with assertions unsettling your minds, it has seemed good to us, being assembled in one body, to choose out men and send them to you with our beloved Barnabas and Paul – men who have hazarded their lives for the name of Our Lord Jesus Christ. We have therefore sent Judas and Silas, who themselves will tell you the same things by word of mouth. For it has seemed good to the Holy Spirit and to us to lay upon you no further burden than these necessary things: that you abstain from things sacrificed to idols, from blood, from things strangled, and from fornication; from which if you keep yourselves you will be doing well. Farewell."[8]

There is much more in these simple phrases than meets the eye.

A few Jews, headed by a former fisherman, announce a decision bound to have wide and lasting consequences. They appeal not to Moses and the prophets, not even to God the Father or to Christ, but to no authority outside themselves under the collective guidance of the Holy Spirit. "It has seemed good to the Holy Spirit and to us."[9] No such assertion had ever been made before in Israel.

The decision itself is no less arresting. These men in effect are abolishing the rite of circumcision which was as important to Jews under the Old Law as Baptism under the New: the rite to which Christ himself had submitted, and which he had given them no command, so far as the New Testament reveals, to do away with. They are also discarding most of the ceremonial precepts; they are announcing, in effect, that they, the Church, are the only authentic religious authority, and that the synagogue and temple no longer have any standing as such.

The method of making known the decision reveals a great deal more about the nature of the Church. In this, her first official document, she indicates a peculiar distrust of documents. The Lord did not commit his teachings to writing. He wrote nothing but those few cryptic words on the floor of the temple. What he did was to gather around him a group of baptized human beings, the unified living society that has been called his Mystical Body. The authority of this organism could not possibly reside in any document, for the New Testament did not yet exist: it is not certain that even Matthew's gospel had been written. Books are made by men, and

---

[8] *ibid*, 15:24-29

[9] ἔδοξεν γάρ τῷ πνεύματι τῷ ἁγίῳ χαί ἡμιν literally, "It has seemed good to the breath of the Spirit and to us."

the ultimate authority is not in a writing, as Father McNabb trenchantly observed, but in a writer. If the New Testament should be destroyed after coming piecemeal into existence, if the Old Testament should be obliterated by catastrophe, the Church would go on teaching by word of mouth, as the apostles taught, as long as human life itself persisted. As if to stress this, the Council does not depend even upon its own letter, for it sends two conciliar legates, Judas and Silas (the first such pair in history) to give the message orally. Important though the document is, it is secondary to them: "they will tell you the same things by word of mouth."

Why is the message entrusted to these two legates, and not to Barnabas and Paul, who are of higher rank in the Church, and have brought the dispute from Antioch to the Council? Why is Paul, the leader of the victorious faction, placed after Barnabas? On the surface, it might seem that the most brilliant intellect and tireless will among the Christians deserves better treatment at the hands of his brethren. But this is to impute petty motives to great and holy men who obviously have solid and just ones. It is to forget, too, that the Holy Spirit guides their decisions, and may see fit to answer, long in advance, the unbelieving exegetes who will exaggerate the position of Paul, to disparage the Church. Paul has great intellectual gifts, but it is Peter who loves Jesus best and Peter whom he has chosen to be head of his Church. However, the Council includes Barnabas and Paul as a delicate compliment for the services they have rendered to truth. But knowing that the Judaizing brethren will surely resent getting the news of their defeat from the hands of those chiefly responsible for it, they commit the message to Judas and Silas, and the wounds in Christ's Mystical Body begin to heal.

Finally, the position of Peter as head of the Church is all the more clear because the writer of the *Acts* makes no attempt to stress it. There is nothing arrogant or dictatorial in Peter's attitude, and he is willing to accept James's amendment.[10] Yet his own calm and majestic speech is clearly the decisive one.

What is not so obvious is the anguish it must have cost the old man to make his choice and to stand by it. For Peter loved his people next only to God, and this, he knew, was farewell. Let Paul

---

[10] The best short analysis of the Council I have seen is that of Father Vincent McNabb, in a paper he read at Oxford during the Church Unity Octave in January 1943, reprinted by Blackfriars in their pamphlet, *The Very Reverend Father Vincent McNabb, O.P., S.I.M.* Oxford, 1943, shortly after his saintly death. I could do no better than try to summarize his thought here, with the kind permission of Blackfriars.

again be spokesman for him and for every Jew who has had to make the same heroic decision: "I speak the truth in Christ – I do not lie, my conscience bearing me witness in the Holy Spirit – that I have a great grief and ceaseless pain in my heart; for I could wish that I myself were anathema from Christ for my brothers' sake, who are my kindred in the flesh, who are Israelites; to whom belong by adoption, and the glory, and the covenants, and the giving of the Law, and the divine worship, and the promises; of whom were the patriarchs, and from whom, as regards the flesh, is the Christ, who is God over all, blessed for all eternity."[11]

On other occasions Paul spoke of the Jews with some asperity as "workers of evil,"[12] "flesh-cutters,"[13] "silly talkers and deceivers,"[14] "the Jews, who put to death the Lord Jesus and the prophets, and drove us out" and are "displeasing to God and opposed to all men by prohibiting us to speak to the gentiles lest they should be saved."[15] These were the complaints of a tired, exasperated man who had done his best in vain. Those who have overstressed their importance have forgotten first that "Jews" in the New Testament usually refers to official Judaism rather than the Jewish people as such, and secondly, that Paul's real thought is to be found in many longer passages, where the subject is treated more deliberately and judiciously. He warned the Roman gentile converts not to lay rash hands on the mystery of Jewish unbelief, since it was a part of a divine plan beyond the powers of human reason to understand. The Jews had rejected God, but he had not rejected them. In his inscrutable wisdom he had even made use of their loss to benefit the very gentiles who denounced them. "I ask you, then, did they so stumble as to fall utterly? Not so! But by their transgression salvation has come to the gentiles in a way to incite themselves to emulation. But if their transgression has enriched the world, and their loss has enriched the gentiles, how much greater enrichment will not their complete conversion bring!"[16] ... "For I do not wish you, brethren, to be ignorant of this mystery – lest you should think too highly of yourselves – that hardening has come upon Israel in part, until the full number of the gentiles enter and so all Israel shall be saved."[17]

---

[11] Rom 9:1-5
[12] Phil 3:2
[13] *ibid* 3:3
[14] Titus 1:10
[15] 1 Thess 2:15-16
[16] Rom 11:11-12
[17] *ibid* 11:16

They were cut off from the original olive tree and the gentiles grafted on. But God could cut off the gentiles and put back the Jews, if they came to believe.[18]

If this was Paul's reasoning, we may be sure it was Peter's also. He had just as good grounds for denouncing the unbelievers – if that was the right way to solve "the Jewish question." He had heard Christ himself excoriate the high priests and pharisees to their faces in terrible and holy words never to be forgotten. It must be significant that with such an example before him, Peter never followed it except in a sentence of his first sermon which he qualified in his second with, "I know, brethren, you did it through ignorance, as did your rulers." It was fitting for Jesus to say what he had said, for the judgment of men had been committed to him as Son of God. Peter was only a man, and though as keeper of the Keys he had the right to forgive or retain sins, he did not regard this apparently, as permission to lay his hands upon this mystery of repudiation. He who had denied his Lord after living in close friendship with him for three years could never bring himself to the point of condemning men with no such advantage, particularly if they had heard of him in their dispersion, and only from his enemies. He does not even mention the Jews in fact, in his two encyclical letters. This is particularly significant considering the vigorous language he employs against heretics within the Church.

It must be more than a coincidence, too, that for nineteen centuries the successors of Peter, numbering nearly three hundred, have followed his example with a consistency to which Jewish scholars have paid generous tribute. The Holy See has never turned its face against the Jews except to perform its obvious duty of protecting Christians from their unbelief. It has repeatedly stood between them and destruction, down to our own time. It forbade their persecution in the Middle Ages, denouncing such lies as those accusing them of ritual murder, or of causing the Black Death by poisoning the wells. Through all their long exile it followed them with the loving and sorrowful eyes of Peter, who had to listen to God rather than to men.

It is a curious fact, too, that although the Church has continued to pray for the conversion of the Jews, she has never made any particular effort to bring it about. The local attempts of individual Catholic zealots in this direction have almost invariably had unfortunate effects both for the Church and for the Jews. Their ex-

---

[18] *ibid* 11:23-24

254

pulsion from Spain, for example, scattered them through Europe to
help promote the disastrous revolt of the sixteenth century. The
Church herself remembered the hint given by the Lord that they
would not be converted until "the times of the nations are completed," presumably in the last days. Not man but God would
remove the scales from their eyes, and in his own time and his own
way. Saint Gregory the Great believed that this would be the
mission of Elijah when he returned to the earth. From this point of
view it would be both futile and criminal to attempt to force a
solution of the mystery. Saint Augustine expressed it very well in
his answer to the Jew-baiting Faustus.[19] He admitted that the Jews
seemed to have been prefigured by Cain wandering through the
world, branded and accursed for the crime of killing his brother.
But he reminded his adversary that God had pronounced a seven-
fold curse on anyone who should kill Cain – or the Jews. As Saint
Bernard headed off a mob bent upon a pogrom, he cried to them,
"You are of your father the devil, and his work you will do!"
Pharisaic Christians have sought to place on the back of the wandering Jew the whole burden of human iniquity. Those who know
Him better say, "It is for him to judge the Jews. All we know is that
we, his friends, betray him daily. There is no excuse for us. He died
for our sins. We are the Christ-killers."

Peter's love for his people even after he parted from them
finds curious confirmation in two extremes of opinion. The
Jew-baiting heretic Marcion, described by Saint Polycarp as "the
first-born of Satan," accused him of being a Judaizer. The Talmud
presents him in the same light, but obviously as a compliment, in an
odd tale which asserts, with a touching sincerity despite certain
fantastic errors, that "twelve wicked men went out … and they
misled Israel, for they said they were apostles of the Crucified; and
they drew to themselves a large number from among the children of
Israel." The elders of Zion were afflicted, and humbling
themselves, confessed their sins to one another, asking God's
direction. "As they finished the prayer, up rose an elder from their
midst, whose name was Simeon Kepha." He learned the ineffable
name, inserted it in his flesh, and went to the metropolis of the
Nazarenes to profess that he was an apostle of Christ. He restored a
leper and raised the dead. When the Nazarenes acknowledged him,
he told them that Christ, though he hated Israel, wished to leave it
as a witness of the Crucifixion, and therefore commanded them

---

[19] Reply to *Faustus the Manichee*, XX.

"that you do no evil to the Jews; and if a Jew says to a Nazarene, 'Go with me one parasang,' let him go with him two parasangs ... And if you do this, you will deserve to sit with him in his portion."

Peter remained with the Nazarenes, eating only the bread of misery and drinking the water of affliction, and lived in a tower till he died.

Other rabbinical writers make him the author of certain liturgical poems repeated for centuries in the synagogues on Sabbaths and feast-days. In still another legend, he is secretly a Jew who entered the Christian community only to destroy it on behalf of Israel. He advised Christians to throw off the law of Moses completely, but he did this craftily, knowing that the Church, when separated from Moses and the Synagogue, would wither away and die.[20]

The truth underlying all this was that Peter did not cease to love the Jews when he committed them to the hands of God until the last days. He grieved for them, but not without hope. In the light of what he now knew there was much consolation in the pages of the Old Testament as he pored over them again and again. "You thought evil against me," said Joseph, prefiguring Christ, as he forgave his brethren, "but God turned it into good, that he might exalt me, as at present you see, and might save many people."[21] And there was that passage in the Book of Deuteronomy where after all his threats and promises to his people, the Lord God had said to Moses:

"Now when all these things shall come upon you, the blessing or the curse, which I have set forth before you, and you shall be touched with repentance of your heart among all the nations into which the Lord your God shall have scattered you, and shall return to him, and obey his commandments, as I command you this day, you and your children, with all your heart, and with all your soul: the Lord your God will bring back again your captivity, and will have mercy on you, and gather you again out of all the nations, into which he scattered you before. If you be driven as far as the poles of heaven, the Lord your God will fetch you back from there, and will take you to himself, and bring you into the land which your fathers possessed, and you shall possess it, and blessing you, he will make you more numerous than were your fathers. The Lord your God will circumcise your heart and the heart of your seed, that you

---

[20] For these and other particulars, see Edersheim, *op. cit.* Vol. II, p. 788, *et. seq.* Appendix XVIII, and his references.
[21] Gen 50:20

may love the Lord your God with all your heart and with all your soul, that you may live. And he will turn all these curses upon your enemies, and upon them that hate and persecute you."[22]

Another of Peter's sorrows must have been the death of the Lord's mother. There are no historical facts as to time or place. An old tradition has it that she had gone to Ephesus with John, returned to Jerusalem with him just before the Council in 49 or 50, and died there. The apostles laid her in a grave, the site of which is still pointed out, in the Garden of Gethsemane. Later, on going to pray there, they found no trace of the body. And millions of Christians have believed that it was borne to heaven at night by angels, there to be united in glory with her immaculate soul. For it was fitting that the virgin mother of the Christ, who had been spared the stain of original sin, should be saved also, as he was, from corruption. After mothering him she had been mother to his infant Church. With the Council of Jerusalem that child had come of age, and her work on earth being done, she had died of love, desiring only to be with the God who had been Father, Spouse, and Son to her.

Peter never mentioned her in his brief and reticent writings. Yet it does not follow that her death left him unmoved, or that he did not kneel at the empty grave to ask the Lily of Israel to pray that the lost sheep would find their way home at last.

---

[22] Deut 30:1-10

31

When he finally returned to Rome, some time after 54 A.D., he must have begun to show his age, which was over sixty. His hair turning white, his keen eyes more blue, his sad face smiling easily, like a child's, he was one to remark and remember. There was something about him at once selfless and intensely personal, very plain yet very distinctive.

He did not go to the ghetto this time. He would not have been welcome there. The breach had been final and definite, and since the riots of 49, the Christians had moved to another part of the Trastevere, or had crossed the river. Many of them had taken over small homes in a rather run-down section on the Aventine. It was higher and more healthy there, and the separate dwellings offered a better opportunity for such a family life as Christians and Jews preferred. Among the settlers there, according to archaeological evidence, were the Jewish Christians Aquila and Priscilla, who were back in town after risking their lives to save Paul's in Ephesus. Their house was the centre of a "congregation" which met presumably for the celebration of the Eucharist.[1] It was probably with them, too, that Peter made his home during this second sojourn in Rome. It was in their simple house that he found the quiet, denied him in the insulae, to write his letters and to rule the universal Church.

Other traditions associate him more or less vaguely with some of the gentile converts who were now becoming so numerous. The slaves he had baptized in the ghetto had converted their masters, and the process was continuing. The next step would be that the masters, perhaps on death-beds, would begin to liberate the slaves. By the fourth century, Saint Melania and many others would be giving freedom to thousands of such before selling their lands and distributing the proceeds among the poor. In this way the Church had already quietly begun the destruction of the vast injustice on which Roman society rested. If Peter and Paul had preached openly against it, they would either have failed dismally, or would have created an anarchy greater than the evil itself. Yet the seed had been planted. And we may be sure that when Peter was called upon to visit the town houses of the more prosperous gentile converts, he looked with no approving eye upon a magnificence sweated from

---

[1] Rom 16:3-5. In Nero's time the rich were beginning to reclaim the Aventine from the poor. Aquila and his wife may have been clients or factors of the Cornelii.

the backs of slaves.

One tradition has it that he offered the Holy Sacrifice in the house of Senator Pudens. Another represents that he baptized young Marcus Acilius Glabrio, scion of a senatorial family, who was to be consul in 91, and a Christian martyr under Domitian. The gardens of his family covered the whole Pincian Hill, over the catacomb of Saint Priscilla on the Via Salaria. The first visit of Peter to such an establishment must have been intensely interesting. For the villa of the Glabrios would be very different from the homes of the rich he had entered with the Lord in Judea. It stood high on the hill, commanding a magnificent view and surrounded by luxuriant gardens. He passed through a vestibule, and then through double doors of bronze to the atrium. This corresponded roughly to the interior court of a Jewish house, but it was roofed over, save for an aperture through which the rain, gathered from the eaves, fell into a basin below known as the peripluvium. It was the reception hall and, as the excavations at Pompeii disclosed, it could be very beautiful. The floor was an intricate mosaic of fine marble, kept immaculate by the frequent use of feather brooms. The walls, too, were of delicately tinted marbles, relieved sometimes by tapestries, sometimes by paintings. Lovely statues in the niches and recesses completed the effect of serene opulence. Through glass windows at the further end of the atrium there was a little vista of a formal garden, where the family frequently gathered and usually dined in fair warm weather.

The whole house corresponded to the elegance Peter had noticed in the atrium. The glass windows, the long sloping-backed chairs that women liked, the comfortable couches used for reading or writing, the bronze chairs, the oil lamps of many curious shapes, the beautiful mirrors – even the copper pots and jars in the kitchen, with their graceful forms and original designs, called attention to the thoroughness with which the Romans did everything.

A family like that of the Glabrios was not necessarily soft and spoiled. The master would arise at dawn or earlier, have a snack of breakfast and spend the morning at work, either at home or in the forum. By nine o'clock his atrium would be full of visitors, waiting to ask him about this business or that. Others would intercept him on the way as he proceeded with a growing attendance of clients before and after. Between five in the morning and noon he usually did a pretty good day's work, while his wife went shopping or visiting. After a light lunch he had his siesta. At four o'clock he was ready for dinner.

The four o'clock dinners were not what Peter would have chosen for himself, but he was no prude, and with the example and words of Christ always in his mind, he doubtless ate and drank such things as were set before him on occasion. He was keenly interested in the family and their friends as they assembled in the garden among the gorgeous flowers and marble statuary under the deep blue sky of late afternoon – the ladies in long and queenly gowns, the men in white tunics after they had laid aside their togas; all chatting and laughing as if they enjoyed being alive. In winter these dinners were held indoors, where the arrangement was quite similar to that of Palestine. There were several square tables, with nine couches at each, three to a side, the fourth side being left open for serving. The most notable difference was that here the ladies had no separate tables. The dinner was excellent, but moderate; the wine very good.

More interesting to an old ascetic like Peter would be the conversation that followed. There would be no political gossip, for that would be dangerous. Nevertheless many hints would be dropped about personalities in the imperial court, and affairs in general. It was gratifying to know that friends of the Glabrios, some of them important persons, were becoming interested in the Church. In Paul's letter to the Romans he greets "the family of Aristobulus" who may have been a nephew of King Herod; "the family of Narcissus," believed to have been a secretary to the Emperor Claudius. In another letter he speaks of the Christians in "Caesar's household."

One thing that Peter undoubtedly disliked about the Roman houses was that there was no place on the roof for observation and prayer. It is likely, too, that walking one morning in the humble garden of Aquila on the Aventine, he saw the sumptuous park of the Caesars on the Vatican Hill opposite, and caught a glimpse of the young emperor driving one of his chariots furiously about his own race track just where Saint Peter's now stands. He was an overgrown blond boy with a low brow, a rather handsome, but pasty and arrogant face, a thick neck, a paunchy body and thin legs. This was Nero, the master of the world.

The Vicar of Christ had heard something, of course, about the death of Claudius in 54 A.D. Having murdered the nymphomaniac Messalina, he had been poisoned by his fourth wife and niece Agrippina, who had then succeeded in having her son raised to the purple, at the age of seventeen, by the Praetorian guards. Not since mad Caligula had such a grotesque choice been made. Nero was a homosexual egomaniac obsessed with the idea that he was an artist such as the world had never seen, nor would again. It was something new but not reassuring for the Roman people to see their emperor strutting on the public stage like any professional singer, reciting his own mediocre poems to the strumming of his harp; or playing on the flute or bagpipes; or displaying his disgusting body in ungainly dances. The mob applauded him wildly, especially after he added a money dole to their free corn and circuses. But although he inhaled the incense of their praise, he did not trust their constancy too far. Whenever he appeared on the stage, a claque of paid "boomers" or "rattlers" was scattered through the audience to stimulate the applause. The doors were locked as soon as the show began, so that no one could leave unless perhaps by pretending to be dead and being carried out.

Unfortunately there was a darker side to this colossal joke on the Roman people. The ambitious Agrippina and two of his tutors, the Spanish philosopher Seneca, and Burrus, head of the imperial police, had exercised a considerable restraint upon Caesar's less attractive impulses during the first years of his reign. These influences he gradually shook off, however, as his art, that is to say himself, became all in all to him. He had his mother strangled, drove the faithful Seneca to exile and perhaps suicide, and probably poisoned Burrus. When anyone incurred his displeasure thereafter, he was likely to send him a little dagger or a bit of poison with a brief note inviting him to commit suicide. He became more and more extravagant. When he needed money, as he often did, he would send some rich man into exile on any convenient pretext: in modern parlance he would "purge" the Senate of him – and confiscate his property. The Senate naturally detested him, but was powerless so long as the Praetorians continued to support him. The mob, stuffed with free corn and hugely amused, applauded wildly, and pretended to regard him as a god.

Peter had seen the pagan grandeur of Herod and the sheikhs of Arabia, but he had never expected to see anything so fantastic as one of those "progresses" with which the imperial buffoon now and then entertained himself and the world. It was like nothing so much as a modern circus parade. It included not only the chariots and litters of some ten to twelve thousand aristocrats and courtiers, spangled with bright colours and festooned with flowers, but blood horses for the races, caged wild animals for the gladiatorial games, clowns, buffoons, slaves and musicians for the shows and concerts with which Augustus would beguile his hours of leisure. At the head of the procession, as it started from Rome down the Appian Way to Antium or Baiae, appeared aloft the Roman Eagles, so hateful to Jewish eyes, together with statues and busts of the gods and of Caesar. Toward the end came a gilded chariot drawn by six white Idumean stallions shod with gold; and there, awaiting the acclaim of the populace, with a toga of amethyst over his white tunic, and a laurel wreath above his pudgy degenerate face, lolled Caesar.

Last of all, on a litter carried by eight huge Negroes, appeared the reclining figure of the woman who was said to be Caesar's wife. Sparkling with jewels and tinted with many rare cosmetics, she had the exotic and disturbing beauty of some oriental goddess, patroness of sins not to be mentioned. She was followed by a long train of wagons containing her servants, slaves, wardrobes, and accessories; and on one occasion at least by a herd of five hundred female asses, to furnish milk for the daily baths which kept her peerless skin so soft and white. This was Poppaea Sabina, who had poisoned her husband to marry Nero, over whom she had great influence. It has been conjectured that she was a Jewess or at least a convert to Judaism, because of the favour she showed to Jews in the court, and because when she died, her remains were not cremated, but were laid intact among the urns of the Emperors. Jews have not found this evidence conclusive, and have never claimed her as their own.

Peter also had something better to do than to watch imperial parades or to relax with aristocrats on the Pincian Hill. He must still visit the poor Christians in the insulae, heal the sick by anointing them with oil in the sacrament we call Anointing of the Sick, distribute food and clothing collected from the more prosperous, settle disputes and reconcile enemies, baptize, preach, console, rebuke, offer the Holy Sacrifice on Sundays and perhaps daily. The task of presiding over a universal Church had grown, moreover, to be a colossal one. He would have welcomed the presence and help of Paul, who often promised to visit Rome on his way to Spain, but was always detained by his work in the cast. The labour in Rome was more than enough for one old man. The gentile believers now outnumbered the Jewish ones. The wonderful success of the Roman Church under Peter's direction had made it celebrated, as Paul wrote generously from Corinth, all over the world. Tacitus referred to the Christians as "a huge multitude."

By this time, too, the Church everywhere stood out plainly in essentially the form it has now. It had all the sacraments of today. For besides anointing with oil and baptizing, the apostles undoubtedly gave absolution by the authority of Christ's words, "Whose sins you forgive, they are forgiven them; whose sins you retain, they are retained." They distributed his sacred Body and Blood under the appearances of bread and wine. They imparted the Holy Spirit, as he had bestowed it on them, in Confirmation. Remembering what he had said of marriage, they joined men and women sacramentally. They transmitted their priestly powers by ordination. Thus twelve simple men without money or political influence, but wielding the seven instruments of grace, were quietly building the indivisible and indestructible texture of the Mystical Body.

Belief in Purgatory was an inheritance from the Old Testament Hebrews, for they prayed for their dead; so did the first century Christians, as many records in the catacombs make plain. The veneration of Mary likewise dates from the earliest days of the Church. Besides the certainty with which Ignatius, disciple of Peter, refers to it in a letter of about 106 A.D., there is the evidence of a striking painting on a wall in the catacomb of Saint Priscilla, in the Pompeian style, and undoubtedly of the first half of the second century. She is holding the Child Jesus, and one of the prophets (Isaiah, perhaps) is shown adoring him and pointing to a star. The apostles originally had universal commissions, all subject to the primacy of Peter as their head, but James the Less had remained in Jerusalem. Peter had centred his episcopal labours in Rome, and the new bishops, now being trained to succeed the twelve, would be found everywhere with local jurisdictions: as, for example, Ignatius of Antioch, Polycarp of Smyrna, Irenaeus of Lyons. Originally there had been one order of apostles. Under them in the new testament appear bishops, priests and deacons. The primacy of the Bishop of Rome did not destroy the prerogatives of the other apostles as bishops; and this distinction between orders and jurisdiction has always been retained. The title of "Pope" would not be given him exclusively for several centuries. Yet he was recognized everywhere as head of the Church and Vicar of Christ. Thus, before the death of Peter, the hierarchical organization was plainly defined and completed. He presided over a widely-spread institution, monarchical in functioning, democratic in its method of renewing its official life from the bottom.

This is quite apparent from Peter's first encyclical letter to the Jewish and other Christians of "Pontus, Galatia, Cappadocia, Asia, and Bithynia," probably about 58 or 59 A.D. A simple old man is walking back and forth in his room, in Aquila's house on the Aventine or some other's, as he dictates slowly and emphatically to his secretary Silas, or to "my son Mark," who sits on the floor cross-legged and writes with a quill pen which he sharpens occasionally with pumice stone, while he holds the parchment or tablet on his knee, often for two hours at a time. Peter's words are rugged and still slightly awkward; yet they have the unmistakable grandeur that speaks in the Hebrew prophets, and that accent of serene majestic certitude that we find in the pronouncements of the Popes for nineteen centuries. Writing from "Babylon," that is to say Rome, this old man speaks with authority and assurance to Christians as far away as Asia. He makes it plain that they belong not to a sect, or to a particular nation, but to a unique society of divine origin. They are the living stones of a spiritual house, the precious cornerstone of which (rejected by the builders) is Jesus Christ, the Son of God.[2] "You are a chosen race, a royal priesthood, a holy nation, a people for God's own possession, that you may celebrate the excellences of him who called you out of darkness into his marvellous light; who once were not a people, but are now the people of God."[3] In this great letter he suggests, at least, all the distinguishing marks of the true Church: she is One, Holy, Apostolic, Roman, and Catholic.

He insists above all that as members of Christ they must be holy, as he is. "It is written, 'You shall be holy because I am holy.'" They were redeemed from "your unprofitable mode of life handed down from your forefathers" not by silver and gold, but by "the precious blood of Christ" Let them therefore "love one another earnestly from the heart ... putting away all malice, and all deceit, pretence, envy, and all slander ... Beloved, I implore you as strangers and pilgrims to refrain from sensual desires which war against the soul. Keep your conduct excellent among the heathen, so that, whereas they slander you as evil doers, they may, by observing the nobility of your actions, glorify God in the day of visitation ... Let none of you deserve to suffer as a murderer, or a thief, or a criminal, or a meddler in others' affairs; but if one suffers as a Christian let him not be ashamed, but let him glorify God in that name ... Be all of

---

[2] 1 Pet 2:5-8
[3] *ibid*, 2:9-10

the same mind, compassionate, brotherly, merciful, humble; not returning wrong for wrong, nor insult for insult, but on the contrary conferring blessings; for you were called to do so, in order that you might inherit a blessing ... The time past was enough for working the will of the heathen, and for living in licentiousness, lusts, drunkenness, revelling, carousing, and abominable idolatries ... Be prudent, therefore, and vigilant in prayer. But before everything have earnest love among yourselves, for love covers a multitude of sins."[4]

It is upon this mutual love that unity depends. Hence domestics must be obedient even to disagreeable masters, following Christ's example. Priests should not "lord it over" their flocks, nor rule them "for sordid gain" but should be models to them. Wives should be submissive to their husbands. Here perhaps Peter is thinking of his mother and of the Lord's. A new note of gentleness and graciousness comes into his words as he addresses the Jewish Christian ladies of the East: "Let not your adornment be of the extreme kind – braided hair, golden jewellery, or special gowns, but let it be the hidden woman of the heart, clad with the incorruptible garment of a quiet and gentle spirit, which in the sight of God is very precious." Likewise husbands must live with their wives "in a reasonable way ... and honour them as equal inheritors of the gift of life."[5] This is the first known expression of the Church's gift of equality to the women of the ancient world.

History takes no notice of "the Apostles' Creed" until the fourth century. It does not follow, however, that the twelve did not hand it down in all its essentials. This first letter of Peter, on the contrary, contains a fairly complete outline of it. It begins with praise of "God, the Father of Our Lord Jesus Christ." It asserts that Christ suffered and died, that he "went and preached to the imprisoned souls who were formerly disobedient," that he rose from the dead, that he ascended to heaven and there sits at the right hand of God. It refers to the Holy Spirit, the communion of saints, the forgiveness of sins, the resurrection of the body and the life everlasting.

In addition to this, Peter warns the faithful that being in the world, they must obey all lawful civil authority, but being not of the world, they must expect to be persecuted, as Christ was, since "your adversary the devil prowls about like a roaring lion, looking for someone to devour." However, "all will soon be over" and after

---

[4] 1 Pet 2, *passim*
[5] *ibid*, 3:1-7

sharing in the sufferings of Christ, they will participate in his glory. Having added his greetings and his son Mark's, he sealed the letter and sent it off on its long journey with his disciple Sylvanus.

Mark remained in Rome to compose another document which reveals a great deal, indirectly, about Peter. The second gospel was written, evidently, to help him convert the sceptical gentiles of that city; and it clearly contains evidence that he inspired it if he did not dictate it. Matthew had stressed the prophecies, for he was writing for Jews; what he had to show was that Jesus fulfilled them. Mark has fewer quotations from the Old Testament, for they would be meaningless to the Romans. On the other hand, he takes pains to explain terms that any Jewish reader will ready understand: the Passover, the Day of Preparation, the location of the Mount of Olives. He makes much of the miracles, knowing that this will impress the gentiles, and describes no fewer than eighteen in the space of his short book. He also wishes them to notice that since Christ is God, all things in heaven and earth are subject to him; hence Peter, his representative, must be believed.

Mark's gospel has all the vivacity and directness of an eye-witness account. It has the triumphant air, too, of one whose personal knowledge of the works of Christ was beyond question. Words like "immediately" or "straightway" suggest that the writer is seeing over again what he is describing.

In this terse and direct gospel we see Peter, in his old age, looking back with longing from the noisy, dirty streets of Rome to the clean sweet hills of Galilee that he will never see again. Aramaic words not used by the other evangelists come ready to his mind: "Boanerges," "Talitha Kumi." He is always thinking of "the sea." The sparkle and the motion of it run through the narrative; we are always coming within sight of it, as Peter was in his dreams. He is humble now, and he has Mark omit things creditable to him, such as his walking on the water, and stress what is discreditable, such as the denial. But he helps him to visualize the Lord with exceptional power and fidelity. He loves to give him details of what he was doing when he said this or that: he "looked roundabout," or "he was walking on before the rest."[6] Twice at least he heard him sigh; he remembers it after thirty years as if it were yesterday. The face, the eyes, the gestures, the voice, the love of Jesus are always with him.

As his duties increased and his energies decreased, Peter looked forward to the long deferred visit of Paul, who would be

---

[6] Pope, *op. cit.* III, p. 201 *et. seq.*

especially valuable in this work of converting the Roman gentiles. But nothing was heard of him until, about 58 A.D., word came of his arrest in Jerusalem. Returning from his third journey, he had been mobbed in the temple in the very act of keeping a Mosaic vow with shaven head, and had barely escaped alive. Proclaiming himself a Roman citizen, he had been taken into protective custody to Caesarea. Two years passed before he was finally sent under guard on a ship sailing for Rome. No more news arrived for several months. Then, suddenly, the Roman Christians got word that he had landed at Puteoli. Many of the brethren, including no doubt his old friends Aquila and Priscilla, started down the Via Appia to meet him. Peter is not mentioned among them. It is possible that he was away on a missionary journey, or that he was ill.[7]

---

[7] Acts 21:17-28:15

32

Paul arrived in chains, under guard; but as a Roman citizen whose only offence had been to displease somebody in Palestine, he was treated with considerable leniency. He was given a room of his own, probably in one of the better insulae, and was allowed to receive his friends there, and to go out about the city, still chained, during the day. On the third day he invited the principal Jews of Rome to confer with him. It was no small tribute to his powers that they did so, and listened to his account of his arrest and captivity. They even agreed to hear his defence of Christianity, though they frankly admitted a bias against it. On an appointed day a good number went to his lodgings, where he preaches to them. "And some believed what was spoken while others disbelieved." A lively dispute followed, and the Jews were unable to agree. Paul then quoted Isaiah at them – 'You shall listen and listen, and by no means understand" – and remarked, "Let it therefore be known to you that this salvation of God has been sent to the gentiles, and they will listen!" With that they departed.[1]

This incident, with which Luke brings the *Acts* to a close, seems favourable at first view to the case against Peter's presence in Rome, particularly as no mention is made of him. It may be argued that the leading Jews would never have assembled to hear Paul if they had definitely broken with Peter. But Luke is concerned only with his object of ending the story of Paul's journey to Rome; and as usual, he omits many known facts. A careful rereading of the passage indicates that Paul did not appeal to the Jews as a Christian, but as a fellow-Jew who had been persecuted by the Romans. With characteristic loyalty they flocked to his assistance. They had no idea who he was, for they told him, "We neither received letters from Judea about you, nor did any of the brethren that came here report or speak any evil of you. But we should like to hear from yourself what your opinions are."[2] It was only when he had them together that he revealed his true purpose. By that time the spell of his words and personality had captivated them sufficiently to make them willing to hear him at length. But before they did so they made a remark that clearly shows they had already come in contact with Christianity and had rejected it. "As regards this sect we know

---

[1] Acts 28:16-28
[2] Acts 28:22

that it is everywhere spoken against." This Jewish testimony is not needed, however, to prove the existence of the Christian community in Rome before Paul's arrival. His own letter to the Romans, with its evidence that he has not yet been among them, does that amply; and other testimony is overwhelming. And since it is plain that Paul did not establish the Roman Church, we come back to the proposition that only Peter could have done so.

The probability is that Peter was one of the first to greet him when he arrived in Rome, but that neither of them, nor their disciples, considered the fact important enough to mention. They were not writing a society column, these stalwart bishops, nor were they much given to handshaking and mutual incensing. Peter was engrossed in the labours mentioned above, and Paul immediately began to make the best of his mild imprisonment. The worst of it was that he had one of the Praetorians with him day and night, whether he walked abroad or lectured in his room. This penance he turned into a blessing of no small dimensions. The guard was changed daily; hence in the course of two years he was able to give some seven hundred of Caesar's soldiers individual answers to the riddle of existence of which they had heard so much from Stoics, peripatetics, and other "seed-pickers" who infested the city; and he wrote triumphantly to his friends in Philippi that "it had been clear to the whole Praetorian Guard and to all the rest that my captivity is for the cause of Christ."[3] He was finally acquitted in 62 A.D. for reasons still obscure. Perhaps Tigellinus the Horrible, the new chief of the Imperial Police, was too busy, "purging" the men with whom Nero was annoyed, to waste time on a trivial dispute from the provinces. At all events Paul was set free.

The voice of many traditions linking him with Peter in Rome will not be cried down merely because history is silent. Christians from the first century always thought of them together. Their names are scrawled together on the walls of the catacombs. Their images appear together on bronze medallions of the second century. The third Bishop of Rome, Clement, who certainly must have known them both, refers to the Roman Church as the fruit of their joint labours.[4] It is taking no liberty with essential truth, then, to imagine them strolling together along the bank of the Tiber or through the human mazes of the Forum, talking earnestly of many things in Greek or Hebrew (for Paul was not much at home in Aramaic),

---

[3] Phil 1:13
[4] *op. cit.* 5:6

while people looked curiously after them, judging from their beards and general appearance that they were two old rabbis.

They were better friends than when they had first met in Jerusalem more than twenty years ago. The little man's heroic sufferings had brought Paul's spiritual and intellectual powers to their splendid maturity. He threw off profound observations and bits of imperishable poetry with no effort; and although his superior may still have found his tense conversation somewhat tiring, he could see how love had increased in the fiery warrior of God those gentler qualities that appear in the fatherly letters to Timothy, and in the one to Philemon, where he pleads tenderly for a fugitive slave; to say nothing of the beautiful clarity of the two admonitions to the Corinthians. Peter also had changed, of course. He had become at last the rock that Christ had sought in him. He had long ago finished with wavering; through his labours and sufferings the Holy Spirit had brought him to the massive equilibrium and lucidity apparent in his final utterances. Two such men, living only in Christ and for Christ, could not help understanding and respecting each other.

One of the subjects they talked about must have been the activities of the other apostles, now scattered throughout the world. Peter remembered with affection those with whom he had lived and travelled for three years in the peripatetic college of Christ. He would naturally be eager for any news he might receive of them particularly of his brother Andrew, whom he had last met, perhaps, at the Council of Jerusalem. Paul, having been so much in the East, and being a more energetic letter-writer, had probably picked up all sorts of information about this one or that one. Certainly both of them heard the sad news of what occurred in Jerusalem in 62 A.D., the year of Paul's release. James the Less, the most lovable of men, pattern of bishops, author of the first liturgy of the Church, a man utterly devoted to God and his fellow creatures, had been stoned to death that April. The High Priest Ananas, true son of old Annas, had become jealous of his growing popularity among Jews, and on some pretext had managed to incite a mob against him, thus granting him the privilege of following in the footsteps of Christ, of Stephen, and of the elder James. Unbelieving Jews mourned him with the Christians, and some of them later attributed the destruction of the city to the crime of his murder.

There are many conflicting and some doubtful traditions about the subsequent lives of the remaining apostles. Yet from the earliest times there has been a consistent agreement that nearly all died as martyrs, confirming the prophecy of Christ that the servant would not escape the fate of the master. Strangely enough the first of the original twelve to die had been Judas, who had loved this life most. Peter's brother Andrew is said to have preached in Greece, Thrace, Asia Minor; and after enduring many trials in the land of the anthropophagi and the burning deserts of Scythia, was crucified at Patriae, in Achaia, on 30 November, 60 A.D.; tied, not nailed to the cross, to make his agony last longer. Thomas the Twin went to Parthia, and thence all over the East, telling what he knew to the Medes, the Persians and the Hyrcanians until, somewhere near the Ganges in India, he was stabbed to death with lances. He may even have gone to Sumatra and Ceylon; the eastern traditions about him are old and strong; and in the sixteenth century the Portuguese navigators found fifteen thousand families of "Thomas Christians" on the Malabar coast. Matthew, who was once Levi the publican, preached in Judea and wrote his gospel there. Then he went to Persia, and is said to have been martyred in Parthia, and buried in Hierapolis. Jude Thaddeus was last heard of in Syria. Simon the Zealous, patron of tanners, preached on the shores of the Black Sea, then in Egypt and North Africa. He was said also to have visited Britain before he was sawn to pieces, either at Caldria or at Suanir in Persia. Bartholemew worked tirelessly in India, Mesopotamia, Persia, Egypt, Armenia, Phrygia, and on the shores of the Black Sea. He died at Albanapolis in Armenia, some say beheaded, others say flayed alive head down, by order of Astyages, for having converted his brother King Polymius. So with all the brethren with the possible exception of John, of whose death tradition has nothing to say, except that it occurred after he had written the Apocalypse on the isle of Patmos, having survived boiling in oil and having toiled as bishop of Ephesus until he was a hundred years old.

When Peter and Paul talked over their missing brethren, and heard of the death of this one or that, they must inevitably have wondered what would happen to the Church when the last had vanished from the earth. Again it is the third Pope, Clement of Rome, who tells us that they anticipated the problem. They chose good successors for the original apostles or bishops. They agreed upon the principle of the apostolic succession, through which the authority granted by Christ has been transmitted from bishop to bishop, by the laying on of hands, down to the present day.

"Christ is from God, and the apostles are from Christ ... and our apostles knew through our Lord Jesus Christ," wrote Saint

Clement about 90 A.D. "that there would be strife over the name of the bishop's office. For this cause therefore, having received complete foreknowledge, they appointed the aforesaid persons and afterwards they provided a continuance, that if these should fall asleep, other approved men should succeed to their ministration." [5]

Another frequent subject of conversation between Peter and Paul, judging by its prominence in their letters and those of James, John, and Jude, was the problem of heresy. Saint Thomas Aquinas defines this as "a species of infidelity in men who, having professed the faith of Christ, corrupt its dogmas."[6] It is a spiritual disease that attacked Jews under the Old Law as it does Christians under the New; for Judaism implied faith in the Christ to come, and it is significant that Josephus accuses the pharisees, sadducees, and essenes of "heresy"[7] – the word that Jewish leaders wrongly applied to Paul and the "sect of the Nazarenes."[8] Literally, in the Greek, it means "picking and choosing." The heretic professes to accept all the divine revelation except those parts that displease him. But in rejecting even one of a hundred such dogmas, he is setting himself up as judge in place of God, thus in effect repudiating his authority. This is what makes the crime so abominable; this is why Balmes called it "implicit atheism"; this, no doubt, is why Christ was so unsparing of those who accepted him "with reservations," calling them children of the devil.

All the apostles whose letters are extant adopted the same un-compromising tone toward the "wolves in sheep's clothing" against whom He had warned them. John advised his flocks to have nothing to do with one whose doctrine was different from that handed down by him: "Do not receive him into your house, and give him no greeting."[9] Jude Thaddeus lamented that "certain men have stealthily crept in ... impious men who pervert the grace of our God into licentiousness, and deny our only sovereign and lord, Jesus Christ ... the ones whose presence stains your love-feasts when they feast with you ... discontented fault-finders ... their mouth utters pompous words; they pay court to persons for the sake of gain ... sensual men, not possessing the spirit."[10] Paul poured the fire of his eloquence on more than one sect of these borers-from-within who were trying to uproot what he had planted. He clearly

[5] *op. cit.* 42, 44
[6] II, II, q 11, a. 1.
[7] *Jewish War* II, VIII, 1; *Ant.* XIII, V, 9.
[8] Acts 14:5; 28:22
[9] 2 John 11
[10] Jude 4:12, 16, 19

indicates in one such group the forerunners of the Manichean sects that were to confuse and devastate Europe in the Middle Ages, "giving assent to seducing spirits and to doctrines of demons through the hypocrisy of men who speak lies, whose consciences are seared, who forbid marriage, and command abstinence from foods which God created to be partaken of." There could be no common ground or interfaith nonsense with those who did not accept Christ wholeheartedly in his Church. "Do not become incongruously yoked with unbelievers," he wrote to the Corinthians: "for what partnership have righteousness and iniquity? or what has light in common with darkness? and what concord has Christ with Belial?"[11] When he parted with Peter about 63 A.D., it was to hasten back to Ephesus, to combat certain wolves who were ravaging his fold there.

Peter's second letter seems to have been written about the same time[12] with a similar purpose. Never in the history of papal pronouncements, and it was the father of many such down to today, have heretics been held up before the flock of Christ in a less fettering light. They are "false prophets"... false teachers who will smuggle in destructive sects, and deny even the master who ransomed them, bringing swift destruction upon themselves. And many will follow their lascivious doings: and on their account the way of truth will be defamed. And out of greed they will trade upon you with delusive talk. Audacious and self-willed men ... these, like unreasoning animals born naturally only for capture and destruction, revile what they do not understand, and shall perish in their own corruption ... They count it pleasure to revel in the daytime; they are spots and blemishes; they revel in their deceits while feasting with you; they have eyes full of adultery that cannot cease from sin; they allure unsteady souls; they have a heart trained in avarice; they are children of malediction ... springs without water, and mists driven by the storm ... For by pompous words of folly, they entice, with the bait of sensual lusts and licentiousness, persons who are just escaping the influence of those living in error. They promise them liberty, while they themselves are slaves of corruption..."

A tradition going back to the second century identifies one of the "false Christs and false prophets" against whom Peter pitted his strength in these last years as Simon Magus, to whom he had said

---

[11] 2 Cor 6:14-16

[12] 2 Pet is generally assigned to about 67 A.D. because in it the author expresses a premonition of his death; Peter might have had this, however, in 63 or 64.

"To hell with you and your money," twenty years before in Samaria. The story is that after his failure to purchase the gifts of the Holy Spirit from the Vicar of Christ, the magician travelled to Rome, where the wealth, corruption, and syncretistic international-ism of the imperial court, offered unusual opportunities for his talents. He was particularly attentive to rich and sentimental women, and played upon their emotions and superstitions so adroitly that he wormed his way even into Caesar's household. Representing himself as "the Power of God" and a beautiful blonde Greek prostitute, Helena, as his "First Intelligence," he is said to have elicited nothing less than worship from some of the courtiers who fawned upon Messalina and Poppaea. According to Eusebius his cult grew so alarmingly that the Christians sent east for Peter, who hastened back to Rome, some time after the Council of Jerusalem, to renew the battle with his ancient foe and to expose him a second time.

Some of the more fantastic variations of this story posit a grand contest of the two Simons before no less a judge than Nero. Simon Magus offered to outdo the miracles of Simon Peter by flying in the air before the whole imperial court. This he proceeded, with the devil's help, to do; but he had reckoned without the prayers of Peter and Paul, who stood watching him, and after soaring some distance he suddenly fell and was dashed to pieces.

These tales unfortunately sound too good to be true. No historical evidence points to any appearance of Peter before Nero, much less to the levitation and other marvels. It does not follow, as certain modem Catholic scholars have concluded, that Simon Magus did not make some sort of stir in Nero's Rome. The insistence of the second- and third-century Christian writers that he was Peter's adversary in the west as well as the east is supported, to some extent at least, by the widespread and undeniable existence of the second century gnostic sect called Simonians, who professed to be his followers. They anticipated the early Manichees in their hatred of the Old Testament, which they attributed to a secondary god, the demiurge; and some of them called the God of Abraham, of Isaac, and of Jacob, a devil. If Peter was not referring to them and to their leader in his denunciation of false teachers and "their lascivious doings" who "out of greed will trade upon you with delusive talk," it is difficult to know whom he could have meant.[13]

---

[13] Father Spencer, in his translation of the New Testament (Macmillan) believes that Peter spoke of false teachers "such as the followers of Simon Magus," etc.

This second letter of Peter's is also his farewell to his flock. He has had a revelation that he will not live long, and he begs them to heed his warnings, "knowing as I do that the striking of my tent is close at hand, as Our Lord Jesus Christ has signified to me." His words glow with lyrical fervour as he recalls the Lord's transfiguration on the mount, of which he and the Boanerges were witnesses; he wants them all to remember this after his death. But they must always be prepared for the second coming of the Lord – and here Peter seems to be speaking across the centuries to men of our age or any age:

"It is important, then, that you should know this – that in the last days scoffers will come with mockery, men living in accordance with their own lusts, who will say 'Where is his promised coming? for since the time our forefathers went to their repose, all things continue as they were from the beginning of creation.' They wilfully suffer this to escape them – that, by the word of God, a firmament existed from of old, and land risen out of water and formed by the action of water; that by means of water also the world of that time perished in a flood; that the heavens and the earth, as they now are, have by the same word been treasured up for fire, reserved until the Day of judgment and destruction for impious men.

But let not this one truth escape your mind, beloved, that with the Lord one day is as a thousand years, and a thousand years as one day. The Lord does not delay his promise as some account delay, but is long-suffering on your account, not wishing that any should perish, but that all should come to repentance. But the day of the Lord shall come like a thief, when the heavens shall pass away with a mighty rush, and the elements shall be dissolved with fervid heat, and the earth and all the works that are upon it shall be consumed. Since therefore all these are to be resolved, what sort of persons ought you to be in holy conduct and piety, while you expect and hasten the coming of the day of God! Because of it the glowing heavens shall be dissolved, and the elements melted with fervid heat. Yet, according to his promise, we look for new heavens and a new earth, in which righteousness will dwell."

After nineteen centuries, the words of the fisherman seem to take on a new and disquieting glow. They are as modern and as urgent as the atomic bomb.

33

Toward sunset on the hot 19 July of 64 A.D., Peter was returning to his house on the Aventine, let us suppose, a tired and lonely old man. It had been a tedious day. Long before sunrise he had attended the funeral of one of his earliest converts, who had been laid according to his wishes, by the side of his Jewish wife and Jewish parents. After consoling the bereaved, the apostle had spent the day in various parts of the city, ministering to the sick and the needy. Now, as he sweltered in the dusk, he remembered gratefully the cool silence of the old catacomb where he had passed the only comfortable hour of the past twenty-four. Perhaps the recollection set up a train of thought.

The two oldest catacombs in Rome had been dug out of the soft tufa by the children of the Jewish prisoners of Pompey. They could not conscientiously cremate their dead, as the pagans did, and land was too expensive; so they went down; and the subterranean passages, about 16 feet wide, with elliptical walls, now ran under large sections of the city. In them the first Christians had been buried secretly by night as Jews. After the Council of Jerusalem, the Christians began digging their own. They would start in the garden of some member of the Church, and go on indefinitely; and for some reason they made their caves straighter and narrower than the Jewish ones, with vertical instead of curved walls, and with the corners at right angles. By the fourth century there were some forty of these tunnels, forming vast inextricable labyrinths, some with as many as five levels, going down 82 feet. Four of these, extending for miles under various parts of Rome, date from Apostolic times: those of Domatilla on the Ardeatina, of Priscilla on the Via Salaria, of Lucina on the Via Appia, and of Commodilla on the Via Astrensis; and in them, in the course of three centuries, two million Christians were buried, one over another, in compartments scooped out of the walls.

One obvious thought was that here was one more debt that the faithful of Christ owed to the Jews.[1] Another was that if ever there

---

[1] Monsignor Barnes holds that the "Jewish" catacombs were dug by Hebrew Christians (*Christianity at Rome,* etc., p. 91) who wanted to be buried in rock, as our Lord was. But He was so interred to conform to Jewish custom! Also, why should Jews have imitated Christians in this matter? Jewish scholars claim six catacombs, one at least, on the Via Portuense, containing no Christian signs or memorials. See H. J. Leon, for example, in *Hebrew Union College Annual,* Vol. V, 1928.

was a persecution in this city, it would not be necessary for people to flee, as they had from Jerusalem before the conversion of Paul. They could hide underground, and it would be difficult to find them all. Furthermore, even a tyrant would hesitate to seek them there, since the *Coemetaria* were inviolable under the Roman law.

While some such reflections pass through Peter's mind, he hears a fanfare, and sees rounding a comer another "progress" of Nero and Poppaea. This one has been hastily assembled and is smaller than usual, for Caesar and his court are fleeing from the suffocating heat, which has come rather suddenly, to his cool villa at Antium by the southern sea. Peter is too hot and tired even to look after them. But he cannot keep out of his mind some words that James the Less wrote in his last letter, just before he was stoned by order of the Sons of Annas:

"Come now, you rich, weep and wail over your impending miseries. Your wealth is rotting and your garments are moth-eaten. Your gold and silver are rusted, and their rust shall become an evidence against you, and shall consume your flesh like fire. A treasure you have laid up for the last days! See! The wages of the workmen who have mowed your lands, wages fraudulently with-held by you, cry out: and the outcries of the reaper have entered the ears of the Lord of Hosts. You have lived delicately and voluptuously on the earth; you have pampered your hearts in a day that reeked of slaughter. You have condemned, you have murdered the class of the righteous, who do not resist you!"

Thus thinking, the Vicar of Christ, we still suppose, went home to his poor supper of lentil soup or dried peas, intending to retire early and sleep if possible.

During the evening he became aware of something unusual stirring in the streets down toward the Forum. The people were always restless on hot nights, but this evening they were more so. Some were leaning limply from windows, some sitting or lying on the crowded pavements. Infants were wailing, dogs howling, heavy carts shaking the dusty walls of the insulae, down below, as they rumbled by with more than their ordinary racket.

From some blocks away the shrieking of women and the deeper shouts of men came through the heavy air. It was an old cry, understood even before it was clearly distinguished. "Fire!" Clouds of smoke were already visible over the Via Ostia and the low districts nearby. Already it could be smelled on the Aventine. People were rushing into the streets running here and there, lugging their furniture into alleys already cluttered.

"The Circus Maximus is afire!"

In an incredibly short time the flames had swept through the poor Jewish quarter near the Capena Gae, had swallowed the shops and houses about the Circus Maximus, and were roaring up the Aventine and Caelian hills. The centre of the city was like a glowing furnace. Caesar's seven thousand watchmen were helpless; there was nothing to be done now but flee. Crowds trampled one another to death; they were burned alive, screaming; they plunged into the Tiber and drowned. Some mounted a hilltop only to meet another wall of fire coming up the opposite side. Thousands somehow reached the fields outside the gates and camped there, watching their homes go up in smoke. The insulae, well dried by the summer heat, were blazing and crackling like so much paper. New fires mysteriously started here and there.

The principal conflagration changed its course as the wind shifted. Drunken gladiators ran about looting and slaying. The sky over the city was a baleful mixture of smoke and blood, lighting up the whole Campagna. And this went on for nine days and nights.

Beyond his presence in the city, tradition has nothing to say of what happened to the apostle Peter during that hellish week or more. Strangely enough there is no mention of the fire in his later writings, or Paul's, or any contemporary Christian's; though pagan testimony establishes the fact beyond any doubt.[2] Peter may have gone across the Tiber to console and help poor Christians and Jews there. For the Trastevere was one of the four out of the fourteen districts that escaped destruction, thanks to the changing of the wind. Or he may have been carried with the swarm of fugitives from the Aventine to some camp in the open fields.

Wherever he was, he heard what people were saying; and as some sanity began to return to the helpless mob, he knew that all of them were speaking bitterly of the same thing. Nero had galloped back from Antium to watch the catastrophe. He had been seen by the glare of it, looming theatrically on top of the Appian Aqueduct like a grotesque caricature of himself in purple and white, singing and strumming on his lute. It was said that he had been labouring of late on an epic description of the burning of Troy. Many now reported having seen his servants running about the Circus Maximus with torches in their hands just before the outbreak of the fire.

---

[2] Tacitus, *Annales* XV, 44; Suetonius, *Nero* 16; Juvenal *Satires* I, 155; Seneca, *Epistles* 14; Dio Cassius, *Roman History* LXII, 16, etc.

Through the homeless crowds, huddling in the fields or jammed in the streets across the Tiber, swept a gust of anger. "Nero set the fire! He hated the city and wanted to rebuild it!" An enormous mob marched up to his palace on the Palatine, and when he appeared on a balcony, called him an incendiary and a matricide to his face.

Caesar's flabby form shook with terror. The usual promises of more bread and circuses would not suffice to appease such vengeful cries as now afflicted his imperial ears. These people meant to have blood. First they must be flattered, then fed, then induced to turn their anger against some other object. How Nero accomplished this purpose is notorious. It took him only a few days, with the help of Tigellinus and other unscrupulous agents, to build up a case in the public mind against the Christians. They were the easiest group in Rome to villify. Though their love for one another had often aroused admiration, they had also been the victims of many slanders. First they had been included in the fear and distrust of the Jews: they too were suspected of ritual murder, cannibalism, worshipping an ass's head, consuming the blood of a Roman child. It was impossible to prove these tales against the Jews of the synagogue, but the Eucharist itself could be made to lend some colour to them where Christians were concerned. "Unless you eat my Body and drink my Blood, you shall not have life in you." What need had they of further testimony? Everyone knew besides that Christians refused to worship Caesar, thus making themselves enemies of the state and of the whole Roman people. Finally, it was well known that they had often prophesied the destruction of Rome and the world by fire.

To Nero and other satanic minds in his court the problem became beautifully simple. The people were panicky; they wanted a victim; all they needed was a plausible suggestion. The thing was done so quickly that one night in late July or early August, Peter heard the tramp of many feet and the clash of hysterical voices. Even at a distance they were as sinister as death, and when they came nearer, the words were like cold steel in his heart:

"Death to the Christians! The Christians to the lions!"

Rough Praetorian hands seized the flock of Christ wherever they could be found – whether sleeping in the fields under the August moon, or digging in the ashes of their homes for the bodies of their dead. Every day more of them were dragged out of cellars, chimneys, gardens, and ruins. Pagan neighbours, eager to propitiate the gods and promised some rare spectacles besides, now helped the

Praetorians round up the victims. The prisons were crowded. New amphitheatres of wood were being thrown up, for the Circus Maximus had been destroyed. Wild beasts were brought in haste from other cities.

The surviving Christians fled wholesale to the catacombs. They were comparatively safe there for the present, since these underground cemeteries were recognized sanctuaries; and they proceeded to make themselves as much at home as they could in such unnatural surroundings. There they slept, ate, dug, gathered in crowds by smoky candle-light to pray and to receive the Eucharist, sent forth spies by night to bring back news of what was happening to their brethren in the prisons, and consoled one another with the singing of hymns. Peter undoubtedly lived there too, walking among them with compassionate eyes, encouraging the women and children, offering the Holy Sacrifice on an improvised altar, sending pieces of the Holy Bread to those waiting for death in the prisons. Tradition has him in the catacomb of Priscilla on the Via Salaria. Probably the most moving of all his unrecorded sermons were those that he delivered to crowds sitting in the dark corridors, their eyes gleaming with sad courage in the flicker of torches as he reminded them that the servant was not greater than the master. "He who loses his life for my sake and the gospel's shall save it.[3] ... And be not afraid of those who kill the body, but are unable to kill the soul."[4]

Sometimes perhaps with Linus, Cletus, or Clement, whom he had ordained, he went above ground through the gardens on the Aventine by night, and next morning mingled with the crowds gathering early to be sure to get seats in the amphitheatre. He gave his blessing quietly to little groups of his people before they were led into the arena; or seeing them already there, he raised his hand in benediction over them. And when afternoon came he knew he had accomplished his task. The time for words had passed: now was the day of action that the Lord had spoken of, and his people were ready. Even cold Poppaea and the Vestal Virgins were startled to see lovely girls kneeling on the bloody sand with parents, brothers, friends, or sweethearts, and to hear their voices raised in a hymn that throbbed with joy and triumph as tawny African lions came bounding out of their cages to sniff, to growl, to devour:

"Christus vincit! Christus regnat! Christus imperat!"

---

[3] Mark 8:35
[4] Matt 10:28

It was incredible, but everyone heard and saw it. Even as the mangled limbs were flung about the sand, these people continued to cry *"Pro Christo!"* till their mouths were stopped by death. Seneca was astonished to notice that one of the men, dying of tortures, "smiled as if there was happiness in his heart."[5]

This was only the beginning, however. Nero had the thoroughness if not the talent of a great artist, and he had no intention of desisting so long as there was any chance that boredom might let the mob remember his own crime. Hence he enchanted them with mythological tableaux in which Hercules perished in real flames, Orpheus was torn by real bears, Ixion was pulled to pieces on a real rack, and Pasiphae was ravished by a real monster, masked like a wild steer and believed by some to be Nero himself. One night he illuminated his parks with the burning bodies of Christian men, women, and children covered with pitch. If the apostle Peter was abroad that evening, he saw the sickening spectacle on the very ground where Saint Peter's now stands. The devil had not stopped with half measures in this first persecution of the Church of Christ by the pagan empire. He had branded her children as horrible criminals. He had driven them underground for an intermittent trial that was to last more than two hundred and fifty years. The first Beast or Antichrist had certainly appeared.

The famous tradition of Peter's flight at the suggestion of Linus and others, his meeting with Christ on the Via Appia, his saying, *Quo Vadis, Domine?* and his return to the city on hearing that the Lord was going there to die again for him, dates from a sermon of St. Ambrose in the fourth century. Peter at once understood that the Lord was to be crucified in his person, thus conferring the honour he had promised long ago on the shore of Galilee. The old Apostle went back to Rome with joy "glorifying God," to tell the brethren the good news. There is no hint of cowardice in this earliest tradition.

Still more probable is the one that he was arrested before the end of the Neronian persecution, and cast into the Mamertime or Tullianum Prison, just off the Forum at the foot of the Capitoline. This was not an ideal residence even for one who welcomed martyrdom. Originally a deep well cut through solid tufa, it was a conical vault consisting of an upper room, with a trap-door in the floor, through which prisoners were pushed into the dungeon below. Many, like King Jugurtha, never returned alive from the

---

[5] Epistle 78.

horrors of that dark damp hole. Others were brought up raving mad or crippled with disease. The only alleviating circumstance in Peter's incarceration was that after a while he was allowed the companionship of Paul, who on returning from the east had been promptly arrested. Peter is said also to have converted two of his jailers.

One day in June, probably in 67 A.D. the two sick and blinking old men were lifted out of the dungeon, and haled before some military court, where they heard their crimes enumerated and were sentenced to death as enemies of Caesar, of the Roman people, and of the human race. The news quickly reached the catacombs, by some mysterious grapevine, and as Peter walked feebly along between two rows of lictors, and became somewhat accustomed to the painful novelty of sunshine, he began to see familiar faces among the curious crowds, quietly blessing and encouraging him. He was going to meet the Lord today, it might be their turn tomorrow. The cross was carried before him by some soldier, for he was obviously too weak to bear it. His eyes rested with a curious affection upon the three beams, and he smiled a little as he remembered the words the risen Christ had spoken to him that evening by the Sea of Galilee:

"When you grow old, you shall stretch out your hands and another shall bind you and carry you where you have no desire to go."[6]

The gruesome little procession filed through one of the city gates into the gloriously green countryside. As it stopped and divided into two parts at a fork of the road, Peter saw that Paul had been walking behind him. The calm eyes of the two brothers in Christ met for a moment in love and understanding. And with that they parted. Paul was taken to a field well outside the walls, and there, being a Roman citizen, was beheaded with a sword.

Peter was dragged on, his cross before him, to a place on or near the Vatican Hill. There he was nailed to the cross, which was then hoisted to the brow of the hill. The tradition persists that he was crucified, at his own request, upside down, on the ground that he was unworthy to die as Christ died. In either case his agony was fierce and long-drawn-out. As fire racked his chest and thirst tore at his fevered throat, his bloodshot eyes saw another hill and another Cross, and words that were not his were on his lips. "Father, forgive them, for they know not what they do." The pain faded into a

---

[6] John 21:18

numbness and the numbness into a joy that was also the white radiance of the face of Jesus.

Peter was buried by some of his flock on the very spot where he had seen Caesar driving his horses and the martyrs blazing in death. The next year Nero was overthrown and died by his own cowardly hand. Two years later the temple of Jupiter Capitolanus, with the sanctuaries of Juno and Minerva, was burned to the ground.

The same year, 70 A.D., after the Christians of Jerusalem had all found safety in Pella, the holy city was destroyed. In the temple of Herod not one stone was left upon another. The survivors were scattered through the world, without temple, priesthood, or sacrifice, until they should discern and worship their own Lion of Judah in the Lamb of God, offered daily on countless altars from the rising to the setting of the sun. "In the world you shall have affliction. But be of good cheer! I have overcome the world!"[7]

---

[7] John 16:33